HINDI

VOCABULARY

FOR ENGLISH SPEAKERS

ENGLISH-
HINDI

The most useful words
To expand your lexicon and sharpen
your language skills

9000 words

Hindi vocabulary for English speakers - 9000 words

By Andrey Taranov

T&P Books vocabularies are intended for helping you learn, memorize and review foreign words. The dictionary is divided into themes, covering all major spheres of everyday activities, business, science, culture, etc.

The process of learning words using T&P Books' theme-based dictionaries gives you the following advantages:

- Correctly grouped source information predetermines success at subsequent stages of word memorization
- Availability of words derived from the same root allowing memorization of word units (rather than separate words)
- Small units of words facilitate the process of establishing associative links needed for consolidation of vocabulary
- Level of language knowledge can be estimated by the number of learned words

T&P Books Publishing
www.tpbooks.com

ISBN: 978-1-78616-538-1

This book is also available in E-book formats.
Please visit www.tpbooks.com or the major online bookstores.

HINDI VOCABULARY
for English speakers

T&P Books vocabularies are intended to help you learn, memorize, and review foreign words. The vocabulary contains over 9000 commonly used words arranged thematically.

- Vocabulary contains the most commonly used words
- Recommended as an addition to any language course
- Meets the needs of beginners and advanced learners of foreign languages
- Convenient for daily use, revision sessions, and self-testing activities
- Allows you to assess your vocabulary

Special features of the vocabulary

- Words are organized according to their meaning, not alphabetically
- Words are presented in three columns to facilitate the reviewing and self-testing processes
- Words in groups are divided into small blocks to facilitate the learning process
- The vocabulary offers a convenient and simple transcription of each foreign word

The vocabulary has 256 topics including:

Basic Concepts, Numbers, Colors, Months, Seasons, Units of Measurement, Clothing & Accessories, Food & Nutrition, Restaurant, Family Members, Relatives, Character, Feelings, Emotions, Diseases, City, Town, Sightseeing, Shopping, Money, House, Home, Office, Working in the Office, Import & Export, Marketing, Job Search, Sports, Education, Computer, Internet, Tools, Nature, Countries, Nationalities and more ...

T&P BOOKS' THEME-BASED DICTIONARIES

The Correct System for Memorizing Foreign Words

Acquiring vocabulary is one of the most important elements of learning a foreign language, because words allow us to express our thoughts, ask questions, and provide answers. An inadequate vocabulary can impede communication with a foreigner and make it difficult to understand a book or movie well.

The pace of activity in all spheres of modern life, including the learning of modern languages, has increased. Today, we need to memorize large amounts of information (grammar rules, foreign words, etc.) within a short period. However, this does not need to be difficult. All you need to do is to choose the right training materials, learn a few special techniques, and develop your individual training system.

Having a system is critical to the process of language learning. Many people fail to succeed in this regard; they cannot master a foreign language because they fail to follow a system comprised of selecting materials, organizing lessons, arranging new words to be learned, and so on. The lack of a system causes confusion and eventually, lowers self-confidence.

T&P Books' theme-based dictionaries can be included in the list of elements needed for creating an effective system for learning foreign words. These dictionaries were specially developed for learning purposes and are meant to help students effectively memorize words and expand their vocabulary.

Generally speaking, the process of learning words consists of three main elements:

- Reception (creation or acquisition) of a training material, such as a word list
- Work aimed at memorizing new words
- Work aimed at reviewing the learned words, such as self-testing

All three elements are equally important since they determine the quality of work and the final result. All three processes require certain skills and a well-thought-out approach.

New words are often encountered quite randomly when learning a foreign language and it may be difficult to include them all in a unified list. As a result, these words remain written on scraps of paper, in book margins, textbooks, and so on. In order to systematize such words, we have to create and continually update a "book of new words." A paper notebook, a netbook, or a tablet PC can be used for these purposes.

This "book of new words" will be your personal, unique list of words. However, it will only contain the words that you came across during the learning process. For example, you might have written down the words "Sunday," "Tuesday," and "Friday." However, there are additional words for days of the week, for example, "Saturday," that are missing, and your list of words would be incomplete. Using a theme dictionary, in addition to the "book of new words," is a reasonable solution to this problem.

The theme-based dictionary may serve as the basis for expanding your vocabulary.

It will be your big "book of new words" containing the most frequently used words of a foreign language already included. There are quite a few theme-based dictionaries available, and you should ensure that you make the right choice in order to get the maximum benefit from your purchase.

Therefore, we suggest using theme-based dictionaries from T&P Books Publishing as an aid to learning foreign words. Our books are specially developed for effective use in the sphere of vocabulary systematization, expansion and review.

Theme-based dictionaries are not a magical solution to learning new words. However, they can serve as your main database to aid foreign-language acquisition. Apart from theme dictionaries, you can have copybooks for writing down new words, flash cards, glossaries for various texts, as well as other resources; however, a good theme dictionary will always remain your primary collection of words.

T&P Books' theme-based dictionaries are specialty books that contain the most frequently used words in a language.

The main characteristic of such dictionaries is the division of words into themes. For example, the *City* theme contains the words "street," "crossroads," "square," "fountain," and so on. The *Talking* theme might contain words like "to talk," "to ask," "question," and "answer".

All the words in a theme are divided into smaller units, each comprising 3–5 words. Such an arrangement improves the perception of words and makes the learning process less tiresome. Each unit contains a selection of words with similar meanings or identical roots. This allows you to learn words in small groups and establish other associative links that have a positive effect on memorization.

The words on each page are placed in three columns: a word in your native language, its translation, and its transcription. Such positioning allows for the use of techniques for effective memorization. After closing the translation column, you can flip through and review foreign words, and vice versa. "This is an easy and convenient method of review – one that we recommend you do often."

Our theme-based dictionaries contain transcriptions for all the foreign words. Unfortunately, none of the existing transcriptions are able to convey the exact nuances of foreign pronunciation. That is why we recommend using the transcriptions only as a supplementary learning aid. Correct pronunciation can only be acquired with the help of sound. Therefore our collection includes audio theme-based dictionaries.

The process of learning words using T&P Books' theme-based dictionaries gives you the following advantages:

- You have correctly grouped source information, which predetermines your success at subsequent stages of word memorization
- Availability of words derived from the same root (lazy, lazily, lazybones), allowing you to memorize word units instead of separate words
- Small units of words facilitate the process of establishing associative links needed for consolidation of vocabulary
- You can estimate the number of learned words and hence your level of language knowledge
- The dictionary allows for the creation of an effective and high-quality revision process
- You can revise certain themes several times, modifying the revision methods and techniques
- Audio versions of the dictionaries help you to work out the pronunciation of words and develop your skills of auditory word perception

The T&P Books' theme-based dictionaries are offered in several variants differing in the number of words: 1.500, 3.000, 5.000, 7.000, and 9.000 words. There are also dictionaries containing 15,000 words for some language combinations. Your choice of dictionary will depend on your knowledge level and goals.

We sincerely believe that our dictionaries will become your trusty assistant in learning foreign languages and will allow you to easily acquire the necessary vocabulary.

TABLE OF CONTENTS

MISCELLANEOUS   248

MAIN 500 VERBS   255

PRONUNCIATION GUIDE

Letter	Hindi example	T&P phonetic alphabet	English example

Vowels

Letter	Hindi example	T&P phonetic alphabet	English example
अ	अक्सर	[a]; [ɑ], [ə]	park; teacher
आ	आगमन	[a:]	calf, palm
इ	इनाम	[i]	shorter than in feet
ई	ईश्वर	[i], [i:]	feet, Peter
उ	उठना	[ʊ]	good, booklet
ऊ	ऊपर	[u:]	pool, room
ऋ	ऋग्वेद	[r, rʲ]	green
ए	एकता	[e:]	longer than in bell
ऐ	ऐनक	[aj]	time, white
ओ	ओला	[o:]	fall, bomb
औ	औरत	[au]	loud, powder
अं	अंजीर	[ŋ]	English, ring
अः	अ से अः	[h]	home, have
ऑ	ऑफिस	[ɒ]	cotton, pocket

Consonants

Letter	Hindi example	T&P phonetic alphabet	English example
क	कमरा	[k]	clock, kiss
ख	खिड़की	[kh]	work hard
ग	गरज	[g]	game, gold
घ	घर	[gh]	g aspirated
ङ	डाकू	[ŋ]	English, ring
च	चक्कर	[ʧ]	church, French
छ	छात्र	[ʧh]	hitchhiker
ज	जाना	[ʤ]	joke, general
झ	झलक	[ʤ]	joke, general
ञ	विज्ञान	[n]	canyon, new
ट	मटर	[t]	tourist, trip
ठ	ठेका	[th]	don't have
ड	डंडा	[d]	day, doctor
ढ	ढलान	[d]	day, doctor
ण	क्षण	[n]	retroflex nasal
त	ताकत	[t]	tourist, trip

Letter	Hindi example	T&P phonetic alphabet	English example
थ	थकना	[th]	don't have
द	दरवाज़ा	[d]	day, doctor
ध	धोना	[d]	day, doctor
न	नाई	[n]	sang, thing
प	पिता	[p]	pencil, private
फ	फल	[f]	face, food
ब	बच्चा	[b]	baby, book
भ	भाई	[b]	baby, book
म	माता	[m]	magic, milk
य	याद	[j]	yes, New York
र	रीछ	[r]	rice, radio
ल	लाल	[l]	lace, people
व	वचन	[v]	very, river
श	शिक्षक	[ʃ]	machine, shark
ष	भाषा	[ʃ]	machine, shark
स	सोना	[s]	city, boss
ह	हज़ार	[h]	home, have

Additional consonants

क़	क़लम	[q]	king, club
ख़	ख़बर	[h]	huge, hat
ड़	लड़का	[r]	rice, radio
ढ़	पढ़ना	[r]	rice, radio
ग़	ग़लती	[ɣ]	between [g] and [h]
ज़	ज़िन्दगी	[z]	zebra, please
झ़	ट्रेझ़र	[ʒ]	forge, pleasure
फ़	फ़ौज	[f]	face, food

ABBREVIATIONS
used in the vocabulary

English abbreviations

ab.	-	about
adj	-	adjective
adv	-	adverb
anim.	-	animate
as adj	-	attributive noun used as adjective
e.g.	-	for example
etc.	-	et cetera
fam.	-	familiar
fem.	-	feminine
form.	-	formal
inanim.	-	inanimate
masc.	-	masculine
math	-	mathematics
mil.	-	military
n	-	noun
pl	-	plural
pron.	-	pronoun
sb	-	somebody
sing.	-	singular
sth	-	something
v aux	-	auxiliary verb
vi	-	intransitive verb
vi, vt	-	intransitive, transitive verb
vt	-	transitive verb

Hindi abbreviations

f	-	feminine noun
f pl	-	feminine plural
m	-	masculine noun
m pl	-	masculine plural

BASIC CONCEPTS

Basic concepts. Part 1

1. Pronouns

I, me	मैं	main
you	तुम	tum
he, she, it	वह	vah
we	हम	ham
you (to a group)	आप	āp
they	बे	ve

2. Greetings. Salutations. Farewells

Hello! (fam.)	नमस्कार!	namaskār!
Hello! (form.)	नमस्ते!	namaste!
Good morning!	नमस्ते!	namaste!
Good afternoon!	नमस्ते!	namaste!
Good evening!	नमस्ते!	namaste!
to say hello	नमस्कार कहना	namaskār kahana
Hi! (hello)	नमस्कार!	namaskār!
greeting (n)	अभिवादन (m)	abhivādan
to greet (vt)	अभिवादन करना	abhivādan karana
How are you?	आप कैसे हैं?	āp kaise hain?
What's new?	क्या हाल है?	kya hāl hai?
Bye-Bye! Goodbye!	अलविदा!	alavida!
See you soon!	फिर मिलेंगे!	fir milenge!
Farewell! (to a friend)	अलिवदा!	alivada!
Farewell! (form.)	अलविदा!	alavida!
to say goodbye	अलविदा कहना	alavida kahana
So long!	अलविदा!	alavida!
Thank you!	धन्यवाद!	dhanyavād!
Thank you very much!	बहुत बहुत शुक्रिया!	bahut bahut shukriya!
You're welcome	कोई बात नहीं	koī bāt nahin
Don't mention it!	कोई बात नहीं	koī bāt nahin
It was nothing	कोई बात नहीं	koī bāt nahin
Excuse me! (fam.)	माफ़ कीजिएगा!	māf kījiega!
Excuse me! (form.)	माफ़ी कीजियेगा!	māfī kījiyega!

to excuse (forgive)	माफ़ करना	māf karana
to apologize (vi)	माफ़ी मांगना	māfī māngana
My apologies	मुझे माफ़ कीजिएगा	mujhe māf kījiega
I'm sorry!	मुझे माफ़ कीजिएगा!	mujhe māf kījiega!
to forgive (vt)	माफ़ करना	māf karana
please (adv)	कृप्या	krpya

Don't forget!	भूलना नहीं!	bhūlana nahin!
Certainly!	ज़रूर!	zarūr!
Of course not!	बिल्कुल नहीं!	bilkul nahin!
Okay! (I agree)	ठीक है!	thīk hai!
That's enough!	बहुत हुआ!	bahut hua!

3. How to address

mister, sir	श्रीमान	shrīmān
ma'am	श्रीमती	shrīmatī
miss	मैम	maim
young man	बेटा	beta
young man (little boy, kid)	बेटा	beta
miss (little girl)	कुमारी	kumārī

4. Cardinal numbers. Part 1

0 zero	ज़ीरो	zīro
1 one	एक	ek
2 two	दो	do
3 three	तीन	tīn
4 four	चार	chār

5 five	पाँच	pānch
6 six	छह	chhah
7 seven	सात	sāt
8 eight	आठ	āth
9 nine	नौ	nau

10 ten	दस	das
11 eleven	ग्यारह	gyārah
12 twelve	बारह	bārah
13 thirteen	तेरह	terah
14 fourteen	चौदह	chaudah

15 fifteen	पन्द्रह	pandrah
16 sixteen	सोलह	solah
17 seventeen	सत्रह	satrah
18 eighteen	अठारह	athārah
19 nineteen	उन्नीस	unnīs
20 twenty	बीस	bīs

21 twenty-one	इक्कीस	ikkīs
22 twenty-two	बाईस	baīs
23 twenty-three	तेईस	teīs
30 thirty	तीस	tīs
31 thirty-one	इकतीस	ikattīs
32 thirty-two	बत्तीस	battīs
33 thirty-three	तैंतीस	taintīs
40 forty	चालीस	chālīs
41 forty-one	इक्तालीस	iktālīs
42 forty-two	बयालीस	bayālīs
43 forty-three	तैंतालीस	taintālīs
50 fifty	पचास	pachās
51 fifty-one	इक्यावन	ikyāvan
52 fifty-two	बावन	bāvan
53 fifty-three	तिरपन	tirapan
60 sixty	साठ	sāth
61 sixty-one	इकसठ	ikasath
62 sixty-two	बासठ	bāsath
63 sixty-three	तिरसठ	tirasath
70 seventy	सत्तर	sattar
71 seventy-one	इकहत्तर	ikahattar
72 seventy-two	बहत्तर	bahattar
73 seventy-three	तिहत्तर	tihattar
80 eighty	अस्सी	assī
81 eighty-one	इक्यासी	ikyāsī
82 eighty-two	बयासी	bayāsī
83 eighty-three	तिरासी	tirāsī
90 ninety	नब्बे	nabbe
91 ninety-one	इक्यानवे	ikyānave
92 ninety-two	बानवे	bānave
93 ninety-three	तिरानवे	tirānave

5. Cardinal numbers. Part 2

100 one hundred	सौ	sau
200 two hundred	दो सौ	do sau
300 three hundred	तीन सौ	tīn sau
400 four hundred	चार सौ	chār sau
500 five hundred	पाँच सौ	pānch sau
600 six hundred	छह सौ	chhah sau
700 seven hundred	सात सो	sāt so
800 eight hundred	आठ सौ	āth sau

900 nine hundred	नौ सौ	nau sau
1000 one thousand	एक हज़ार	ek hazār
2000 two thousand	दो हज़ार	do hazār
3000 three thousand	तीन हज़ार	tīn hazār
10000 ten thousand	दस हज़ार	das hazār
one hundred thousand	एक लाख	ek lākh
million	दस लाख (m)	das lākh
billion	अरब (m)	arab

6. Ordinal numbers

first (adj)	पहला	pahala
second (adj)	दूसरा	dūsara
third (adj)	तीसरा	tīsara
fourth (adj)	चौथा	chautha
fifth (adj)	पाँचवाँ	pānchavān
sixth (adj)	छठा	chhatha
seventh (adj)	सातवाँ	sātavān
eighth (adj)	आठवाँ	āthavān
ninth (adj)	नौवाँ	nauvān
tenth (adj)	दसवाँ	dasavān

7. Numbers. Fractions

fraction	अपूर्णांक (m)	apūrnānk
one half	आधा	ādha
one third	एक तीहाई	ek tīhaī
one quarter	एक चौथाई	ek chauthaī
one eighth	आठवां हिस्सा	āthavān hissa
one tenth	दसवां हिस्सा	dasavān hissa
two thirds	दो तिहाई	do tihaī
three quarters	पौना	pauna

8. Numbers. Basic operations

subtraction	घटाव (m)	ghatāv
to subtract (vi, vt)	घटाना	ghatāna
division	विभाजन (m)	vibhājan
to divide (vt)	विभाजित करना	vibhājit karana
addition	जोड़ (m)	jor
to add up (vt)	जोड़ करना	jor karana
to add (vi, vt)	जोड़ना	jorana
multiplication	गुणन (m)	gunan
to multiply (vt)	गुणा करना	guna karana

9. Numbers. Miscellaneous

digit, figure	अंक (m)	ank
number	संख्या (f)	sankhya
numeral	संख्यावाचक (m)	sankhyāvāchak
minus sign	घटाव चिह्न (m)	ghatāv chihn
plus sign	जोड़ चिह्न (m)	jor chihn
formula	फ़ारमूला (m)	fāramūla
calculation	गणना (f)	ganana
to count (vi, vt)	गिनना	ginana
to count up	गिनती करना	ginatī karana
to compare (vt)	तुलना करना	tulana karana
How much?	कितना?	kitana?
sum, total	कुल (m)	kul
result	नतीजा (m)	natīja
remainder	शेष (m)	shesh
a few (e.g., ~ years ago)	कुछ	kuchh
little (I had ~ time)	थोड़ा ...	thora ...
the rest	बाक़ी	bāqī
one and a half	डेढ़	derh
dozen	दर्जन (m)	darjan
in half (adv)	दो भागों में	do bhāgon men
equally (evenly)	बराबर	barābar
half	आधा (m)	ādha
time (three ~s)	बार (m)	bār

10. The most important verbs. Part 1

to advise (vt)	सलाह देना	salāh dena
to agree (say yes)	राज़ी होना	rāzī hona
to answer (vi, vt)	जवाब देना	javāb dena
to apologize (vi)	माफ़ी मांगना	māfī māngana
to arrive (vi)	पहुँचना	pahunchana
to ask (~ oneself)	पूछना	pūchhana
to ask (~ sb to do sth)	मांगना	māngana
to be (vi)	होना	hona
to be afraid	डरना	darana
to be hungry	भूख लगाना	bhūkh lagana
to be interested in ...	रुचि लेना	ruchi lena
to be needed	आवश्यक होना	āvashyak hona
to be surprised	हैरान होना	hairān hona
to be thirsty	प्यास लगाना	pyās lagana
to begin (vt)	शुरू करना	shurū karana

to belong to …	स्वामी होना	svāmī hona
to boast (vi)	डींग मारना	dīng mārana
to break (split into pieces)	तोड़ना	torana
to call (~ for help)	बुलाना	bulāna
can (v aux)	सकना	sakana
to catch (vt)	पकड़ना	pakarana
to change (vt)	बदलना	badalana
to choose (select)	चुनना	chunana
to come down (the stairs)	उतरना	utarana
to compare (vt)	तुलना करना	tulana karana
to complain (vi, vt)	शिकायत करना	shikāyat karana
to confuse (mix up)	गड़बड़ा जाना	garabara jāna
to continue (vt)	जारी रखना	jārī rakhana
to control (vt)	नियंत्रित करना	niyantrit karana
to cook (dinner)	खाना बनाना	khāna banāna
to cost (vt)	दाम होना	dām hona
to count (add up)	गिनना	ginana
to count on …	भरोसा रखना	bharosa rakhana
to create (vt)	बनाना	banāna
to cry (weep)	रोना	rona

11. The most important verbs. Part 2

to deceive (vi, vt)	धोखा देना	dhokha dena
to decorate (tree, street)	सजाना	sajāna
to defend (a country, etc.)	रक्षा करना	raksha karana
to demand (request firmly)	माँगना	māngana
to dig (vt)	खोदना	khodana
to discuss (vt)	चर्चा करना	charcha karana
to do (vt)	करना	karana
to doubt (have doubts)	शक करना	shak karana
to drop (let fall)	गिराना	girāna
to enter	अंदर आना	andar āna
(room, house, etc.)		
to exist (vi)	होना	hona
to expect (foresee)	उम्मीद करना	ummīd karana
to explain (vt)	समझाना	samajhāna
to fall (vi)	गिरना	girana
to find (vt)	ढूढ़ना	dhūrhana
to finish (vt)	खत्म करना	khatm karana
to fly (vi)	उड़ना	urana
to follow … (come after)	पीछे चलना	pīchhe chalana
to forget (vi, vt)	भूलना	bhūlana
to forgive (vt)	क्षमा करना	kshama karana

to give (vt)	देना	dena
to give a hint	इशारा करना	ishāra karana
to go (on foot)	जाना	jāna
to go for a swim	तैरना	tairana
to go out (for dinner, etc.)	बाहर जाना	bāhar jāna
to guess (the answer)	अंदाज़ा लगाना	andāza lagāna
to have (vt)	होना	hona
to have breakfast	नाश्ता करना	nāshta karana
to have dinner	रात्रिभोज करना	rātribhoj karana
to have lunch	दोपहर का भोजन करना	dopahar ka bhojan karana
to hear (vt)	सुनना	sunana
to help (vt)	मदद करना	madad karana
to hide (vt)	छिपाना	chhipāna
to hope (vi, vt)	आशा करना	āsha karana
to hunt (vi, vt)	शिकार करना	shikār karana
to hurry (vi)	जल्दी करना	jaldī karana

12. The most important verbs. Part 3

to inform (vt)	खबर देना	khabar dena
to insist (vi, vt)	आग्रह करना	āgrah karana
to insult (vt)	अपमान करना	apamān karana
to invite (vt)	आमंत्रित करना	āmantrit karana
to joke (vi)	मज़ाक करना	mazāk karana
to keep (vt)	रखना	rakhana
to keep silent	चुप रहना	chup rahana
to kill (vt)	मार डालना	mār dālana
to know (sb)	जानना	jānana
to know (sth)	मालूम होना	mālūm hona
to laugh (vi)	हंसना	hansana
to liberate (city, etc.)	आज़ाद करना	āzād karana
to like (I like ...)	पसंद करना	pasand karana
to look for ... (search)	तलाश करना	talāsh karana
to love (sb)	प्यार करना	pyār karana
to make a mistake	गलती करना	galatī karana
to manage, to run	प्रबंधन करना	prabandhan karana
to mean (signify)	अर्थ होना	arth hona
to mention (talk about)	उल्लेख करना	ullekh karana
to miss (school, etc.)	ग़ैर-हाज़िर होना	gair-hāzir hona
to notice (see)	देखना	dekhana
to object (vi, vt)	एतराज़ करना	etarāz karana
to observe (see)	देखना	dekhana
to open (vt)	खोलना	kholana

to order (meal, etc.)	ऑर्डर करना	ordar karana
to order (mil.)	हुक्म देना	hukm dena
to own (possess)	मालिक होना	mālik hona

to participate (vi)	भाग लेना	bhāg lena
to pay (vi, vt)	दाम चुकाना	dām chukāna
to permit (vt)	अनुमति देना	anumati dena
to plan (vt)	योजना बनाना	yojana banāna
to play (children)	खेलना	khelana

to pray (vi, vt)	दुआ देना	dua dena
to prefer (vt)	तरजीह देना	tarajīh dena
to promise (vt)	वचन देना	vachan dena
to pronounce (vt)	उच्चारण करना	uchchāran karana
to propose (vt)	प्रस्ताव रखना	prastāv rakhana
to punish (vt)	सज़ा देना	saza dena

13. The most important verbs. Part 4

to read (vi, vt)	पढ़ना	parhana
to recommend (vt)	सिफ़ारिश करना	sifārish karana
to refuse (vi, vt)	इन्कार करना	inkār karana
to regret (be sorry)	अफ़सोस जताना	afasos jatāna
to rent (sth from sb)	किराए पर लेना	kirae par lena

to repeat (say again)	दोहराना	doharāna
to reserve, to book	बुक करना	buk karana
to run (vi)	दौड़ना	daurana
to save (rescue)	बचाना	bachāna
to say (~ thank you)	कहना	kahana

to scold (vt)	डाँटना	dāntana
to see (vt)	देखना	dekhana
to sell (vt)	बेचना	bechana
to send (vt)	भेजना	bhejana
to shoot (vi)	गोली चलाना	golī chalāna

to shout (vi)	चिल्लाना	chillāna
to show (vt)	दिखाना	dikhāna
to sign (document)	हस्ताक्षर करना	hastākshar karana
to sit down (vi)	बैठना	baithana

to smile (vi)	मुस्कुराना	muskurāna
to speak (vi, vt)	बोलना	bolana
to steal (money, etc.)	चुराना	churāna
to stop (for pause, etc.)	रुकना	rukana
to stop (please ~ calling me)	बंद करना	band karana
to study (vt)	पढ़ाई करना	parhaī karana
to swim (vi)	तैरना	tairana

to take (vt)	लेना	lena
to think (vi, vt)	सोचना	sochana
to threaten (vt)	धमकाना	dhamakāna
to touch (with hands)	छूना	chhūna
to translate (vt)	अनुवाद करना	anuvād karana
to trust (vt)	यकीन करना	yakīn karana
to try (attempt)	कोशिश करना	koshish karana
to turn (e.g., ~ left)	मुड़ जाना	mur jāna
to underestimate (vt)	कम मूल्यांकन करना	kam mūlyānkan karana
to understand (vt)	समझना	samajhana
to unite (vt)	संयुक्त करना	sanyukt karana
to wait (vt)	इंतज़ार करना	intazār karana
to want (wish, desire)	चाहना	chāhana
to warn (vt)	चेतावनी देना	chetāvanī dena
to work (vi)	काम करना	kām karana
to write (vt)	लिखना	likhana
to write down	लिख लेना	likh lena

14. Colors

color	रंग (m)	rang
shade (tint)	रंग (m)	rang
hue	रंग (m)	rang
rainbow	इन्द्रधनुष (f)	indradhanush
white (adj)	सफ़ेद	safed
black (adj)	काला	kāla
gray (adj)	धूसर	dhūsar
green (adj)	हरा	hara
yellow (adj)	पीला	pīla
red (adj)	लाल	lāl
blue (adj)	नीला	nīla
light blue (adj)	हल्का नीला	halka nīla
pink (adj)	गुलाबी	gulābī
orange (adj)	नारंगी	nārangī
violet (adj)	बैंगनी	bainganī
brown (adj)	भूरा	bhūra
golden (adj)	सुनहरा	sunahara
silvery (adj)	चांदी-जैसा	chāndī-jaisa
beige (adj)	हल्का भूरा	halka bhūra
cream (adj)	क्रीम	krīm
turquoise (adj)	फ़ीरोज़ी	fīrozī
cherry red (adj)	चेरी जैसा लाल	cherī jaisa lāl

| lilac (adj) | हल्का बैंगनी | halka bainganī |
| crimson (adj) | गहरा लाल | gahara lāl |

light (adj)	हल्का	halka
dark (adj)	गहरा	gahara
bright, vivid (adj)	चमकीला	chamakīla

colored (pencils)	रंगीन	rangīn
color (e.g., ~ film)	रंगीन	rangīn
black-and-white (adj)	काला-सफ़ेद	kāla-safed
plain (one-colored)	एक रंग का	ek rang ka
multicolored (adj)	बहुरंगी	bahurangī

15. Questions

Who?	कौन?	kaun?
What?	क्या?	kya?
Where? (at, in)	कहाँ?	kahān?
Where (to)?	किधर?	kidhar?
From where?	कहाँ से?	kahān se?
When?	कब?	kab?
Why? (What for?)	क्यों?	kyon?
Why? (~ are you crying?)	क्यों?	kyon?

What for?	किस लिये?	kis liye?
How? (in what way)	कैसे?	kaise?
What? (What kind of ...?)	कौन-सा?	kaun-sa?
Which?	कौन-सा?	kaun-sa?

To whom?	किसको?	kisako?
About whom?	किसके बारे में?	kisake bāre men?
About what?	किसके बारे में?	kisake bāre men?
With whom?	किसके?	kisake?

| How many? How much? | कितना? | kitana? |
| Whose? | किसका? | kisaka? |

16. Prepositions

with (accompanied by)	के साथ	ke sāth
without	के बिना	ke bina
to (indicating direction)	की तरफ़	kī taraf
about (talking ~ ...)	के बारे में	ke bāre men
before (in time)	के पहले	ke pahale
in front of ...	के सामने	ke sāmane

| under (beneath, below) | के नीचे | ke nīche |
| above (over) | के ऊपर | ke ūpar |

on (atop)	पर	par
from (off, out of)	से	se
of (made from)	से	se
in (e.g., ~ ten minutes)	में	men
over (across the top of)	के ऊपर चढ़कर	ke ūpar charhakar

17. Function words. Adverbs. Part 1

Where? (at, in)	कहाँ?	kahān?
here (adv)	यहाँ	yahān
there (adv)	वहां	vahān
somewhere (to be)	कहीं	kahīn
nowhere (not anywhere)	कहीं नहीं	kahīn nahin
by (near, beside)	के पास	ke pās
by the window	खिड़की के पास	khirakī ke pās
Where (to)?	किधर?	kidhar?
here (e.g., come ~!)	इधर	idhar
there (e.g., to go ~)	उधर	udhar
from here (adv)	यहां से	yahān se
from there (adv)	वहां से	vahān se
close (adv)	पास	pās
far (adv)	दूर	dūr
near (e.g., ~ Paris)	निकट	nikat
nearby (adv)	पास	pās
not far (adv)	दूर नहीं	dūr nahin
left (adj)	बायाँ	bāyān
on the left	बायीं तरफ़	bāyīn taraf
to the left	बायीं तरफ़	bāyīn taraf
right (adj)	दायां	dāyān
on the right	दायीं तरफ़	dāyīn taraf
to the right	दायीं तरफ़	dāyīn taraf
in front (adv)	सामने	sāmane
front (as adj)	सामने का	sāmane ka
ahead (the kids ran ~)	आगे	āge
behind (adv)	पीछे	pīchhe
from behind	पीछे से	pīchhe se
back (towards the rear)	पीछे	pīchhe
middle	बीच (m)	bīch
in the middle	बीच में	bīch men

at the side	कोने में	kone men
everywhere (adv)	सभी	sabhī
around (in all directions)	आस-पास	ās-pās
from inside	अंदर से	andar se
somewhere (to go)	कहीं	kahīn
straight (directly)	सीधे	sīdhe
back (e.g., come ~)	वापस	vāpas
from anywhere	कहीं से भी	kahīn se bhī
from somewhere	कहीं से	kahīn se
firstly (adv)	पहले	pahale
secondly (adv)	दूसरा	dūsara
thirdly (adv)	तीसरा	tīsara
suddenly (adv)	अचानक	achānak
at first (in the beginning)	शुरू में	shurū men
for the first time	पहली बार	pahalī bār
long before ...	बहुत समय पहले ...	bahut samay pahale ...
anew (over again)	नई शुरूआत	naī shurūāt
for good (adv)	हमेशा के लिए	hamesha ke lie
never (adv)	कभी नहीं	kabhī nahin
again (adv)	फिर से	fir se
now (adv)	अब	ab
often (adv)	अकसर	akasar
then (adv)	तब	tab
urgently (quickly)	तत्काल	tatkāl
usually (adv)	आमतौर पर	āmataur par
by the way, ...	प्रसंगवश	prasangavash
possible (that is ~)	मुमकिन	mumakin
probably (adv)	संभव	sambhav
maybe (adv)	शायद	shāyad
besides ...	इस के अलावा	is ke alāva
that's why ...	इस लिए	is lie
in spite of ...	फिर भी ...	fir bhī ...
thanks to ...	... की मेहरबानी से	... kī meharabānī se
what (pron.)	क्या	kya
that (conj.)	कि	ki
something	कुछ	kuchh
anything (something)	कुछ भी	kuchh bhī
nothing	कुछ नहीं	kuchh nahin
who (pron.)	कौन	kaun
someone	कोई	koī
somebody	कोई	koī
nobody	कोई नहीं	koī nahin
nowhere (a voyage to ~)	कहीं नहीं	kahīn nahin

nobody's	किसी का नहीं	kisī ka nahin
somebody's	किसी का	kisī ka
so (I'm ~ glad)	कितना	kitana
also (as well)	भी	bhī
too (as well)	भी	bhī

18. Function words. Adverbs. Part 2

Why?	क्यों?	kyon?
for some reason	किसी कारणवश	kisī kāranavash
because ...	क्यों कि ...	kyon ki ...
for some purpose	किसी वजह से	kisī vajah se
and	और	aur
or	या	ya
but	लेकिन	lekin
for (e.g., ~ me)	के लिए	ke lie
too (~ many people)	ज़्यादा	zyāda
only (exclusively)	सिर्फ़	sirf
exactly (adv)	ठीक	thīk
about (more or less)	करीब	karīb
approximately (adv)	लगभग	lagabhag
approximate (adj)	अनुमानित	anumānit
almost (adv)	करीब	karīb
the rest	बाक़ी	bāqī
each (adj)	हर एक	har ek
any (no matter which)	कोई	koī
many, much (a lot of)	बहुत	bahut
many people	बहुत लोग	bahut log
all (everyone)	सभी	sabhī
in return for ...	... के बदले में	... ke badale men
in exchange (adv)	की जगह	kī jagah
by hand (made)	हाथ से	hāth se
hardly (negative opinion)	शायद ही	shāyad hī
probably (adv)	शायद	shāyad
on purpose (intentionally)	जानबूझकर	jānabūjhakar
by accident (adv)	संयोगवश	sanyogavash
very (adv)	बहुत	bahut
for example (adv)	उदाहरण के लिए	udāharan ke lie
between	के बीच	ke bīch
among	में	men
so much (such a lot)	इतना	itana
especially (adv)	ख़ासतौर पर	khāsataur par

Basic concepts. Part 2

19. Weekdays

Monday	सोमवार (m)	somavār
Tuesday	मंगलवार (m)	mangalavār
Wednesday	बुधवार (m)	budhavār
Thursday	गुरूवार (m)	gurūvār
Friday	शुक्रवार (m)	shukravār
Saturday	शनिवार (m)	shanivār
Sunday	रविवार (m)	ravivār
today (adv)	आज	āj
tomorrow (adv)	कल	kal
the day after tomorrow	परसों	parason
yesterday (adv)	कल	kal
the day before yesterday	परसों	parason
day	दिन (m)	din
working day	कार्यदिवस (m)	kāryadivas
public holiday	सार्वजनिक छुट्टी (f)	sārvajanik chhuttī
day off	छुट्टी का दिन (m)	chhuttī ka din
weekend	सप्ताहांत (m)	saptāhānt
all day long	सारा दिन	sāra din
the next day (adv)	अगला दिन	agala din
two days ago	दो दिन पहले	do din pahale
the day before	एक दिन पहले	ek din pahale
daily (adj)	दैनिक	dainik
every day (adv)	हर दिन	har din
week	हफ़ता (f)	hafata
last week (adv)	पिछले हफ़ते	pichhle hafate
next week (adv)	अगले हफ़ते	agale hafate
weekly (adj)	सप्ताहिक	saptāhik
every week (adv)	हर हफ़ते	har hafate
twice a week	हफ़ते में दो बार	hafate men do bār
every Tuesday	हर मंगलवार को	har mangalavār ko

20. Hours. Day and night

morning	सुबह (m)	subah
in the morning	सुबह में	subah men
noon, midday	दोपहर (m)	dopahar

in the afternoon	दोपहर में	dopahar men
evening	शाम (m)	shām
in the evening	शाम में	shām men
night	रात (f)	rāt
at night	रात में	rāt men
midnight	आधी रात (f)	ādhī rāt

second	सेकन्ड (m)	sekand
minute	मिनट (m)	minat
hour	घंटा (m)	ghanta
half an hour	आधा घंटा	ādha ghanta
a quarter-hour	सवा	sava
fifteen minutes	पंद्रह मीनट	pandrah mīnat
24 hours	24 घंटे (m)	chaubīs ghante

sunrise	सूर्योदय (m)	sūryoday
dawn	सूर्योदय (m)	sūryoday
early morning	प्रातःकाल (m)	prātahkāl
sunset	सूर्यास्त (m)	sūryāst

early in the morning	सुबह-सवेरे	subah-savere
this morning	इस सुबह	is subah
tomorrow morning	कल सुबह	kal subah

this afternoon	आज शाम	āj shām
in the afternoon	दोपहर में	dopahar men
tomorrow afternoon	कल दोपहर	kal dopahar

tonight (this evening)	आज शाम	āj shām
tomorrow night	कल रात	kal rāt

at 3 o'clock sharp	ठीक तीन बजे में	thīk tīn baje men
about 4 o'clock	लगभग चार बजे	lagabhag chār baje
by 12 o'clock	बारह बजे तक	bārah baje tak

in 20 minutes	बीस मीनट में	bīs mīnat men
in an hour	एक घंटे में	ek ghante men
on time (adv)	ठीक समय पर	thīk samay par

a quarter of ...	पौने ... बजे	paune ... baje
within an hour	एक घंटे के अंदर	ek ghante ke andar
every 15 minutes	हर पंद्रह मीनट	har pandrah mīnat
round the clock	दिन-रात (m pl)	din-rāt

21. Months. Seasons

January	जनवरी (m)	janavarī
February	फ़रवरी (m)	faravarī
March	मार्च (m)	mārch
April	अप्रैल (m)	aprail

May	माई (m)	maī
June	जून (m)	jūn
July	जुलाई (m)	julaī
August	अगस्त (m)	agast
September	सितम्बर (m)	sitambar
October	अक्तूबर (m)	aktūbar
November	नवम्बर (m)	navambar
December	दिसम्बर (m)	disambar
spring	वसन्त (m)	vasant
in spring	वसन्त में	vasant men
spring (as adj)	वसन्त	vasant
summer	गरमी (f)	garamī
in summer	गरमियों में	garamiyon men
summer (as adj)	गरमी	garamī
fall	शरद (m)	sharad
in fall	शरद में	sharad men
fall (as adj)	शरद	sharad
winter	सर्दी (f)	sardī
in winter	सर्दियों में	sardiyon men
winter (as adj)	सर्दी	sardī
month	महीना (m)	mahīna
this month	इस महीने	is mahīne
next month	अगले महीने	agale mahīne
last month	पिछले महीने	pichhale mahīne
a month ago	एक महीने पहले	ek mahīne pahale
in a month (a month later)	एक महीने में	ek mahīne men
in 2 months (2 months later)	दो महीने में	do mahīne men
the whole month	पूरे महीने	pūre mahīne
all month long	पूरे महीने	pūre mahīne
monthly (~ magazine)	मासिक	māsik
monthly (adv)	हर महीने	har mahīne
every month	हर महीने	har mahīne
twice a month	महीने में दो बार	mahine men do bār
year	वर्ष (m)	varsh
this year	इस साल	is sāl
next year	अगले साल	agale sāl
last year	पिछले साल	pichhale sāl
a year ago	एक साल पहले	ek sāl pahale
in a year	एक साल में	ek sāl men
in two years	दो साल में	do sāl men
the whole year	पूरा साल	pūra sāl

all year long	पूरा साल	pūra sāl
every year	हर साल	har sāl
annual (adj)	वार्षिक	vārshik
annually (adv)	वार्षिक	vārshik
4 times a year	साल में चार बार	sāl men chār bār

date (e.g., today's ~)	तारीख़ (f)	tārīkh
date (e.g., ~ of birth)	तारीख़ (f)	tārīkh
calendar	कैलेन्डर (m)	kailendar

half a year	आधे वर्ष (m)	ādhe varsh
six months	छमाही (f)	chhamāhī
season (summer, etc.)	मौसम (m)	mausam
century	शताबदी (f)	shatābadī

22. Time. Miscellaneous

time	वक्त (m)	vakt
moment	क्षण (m)	kshan
instant (n)	क्षण (m)	kshan
instant (adj)	तुरंत	turant
lapse (of time)	बीता (m)	bīta
life	जीवन (m)	jīvan
eternity	शाश्वतता (f)	shāshvatata

epoch	युग (f)	yug
era	सम्वत् (f)	samvat
cycle	काल (m)	kāl
period	काल (m)	kāl
term (short-~)	समय (m)	samay

the future	भविष्य (m)	bhavishy
future (as adj)	आगामी	āgāmī
next time	अगली बार	agalī bār
the past	भूतकाल (m)	bhūtakāl
past (recent)	पिछला	pichhala
last time	पिछली बार	pichhalī bār

later (adv)	बाद में	bād men
after (prep.)	के बाद	ke bād
nowadays (adv)	आजकाल	ājakāl
now (adv)	अभी	abhī
immediately (adv)	तुरंत	turant
soon (adv)	थोड़ी ही देर में	thorī hī der men
in advance (beforehand)	पहले से	pahale se

a long time ago	बहुत समय पहले	bahut samay pahale
recently (adv)	हाल ही में	hāl hī men
destiny	भाग्य (f)	bhāgy
memories (childhood ~)	यादगार (f)	yādagār

archives	पुरालेखागार (m)	purālekhāgār
during …	… के दौरान	… ke daurān
long, a long time (adv)	ज़्यादा समय	zyāda samay
not long (adv)	ज़्यादा समय नहीं	zyāda samay nahin
early (in the morning)	जल्दी	jaldī
late (not early)	देर	der

forever (for good)	सदा के लिए	sada ke lie
to start (begin)	शुरू करना	shurū karana
to postpone (vt)	स्थगित करना	sthagit karana

at the same time	एक ही समय पर	ek hī samay par
permanently (adv)	स्थायी रूप से	sthāyī rūp se
constant (noise, pain)	लगातार	lagātār
temporary (adj)	अस्थायी रूप से	asthāyī rūp se

sometimes (adv)	कभी-कभी	kabhī-kabhī
rarely (adv)	शायद ही	shāyad hī
often (adv)	अक्सर	aksar

23. Opposites

| rich (adj) | अमीर | amīr |
| poor (adj) | ग़रीब | garīb |

| ill, sick (adj) | बीमार | bīmār |
| well (not sick) | तंदरुस्त | tandarūst |

| big (adj) | बड़ा | bara |
| small (adj) | छोटा | chhota |

| quickly (adv) | जल्दी से | jaldī se |
| slowly (adv) | धीरे | dhīre |

| fast (adj) | तेज़ | tez |
| slow (adj) | धीमा | dhīma |

| glad (adj) | हँसमुख | hansamukh |
| sad (adj) | उदास | udās |

| together (adv) | साथ-साथ | sāth-sāth |
| separately (adv) | अलग-अलग | alag-alag |

| aloud (to read) | बोलकर | bolakar |
| silently (to oneself) | मन ही मन | man hī man |

tall (adj)	लंबा	lamba
low (adj)	नीचा	nīcha
deep (adj)	गहरा	gahara
shallow (adj)	छिछला	chhichhala

yes	हाँ	hān
no	नहीं	nahin
distant (in space)	दूर	dūr
nearby (adj)	निकट	nikat
far (adv)	दूर	dūr
nearby (adv)	पास	pās
long (adj)	लंबा	lamba
short (adj)	छोटा	chhota
good (kindhearted)	नेक	nek
evil (adj)	दुष्ट	dusht
married (adj)	शादीशुदा	shādīshuda
single (adj)	अविवाहित	avivāhit
to forbid (vt)	प्रतिबंधित करना	pratibandhit karana
to permit (vt)	अनुमति देना	anumati dena
end	अंत (m)	ant
beginning	शुरू (m)	shurū
left (adj)	बायाँ	bāyān
right (adj)	दायां	dāyān
first (adj)	पहला	pahala
last (adj)	आखिरी	ākhirī
crime	जुर्म (m)	jurm
punishment	सज़ा (f)	saza
to order (vt)	हुक्म देना	hukm dena
to obey (vi, vt)	मानना	mānana
straight (adj)	सीधा	sīdha
curved (adj)	टेढ़ा	terha
paradise	जन्नत (m)	jannat
hell	नरक (m)	narak
to be born	जन्म होना	janm hona
to die (vi)	मरना	marana
strong (adj)	शक्तिशाली	shaktishālī
weak (adj)	कमज़ोर	kamazor
old (adj)	बूढ़ा	būrha
young (adj)	जवान	javān
old (adj)	पुराना	purāna
new (adj)	नया	naya

hard (adj)	कठोर	kathor
soft (adj)	नरम	naram
warm (tepid)	गरम	garam
cold (adj)	ठंडा	thanda
fat (adj)	मोटा	mota
thin (adj)	दुबला	dubala
narrow (adj)	तंग	tang
wide (adj)	चौड़ा	chaura
good (adj)	अच्छा	achchha
bad (adj)	बुरा	bura
brave (adj)	बहादुर	bahādur
cowardly (adj)	कायर	kāyar

24. Lines and shapes

square	चतुष्कोण (m)	chatushkon
square (as adj)	चौकोना	chaukona
circle	घेरा (m)	ghera
round (adj)	गोलाकार	golākār
triangle	त्रिकोण (m)	trikon
triangular (adj)	त्रिकोना	trikona
oval	ओवल (m)	oval
oval (as adj)	ओवल	oval
rectangle	आयत (m)	āyat
rectangular (adj)	आयताकार	āyatākār
pyramid	शुंडाकार स्तंभ (m)	shundākār stambh
rhombus	रोम्बस (m)	rombas
trapezoid	विषम चतुर्भुज (m)	visham chaturbhuj
cube	घनक्षेत्र (m)	ghanakshetr
prism	क्रकच आयत (m)	krakach āyat
circumference	परिधि (f)	paridhi
sphere	गोला (m)	gola
ball (solid sphere)	गोला (m)	gola
diameter	व्यास (m)	vyās
radius	व्यासार्ध (m)	vyāsārdh
perimeter (circle's ~)	परिणिति (f)	pariniti
center	केन्द्र (m)	kendr
horizontal (adj)	क्षैतिज	kshaitij
vertical (adj)	ऊर्ध्व	ūrdhv
parallel (n)	समांतर-रेखा (f)	samāntar-rekha
parallel (as adj)	समानान्तर	samānāntar

line	रेखा (f)	rekha
stroke	लकीर (f)	lakīr
straight line	सीधी रेखा (f)	sīdhī rekha
curve (curved line)	टेढ़ी रेखा (f)	terhī rekha
thin (line, etc.)	पतली	patalī
contour (outline)	परिरेखा (f)	parirekha

intersection	प्रतिच्छेदन (f)	pratichchhedan
right angle	समकोण (m)	samakon
segment	खंड (m)	khand
sector	क्षेत्र (m)	kshetr
side (of triangle)	साइड (m)	said
angle	कोण (m)	kon

25. Units of measurement

weight	वज़न (m)	vazan
length	लम्बाई (f)	lambaī
width	चौड़ाई (f)	chauraī
height	ऊंचाई (f)	ūnchaī
depth	गहराई (f)	gaharaī
volume	घनत्व (f)	ghanatv
area	क्षेत्रफल (m)	kshetrafal

gram	ग्राम (m)	grām
milligram	मिलीग्राम (m)	milīgrām
kilogram	किलोग्राम (m)	kilogrām
ton	टन (m)	tan
pound	पौण्ड (m)	paund
ounce	औन्स (m)	auns

meter	मीटर (m)	mītar
millimeter	मिलीमीटर (m)	milīmītar
centimeter	सेंटीमीटर (m)	sentīmītar
kilometer	किलोमीटर (m)	kilomītar
mile	मील (m)	mīl

inch	इंच (m)	inch
foot	फुट (m)	fut
yard	गज (m)	gaj

square meter	वर्ग मीटर (m)	varg mītar
hectare	हेक्टेयर (m)	hekteyar

liter	लीटर (m)	lītar
degree	डिग्री (m)	digrī
volt	वोल्ट (m)	volt
ampere	ऐम्पेयर (m)	aimpeyar
horsepower	अश्व शक्ति (f)	ashv shakti
quantity	मात्रा (f)	mātra

a little bit of ...	कुछ ...	kuchh ...
half	आधा (m)	ādha
dozen	दर्जन (m)	darjan
piece (item)	टुकड़ा (m)	tukara
size	माप (m)	māp
scale (map ~)	पैमाना (m)	paimāna
minimal (adj)	न्यूनतम	nyūnatam
the smallest (adj)	सब से छोटा	sab se chhota
medium (adj)	मध्य	madhy
maximal (adj)	अधिकतम	adhikatam
the largest (adj)	सबसे बड़ा	sabase bara

26. Containers

canning jar (glass ~)	शीशी (f)	shīshī
can	डिब्बा (m)	dibba
bucket	बाल्टी (f)	bāltī
barrel	पीपा (m)	pīpa
wash basin (e.g., plastic ~)	चिलमची (f)	chilamachī
tank (100L water ~)	कुण्ड (m)	kund
hip flask	फ्लास्क (m)	flāsk
jerrycan	जेरिकैन (m)	jerikain
tank (e.g., tank car)	टंकी (f)	tankī
mug	मग (m)	mag
cup (of coffee, etc.)	प्याली (f)	pyālī
saucer	सॉसर (m)	sosar
glass (tumbler)	गिलास (m)	gilās
wine glass	वाइन गिलास (m)	vain gilās
stock pot (soup pot)	सॉसपैन (m)	sosapain
bottle (~ of wine)	बोतल (f)	botal
neck (of the bottle, etc.)	गला (m)	gala
carafe (decanter)	जग (m)	jag
pitcher	सुराही (f)	surāhī
vessel (container)	बरतन (m)	baratan
pot (crock, stoneware ~)	घड़ा (m)	ghara
vase	फूलदान (m)	fūladān
bottle (perfume ~)	शीशी (f)	shīshī
vial, small bottle	शीशी (f)	shīshī
tube (of toothpaste)	ट्यूब (m)	tyūb
sack (bag)	थैला (m)	thaila
bag (paper ~, plastic ~)	थैली (f)	thailī
pack (of cigarettes, etc.)	पैकेट (f)	paiket

box (e.g., shoebox)	डिब्बा (m)	dibba
crate	डिब्बा (m)	dibba
basket	टोकरी (f)	tokarī

27. Materials

material	सामग्री (f)	sāmagrī
wood (n)	लकड़ी (f)	lakarī
wood-, wooden (adj)	लकड़ी का बना	lakarī ka bana
glass (n)	कांच (f)	kānch
glass (as adj)	काँच का	kānch ka
stone (n)	पत्थर (m)	patthar
stone (as adj)	पत्थर का	patthar ka
plastic (n)	प्लास्टिक (m)	plāstik
plastic (as adj)	प्लास्टिक का	plāstik ka
rubber (n)	रबड़ (f)	rabar
rubber (as adj)	रबड़ का	rabar ka
cloth, fabric (n)	कपड़ा (m)	kapara
fabric (as adj)	कपड़े का	kapare ka
paper (n)	काग़ज़ (m)	kāgaz
paper (as adj)	काग़ज़ का	kāgaz ka
cardboard (n)	दफ़ती (f)	dafatī
cardboard (as adj)	दफ़ती का	dafatī ka
polyethylene	पॉलीएथीलीन (m)	polīethīlīn
cellophane	सेल्लोफ़ेन (m)	sellofen
plywood	प्लाईवुड (m)	plaīvud
porcelain (n)	चीनी मिट्टी (f)	chīnī mittī
porcelain (as adj)	चीनी मिट्टी का	chīnī mittī ka
clay (n)	मिट्टी (f)	mittī
clay (as adj)	मिट्टी का	mittī ka
ceramic (n)	चीनी मिट्टी (f)	chīnī mittī
ceramic (as adj)	चीनी मिट्टी का	chīnī mittī ka

28. Metals

metal (n)	धातु (m)	dhātu
metal (as adj)	धात्वीय	dhātvīy
alloy (n)	मिश्रधातु (m)	mishradhātu
gold (n)	सोना (m)	sona

gold, golden (adj)	सोना	sona
silver (n)	चाँदी (f)	chāndī
silver (as adj)	चाँदी का	chāndī ka
iron (n)	लोहा (m)	loha
iron-, made of iron (adj)	लोहे का बना	lohe ka bana
steel (n)	इस्पात (f)	ispāt
steel (as adj)	इस्पात का	ispāt ka
copper (n)	ताँबा (f)	tānba
copper (as adj)	ताँबे का	tānbe ka
aluminum (n)	अल्यूमीनियम (m)	alyumīniyam
aluminum (as adj)	अलुमीनियम का बना	alumīniyam ka bana
bronze (n)	काँसा (f)	kānsa
bronze (as adj)	काँसे का	kānse ka
brass	पीतल (f)	pītal
nickel	निकल (m)	nikal
platinum	प्लैटिनम (m)	plaitinam
mercury	पारा (f)	pāra
tin	टिन (m)	tin
lead	सीसा (f)	sīsa
zinc	जस्ता (m)	jasta

HUMAN BEING

Human being. The body

29. Humans. Basic concepts

human being	मनुष्य (m)	munashy
man (adult male)	आदमी (m)	ādamī
woman	औरत (f)	aurat
child	बच्चा (m)	bachcha
girl	लड़की (f)	larakī
boy	लड़का (m)	laraka
teenager	किशोर (m)	kishor
old man	बूढ़ा (m)	būrha
old woman	बूढ़िया (f)	būrhiya

30. Human anatomy

organism (body)	शरीर (m)	sharīr
heart	दिल (m)	dil
blood	खून (f)	khūn
artery	धमनी (f)	dhamanī
vein	नस (f)	nas
brain	मास्तिष्क (m)	māstishk
nerve	नस (f)	nas
nerves	नसें (f)	nasen
vertebra	कशेरुका (m)	kasheruka
spine (backbone)	रीढ़ की हड्डी	rīrh kī haddī
stomach (organ)	पेट (m)	pet
intestines, bowels	आँतें (f)	ānten
intestine (e.g., large ~)	आँत (f)	ānt
liver	जिगर (f)	jigar
kidney	गुर्दा (f)	gurda
bone	हड्डी (f)	haddī
skeleton	कंकाल (m)	kankāl
rib	पसली (f)	pasalī
skull	खोपड़ी (f)	khoparī
muscle	मांसपेशी (f)	mānsapeshī
biceps	बाइसेप्स (m)	baiseps

triceps	ट्राईसेप्स (m)	traĩseps
tendon	कंडरा (m)	kandara
joint	जोड़ (m)	jor
lungs	फेफड़े (m pl)	fefare
genitals	गुप्तांग (m)	guptāng
skin	त्वचा (f)	tvacha

31. Head

head	सिर (m)	sir
face	चेहरा (m)	chehara
nose	नाक (f)	nāk
mouth	मुँह (m)	munh

eye	आँख (f)	ānkh
eyes	आँखें (f)	ānkhen
pupil	आँख की पुतली (f)	ānkh kī putalī
eyebrow	भौंह (f)	bhaunh
eyelash	बरौनी (f)	baraunī
eyelid	पलक (m)	palak

tongue	जीभ (m)	jībh
tooth	दाँत (f)	dānt
lips	होठ (m)	honth
cheekbones	गाल की हड्डी (f)	gāl kī haddī
gum	मसूड़ा (m)	masūra
palate	तालु (m)	tālu

nostrils	नथने (m pl)	nathane
chin	ठोड़ी (f)	thorī
jaw	जबड़ा (m)	jabara
cheek	गाल (m)	gāl

forehead	माथा (m)	mātha
temple	कनपट्टी (f)	kanapattī
ear	कान (m)	kān
back of the head	सिर का पिछला हिस्सा (m)	sir ka pichhala hissa
neck	गरदन (m)	garadan
throat	गला (m)	gala

hair	बाल (m pl)	bāl
hairstyle	हेयरस्टाइल (m)	heyarastail
haircut	हेयरकट (m)	heyarakat
wig	नकली बाल (m)	nakalī bāl

mustache	मूँछें (f pl)	mūnchhen
beard	दाढ़ी (f)	dārhī
to have (a beard, etc.)	होना	hona
braid	चोटी (f)	chotī
sideburns	गलमुच्छा (m)	galamuchcha

red-haired (adj)	लाल बाल	lāl bāl
gray (hair)	सफ़ेद बाल	safed bāl
bald (adj)	गंजा	ganja
bald patch	गंजाई (f)	ganjaī

| ponytail | पोनी-टेल (f) | ponī-tel |
| bangs | बेंग (m) | beng |

32. Human body

| hand | हाथ (m) | hāth |
| arm | बाँह (m) | bānh |

finger	उँगली (m)	ungalī
thumb	अँगूठा (m)	angūtha
little finger	छोटी उंगली (f)	chhotī ungalī
nail	नाखून (m)	nākhūn

fist	मुट्ठी (m)	mutthī
palm	हथेली (f)	hathelī
wrist	कलाई (f)	kalaī
forearm	प्रकोष्ठ (m)	prakoshth
elbow	कोहनी (f)	kohanī
shoulder	कंधा (m)	kandha

leg	टाँग (f)	tāng
foot	पैर का तलवा (m)	pair ka talava
knee	घुटना (m)	ghutana
calf (part of leg)	पिंडली (f)	pindalī
hip	जाँघ (f)	jāngh
heel	एड़ी (f)	erī

body	शरीर (m)	sharīr
stomach	पेट (m)	pet
chest	सीना (m)	sīna
breast	स्तन (f)	stan
flank	कूल्हा (m)	kūlha
back	पीठ (f)	pīth
lower back	पीठ का निचला हिस्सा (m)	pīth ka nichala hissa
waist	कमर (f)	kamar

navel (belly button)	नाभी (f)	nābhī
buttocks	नितंब (m pl)	nitamb
bottom	नितम्ब (m)	nitamb

beauty mark	सौंदर्य चिन्ह (f)	saundary chinh
birthmark	जन्म चिह्न (m)	janm chihn
(café au lait spot)		

| tattoo | टैटू (m) | taitū |
| scar | घाव का निशान (m) | ghāv ka nishān |

Clothing & Accessories

33. Outerwear. Coats

clothes	कपड़े (m)	kapare
outerwear	बाहरी पोशाक (m)	bāharī poshāk
winter clothing	सर्दियों की पोशक (f)	sardiyon kī poshak
coat (overcoat)	ओवरकोट (m)	ovarakot
fur coat	फरकोट (m)	farakot
fur jacket	फ़र की जैकेट (f)	far kī jaiket
down coat	फ़ेदर कोट (m)	fedar kot
jacket (e.g., leather ~)	जैकेट (f)	jaiket
raincoat (trenchcoat, etc.)	बरसाती (f)	barasātī
waterproof (adj)	जलरोधक	jalarodhak

34. Men's & women's clothing

shirt (button shirt)	कमीज़ (f)	kamīz
pants	पैंट (m)	paint
jeans	जीन्स (m)	jīns
suit jacket	कोट (m)	kot
suit	सूट (m)	sūt
dress (frock)	फ़्रॉक (f)	frok
skirt	स्कर्ट (f)	skart
blouse	ब्लाउज़ (f)	blauz
knitted jacket (cardigan, etc.)	कार्डिगन (f)	kārdigan
jacket (of woman's suit)	जैकेट (f)	jaiket
T-shirt	टी-शर्ट (f)	tī-shart
shorts (short trousers)	शोट्र्स (m pl)	shorts
tracksuit	ट्रैक सूट (m)	traik sūt
bathrobe	बाथ रोब (m)	bāth rob
pajamas	पजामा (m)	pajāma
sweater	सूटर (m)	sūtar
pullover	पुलोवर (m)	pulovar
vest	बण्डी (m)	bandī
tailcoat	टेल-कोट (m)	tel-kot
tuxedo	डिनर-जैकेट (f)	dinar-jaiket

uniform	वर्दी (f)	vardī
workwear	वर्दी (f)	vardī
overalls	ओवरऑल्स (m)	ovarols
coat (e.g., doctor's smock)	कोट (m)	kot

35. Clothing. Underwear

underwear	अंगवस्त्र (m)	angavastr
undershirt (A-shirt)	बनियान (f)	baniyān
socks	मोज़े (m pl)	moze
nightgown	नाइट गाउन (m)	nait gaun
bra	ब्रा (f)	bra
knee highs (knee-high socks)	घुटनों तक के मोज़े (m)	ghutanon tak ke moze
pantyhose	टाइट्स (m pl)	taits
stockings (thigh highs)	स्टॉकिंग (m pl)	stāking
bathing suit	स्विम सूट (m)	svim sūt

36. Headwear

hat	टोपी (f)	topī
fedora	हैट (f)	hait
baseball cap	बैस्बॉल कैप (f)	baisbol kaip
flatcap	फ़्लैट कैप (f)	flait kaip
beret	बेरेट (m)	beret
hood	हुड (m)	hūd
panama hat	पनामा हैट (m)	panāma hait
knit cap (knitted hat)	बुनी हुई टोपी (f)	bunī huī topī
headscarf	सिर का स्कार्फ़ (m)	sir ka skārf
women's hat	महिलाओं की टोपी (f)	mahilaon kī topī
hard hat	हेलमेट (f)	helamet
garrison cap	पुलिसीया टोपी (f)	pulisīya topī
helmet	हेलमेट (f)	helamet
derby	बॉलर हैट (m)	bolar hait
top hat	टॉप हैट (m)	top hait

37. Footwear

footwear	पनही (f)	panahī
shoes (men's shoes)	जूते (m pl)	jūte
shoes (women's shoes)	जूते (m pl)	jūte

boots (e.g., cowboy ~)	बूट (m pl)	būt
slippers	चप्पल (f pl)	chappal
tennis shoes (e.g., Nike ~)	टेनिस के जूते (m)	tenis ke jūte
sneakers (e.g., Converse ~)	स्नीकर्स (m)	snīkars
sandals	सैन्डल (f)	saindal
cobbler (shoe repairer)	मोची (m)	mochī
heel	एड़ी (f)	erī
pair (of shoes)	जोड़ा (m)	jora
shoestring	जूते का फ़ीता (m)	jūte ka fīta
to lace (vt)	फ़ीता बाँधना	fīta bāndhana
shoehorn	शू-होर्न (m)	shū-horn
shoe polish	बूट-पालिश (m)	būt-pālish

38. Textile. Fabrics

cotton (n)	कपास (m)	kapās
cotton (as adj)	सूती	sūtī
flax (n)	प्लैक्स (m)	flaiks
flax (as adj)	प्लैक्स का	flaiks ka
silk (n)	रेशम (f)	resham
silk (as adj)	रेशमी	reshamī
wool (n)	ऊन (m)	ūn
wool (as adj)	ऊनी	ūnī
velvet	मख़मल (m)	makhamal
suede	स्वैड (m)	svaid
corduroy	कॉरडरॉय (m)	koradaroy
nylon (n)	नायलॉन (m)	nāyalon
nylon (as adj)	नायलॉन का	nāyalon ka
polyester (n)	पॉलिएस्टर (m)	poliestar
polyester (as adj)	पॉलिएस्टर का	poliestar ka
leather (n)	चमड़ा (m)	chamara
leather (as adj)	चमड़े का	chamare ka
fur (n)	फ़र (m)	far
fur (e.g., ~ coat)	फ़र का	far ka

39. Personal accessories

gloves	दस्ताने (m pl)	dastāne
mittens	दस्ताने (m pl)	dastāne
scarf (muffler)	मफ़लर (m)	mafalar

glasses (eyeglasses)	ऐनक (m pl)	ainak
frame (eyeglass ~)	चश्मे का फ्रेम (m)	chashme ka frem
umbrella	छतरी (f)	chhatarī
walking stick	छड़ी (f)	chharī
hairbrush	ब्रश (m)	brash
fan	पंखा (m)	pankha

tie (necktie)	टाई (f)	taī
bow tie	बो टाई (f)	bo taī
suspenders	पतलून बाँधने का फ़ीता (m)	patalūn bāndhane ka fīta
handkerchief	रूमाल (m)	rūmāl

comb	कंघा (m)	kangha
barrette	बालपिन (f)	bālapin
hairpin	हेयरक्लीप (f)	heyaraklīp
buckle	बकसुआ (m)	bakasua

| belt | बेल्ट (m) | belt |
| shoulder strap | कंधे का पट्टा (m) | kandhe ka patta |

bag (handbag)	बैग (m)	baig
purse	पर्स (m)	pars
backpack	बैकपैक (m)	baikapaik

40. Clothing. Miscellaneous

fashion	फ़ैशन (m)	faishan
in vogue (adj)	प्रचलन में	prachalan men
fashion designer	फ़ैशन डिज़ाइनर (m)	faishan dizainar

collar	कॉलर (m)	kolar
pocket	जेब (m)	jeb
pocket (as adj)	जेब	jeb
sleeve	आस्तीन (f)	āstīn
hanging loop	हैंगिंग लूप (f)	hainging lūp
fly (on trousers)	ज़िप (f)	zip

zipper (fastener)	ज़िप (f)	zip
fastener	हुक (m)	huk
button	बटन (m)	batan
buttonhole	बटन का काज (m)	batan ka kāj
to come off (ab. button)	निकल जाना	nikal jāna

to sew (vi, vt)	सीना	sīna
to embroider (vi, vt)	काढ़ना	kārhana
embroidery	कढ़ाई (f)	karhaī
sewing needle	सूई (f)	sūī
thread	धागा (m)	dhāga
seam	सीवन (m)	sīvan
to get dirty (vi)	मैला होना	maila hona

stain (mark, spot)	धब्बा (m)	dhabba
to crease, crumple (vi)	शिकन पड़ जाना	shikan par jāna
to tear, to rip (vt)	फट जाना	fat jāna
clothes moth	कपड़ों के कीड़े (m)	kaparon ke kīre

41. Personal care. Cosmetics

toothpaste	टूथपेस्ट (m)	tūthapest
toothbrush	टूथब्रश (m)	tūthabrash
to brush one's teeth	दाँत साफ़ करना	dānt sāf karana
razor	रेज़र (f)	rezar
shaving cream	हजामत का क्रीम (m)	hajāmat ka krīm
to shave (vi)	शेव करना	shev karana
soap	साबुन (m)	sābun
shampoo	शैम्पू (m)	shaimpū
scissors	कैंची (f pl)	kainchī
nail file	नाख़ून घिसनी (f)	nākhūn ghisanī
nail clippers	नाख़ून कतरनी (f)	nākhūn kataranī
tweezers	ट्वीज़र्स (f)	tvīzars
cosmetics	श्रृंगार-सामग्री (f)	shrrngār-sāmagrī
face mask	चेहरे का लेप (m)	chehare ka lep
manicure	मैनीक्योर (m)	mainīkyor
to have a manicure	मैनीक्योर करवाना	mainīkyor karavāna
pedicure	पेडिक्यूर (m)	pedikyūr
make-up bag	श्रृंगार थैली (f)	shrrngār thailī
face powder	पाउडर (m)	paudar
powder compact	कॉम्पैक्ट पाउडर (m)	kompaikt paudar
blusher	ब्लशर (m)	blashar
perfume (bottled)	ख़ुशबू (f)	khushabū
toilet water (lotion)	टॉयलेट वॉटर (m)	tāyalet votar
lotion	लोशन (m)	loshan
cologne	कोलोन (m)	kolon
eyeshadow	आई-शैडो (m)	āī-shaido
eyeliner	आई-पेंसिल (f)	āī-pensil
mascara	मस्कारा (m)	maskāra
lipstick	लिपस्टिक (m)	lipastik
nail polish, enamel	नेल पॉलिश (f)	nel polish
hair spray	हेयर स्प्रे (m)	heyar spre
deodorant	डिओडरेन्ट (m)	diodarent
cream	क्रीम (m)	krīm
face cream	चेहरे की क्रीम (f)	chehare kī krīm

hand cream	हाथ की क्रीम (f)	hāth kī krīm
anti-wrinkle cream	एंटी रिंकल क्रीम (f)	entī rinkal krīm
day (as adj)	दिन का	din ka
night (as adj)	रात का	rāt ka

tampon	टैम्पन (m)	taimpan
toilet paper (toilet roll)	टॉयलेट पेपर (m)	toyalet pepar
hair dryer	हेयर ड्रायर (m)	heyar drāyar

42. Jewelry

jewelry	ज़ेवर (m pl)	zevar
precious (e.g., ~ stone)	बहुमूल्य	bahumūly
hallmark stamp	छाप (m)	chhāp

ring	अंगूठी (f)	angūthī
wedding ring	शादी की अंगूठी (f)	shādī kī angūthī
bracelet	चूड़ी (m)	chūrī

earrings	कान की रिंग (f)	kān kī ring
necklace (~ of pearls)	माला (f)	māla
crown	ताज (m)	tāj
bead necklace	मोती की माला (f)	motī kī māla

diamond	हीरा (m)	hīra
emerald	पन्ना (m)	panna
ruby	माणिक (m)	mānik
sapphire	नीलम (m)	nīlam
pearl	मुक्ताफल (m)	muktāfal
amber	ऐम्बर (m)	embar

43. Watches. Clocks

watch (wristwatch)	घड़ी (f pl)	gharī
dial	डायल (m)	dāyal
hand (of clock, watch)	सुई (f)	suī
metal watch band	धातु से बनी घड़ी का पट्टा (m)	dhātu se banī gharī ka patta
watch strap	घड़ी का पट्टा (m)	gharī ka patta

battery	बैटेरी (f)	baiterī
to be dead (battery)	ख़त्म हो जाना	khatm ho jāna
to change a battery	बैटेरी बदलना	baiterī badalana
to run fast	तेज़ चलना	tez chalana
to run slow	धीमी चलना	dhīmī chalana

| wall clock | दीवार-घड़ी (f pl) | dīvār-gharī |
| hourglass | रेत-घड़ी (f pl) | ret-gharī |

sundial	सूरज-घड़ी (f pl)	sūraj-gharī
alarm clock	अलार्म घड़ी (f)	alārm gharī
watchmaker	घड़ीसाज़ (m)	gharīsāz
to repair (vt)	मरम्मत करना	marammat karana

Food. Nutricion

44. Food

meat	गोश्त (m)	gosht
chicken	चीकन (m)	chīkan
Rock Cornish hen (poussin)	रॉक कोर्निश मुर्गी (f)	rok kornish murgī
duck	बत्तख़ (f)	battakh
goose	हंस (m)	hans
game	शिकार के पशुपक्षी (f)	shikār ke pashupakshī
turkey	टर्की (m)	tarkī
pork	सुअर का गोश्त (m)	suar ka gosht
veal	बछड़े का गोश्त (m)	bachhare ka gosht
lamb	भेड़ का गोश्त (m)	bher ka gosht
beef	गाय का गोश्त (m)	gāy ka gosht
rabbit	खरगोश (m)	kharagosh
sausage (bologna, pepperoni, etc.)	सॉसेज (f)	sosej
vienna sausage (frankfurter)	वियना सॉसेज (m)	viyana sosej
bacon	बेकन (m)	bekan
ham	हैम (m)	haim
gammon	सुअर की जांघ (f)	suar kī jāngh
pâté	पिसा हुआ गोश्त (m)	pisa hua gosht
liver	जिगर (f)	jigar
hamburger (ground beef)	कीमा (m)	kīma
tongue	जीभ (m)	jībh
egg	अंडा (m)	anda
eggs	अंडे (m pl)	ande
egg white	अंडे की सफ़ेदी (m)	ande kī safedī
egg yolk	अंडे की ज़र्दी (m)	ande kī zardī
fish	मछली (f)	machhalī
seafood	समुद्री खाना (m)	samudrī khāna
caviar	मछली के अंडे (m)	machhalī ke ande
crab	केकड़ा (m)	kekara
shrimp	चिंगड़ा (m)	chingara
oyster	सीप (m)	sīp
spiny lobster	लोबस्टर (m)	lobastar
octopus	ओक्टोपस (m)	oktopas

squid	स्कीड (m)	skīd
sturgeon	स्टर्जन (f)	starjan
salmon	सालमन (m)	sālaman
halibut	हैलिबट (f)	hailibat
cod	कॉड (f)	kod
mackerel	माक्रैल (f)	mākrail
tuna	टूना (f)	tūna
eel	बाम मछली (f)	bām machhalī
trout	ट्राउट मछली (f)	traut machhalī
sardine	सार्डीन (f)	sārdīn
pike	पाइक (f)	paik
herring	हेरिंग मछली (f)	hering machhalī
bread	ब्रेड (f)	bred
cheese	पनीर (m)	panīr
sugar	चीनी (f)	chīnī
salt	नमक (m)	namak
rice	चावल (m)	chāval
pasta (macaroni)	पास्ता (m)	pāsta
noodles	नूडल्स (m)	nūdals
butter	मक्खन (m)	makkhan
vegetable oil	तेल (m)	tel
sunflower oil	सूरजमुखी तेल (m)	sūrajamukhī tel
margarine	नकली मक्खन (m)	nakalī makkhan
olives	जैतून (m)	jaitūn
olive oil	जैतून का तेल (m)	jaitūn ka tel
milk	दूध (m)	dūdh
condensed milk	रबड़ी (f)	rabarī
yogurt	दही (m)	dahī
sour cream	खट्टी क्रीम (f)	khattī krīm
cream (of milk)	मलाई (f pl)	malaī
mayonnaise	मेयोनेज़ (m)	meyonez
buttercream	क्रीम (m)	krīm
cereal grains (wheat, etc.)	अनाज के दाने (m)	anāj ke dāne
flour	आटा (m)	āta
canned food	डिब्बाबन्द खाना (m)	dibbāband khāna
cornflakes	कॉर्नफ्लेक्स (m)	kornafleks
honey	शहद (m)	shahad
jam	जैम (m)	jaim
chewing gum	चूइन्ग गम (m)	chūing gam

45. Drinks

water	पानी (m)	pānī
drinking water	पीने का पानी (f)	pīne ka pānī
mineral water	मिनरल वॉटर (m)	minaral votar
still (adj)	स्टिल वॉटर	stil votar
carbonated (adj)	कार्बोनेटेड	kārboneted
sparkling (adj)	स्पार्कलिंग	spārkaling
ice	बर्फ़ (m)	barf
with ice	बर्फ़ के साथ	barf ke sāth
non-alcoholic (adj)	शराब रहित	sharāb rahit
soft drink	कोल्ड ड्रिंक (f)	kold drink
refreshing drink	शीतलक ड्रिंक (f)	shītalak drink
lemonade	लेमोनेड (m)	lemoned
liquors	शराब (m pl)	sharāb
wine	वाइन (f)	vain
white wine	सफ़ेद वाइन (f)	safed vain
red wine	लाल वाइन (f)	lāl vain
liqueur	लिकर (m)	likar
champagne	शैम्पेन (f)	shaimpen
vermouth	वर्माउथ (f)	varmauth
whiskey	विस्की (f)	viskī
vodka	वोडका (m)	vodaka
gin	जिन (f)	jin
cognac	कोन्याक (m)	konyāk
rum	रम (m)	ram
coffee	कॉफ़ी (f)	kofī
black coffee	काली कॉफ़ी (f)	kālī kofī
coffee with milk	दूध के साथ कॉफ़ी (f)	dūdh ke sāth kofī
cappuccino	कैपूचिनो (f)	kaipūchino
instant coffee	इन्सटेन्ट-काफ़ी (f)	insatent-kāfī
milk	दूध (m)	dūdh
cocktail	कॉकटेल (m)	kokatel
milkshake	मिल्कशेक (m)	milkashek
juice	रस (m)	ras
tomato juice	टमाटर का रस (m)	tamātar ka ras
orange juice	संतरे का रस (m)	santare ka ras
freshly squeezed juice	ताज़ा रस (m)	tāza ras
beer	बियर (m)	biyar
light beer	हल्का बियर (m)	halka biyar
dark beer	डार्क बियर (m)	dārk biyar
tea	चाय (f)	chāy

| black tea | काली चाय (f) | kālī chāy |
| green tea | हरी चाय (f) | harī chāy |

46. Vegetables

| vegetables | सब्जियाँ (f pl) | sabziyān |
| greens | हरी सब्जियाँ (f) | harī sabziyān |

tomato	टमाटर (m)	tamātar
cucumber	खीरा (m)	khīra
carrot	गाजर (f)	gājar
potato	आलू (m)	ālū
onion	प्याज़ (m)	pyāz
garlic	लहसुन (m)	lahasun

cabbage	पत्ता गोभी (f)	patta gobhī
cauliflower	फूल गोभी (f)	fūl gobhī
Brussels sprouts	ब्रसेल्स स्प्राउट्स (m)	brasels sprauts
broccoli	ब्रोकोली (f)	brokolī

beetroot	चुकन्दर (m)	chukandar
eggplant	बैंगन (m)	baingan
zucchini	तुरई (f)	turī
pumpkin	कद्दू	kaddū
turnip	शलजम (f)	shalajam

parsley	अजमोद (f)	ajamod
dill	सोआ (m)	soa
lettuce	सलाद पत्ता (m)	salād patta
celery	सेलरी (m)	selarī
asparagus	एस्पैरेगस (m)	espairegas
spinach	पालक (m)	pālak

pea	मटर (m)	matar
beans	फली (f pl)	falī
corn (maize)	मकई (f)	makī
kidney bean	राजमा (f)	rājama

bell pepper	शिमला मिर्च (m)	shimala mirch
radish	मूली (f)	mūlī
artichoke	हाथीचक (m)	hāthīchak

47. Fruits. Nuts

fruit	फल (m)	fal
apple	सेब (m)	seb
pear	नाशपाती (f)	nāshapātī
lemon	नींबू (m)	nīmbū

orange	संतरा (m)	santara
strawberry (garden ~)	स्ट्रॉबेरी (f)	stroberī
mandarin	नारंगी (m)	nārangī
plum	आलूबुखारा (m)	ālūbukhāra
peach	आड़ू (m)	ārū
apricot	खूबानी (f)	khūbānī
raspberry	रसभरी (f)	rasabharī
pineapple	अनानास (m)	anānās
banana	केला (m)	kela
watermelon	तरबूज़ (m)	tarabūz
grape	अंगूर (m)	angūr
cherry	चेरी (f)	cherī
melon	खरबूज़ा (f)	kharabūza
grapefruit	ग्रेपफ्रूट (m)	grepafrūt
avocado	एवोकांडो (m)	evokādo
papaya	पपीता (f)	papīta
mango	आम (m)	ām
pomegranate	अनार (m)	anār
redcurrant	लाल किशमिश (f)	lāl kishamish
blackcurrant	काली किशमिश (f)	kālī kishamish
gooseberry	आमला (f)	āmala
bilberry	बिलबेरी (f)	bilaberī
blackberry	ब्लैकबेरी (f)	blaikaberī
raisin	किशमिश (m)	kishamish
fig	अंजीर (m)	anjīr
date	खजूर (m)	khajūr
peanut	मूँगफली (m)	mūngafalī
almond	बादाम (f)	bādām
walnut	अखरोट (m)	akharot
hazelnut	हेज़लनट (m)	hezalanat
coconut	नारियल (m)	nāriyal
pistachios	पिस्ता (m)	pista

48. Bread. Candy

bakers' confectionery (pastry)	मिठाई (f pl)	mithaī
bread	ब्रेड (f)	bred
cookies	बिस्कुट (m)	biskut
chocolate (n)	चॉकलेट (m)	chokalet
chocolate (as adj)	चॉकलेटी	chokaletī
candy (wrapped)	टॉफ़ी (f)	tofī
cake (e.g., cupcake)	पेस्ट्री (f)	pestrī

cake (e.g., birthday ~)	केक (m)	kek
pie (e.g., apple ~)	पाई (m)	paī
filling (for cake, pie)	फ़िलिंग (f)	filing
jam (whole fruit jam)	जैम (m)	jaim
marmalade	मुरब्बा (m)	murabba
waffles	वैफ़र (m pl)	vefar
ice-cream	आईस-क्रीम (f)	āīs-krīm

49. Cooked dishes

course, dish	पकवान (m)	pakavān
cuisine	व्यंजन (m)	vyanjan
recipe	रैसीपी (f)	raisīpī
portion	भाग (m)	bhāg
salad	सलाद (m)	salād
soup	सूप (m)	sūp
clear soup (broth)	यख़नी (f)	yakhanī
sandwich (bread)	सैन्डविच (m)	saindavich
fried eggs	आमलेट (m)	āmalet
hamburger (beefburger)	हैमबर्गर (m)	haimabargar
beefsteak	बीफ़स्टीक (m)	bīfastīk
side dish	साइड डिश (f)	said dish
spaghetti	स्पेघेटी (f)	speghetī
mashed potatoes	आलू भरता (f)	ālū bharata
pizza	पीट्ज़ा (f)	pītza
porridge (oatmeal, etc.)	दलिया (f)	daliya
omelet	आमलेट (m)	āmalet
boiled (e.g., ~ beef)	उबला	ubala
smoked (adj)	धुएँ में पकाया हुआ	dhuen men pakāya hua
fried (adj)	भुना	bhuna
dried (adj)	सूखा	sūkha
frozen (adj)	फ़्रोज़न	frozan
pickled (adj)	अचार	achār
sweet (sugary)	मीठा	mītha
salty (adj)	नमकीन	namakīn
cold (adj)	ठंडा	thanda
hot (adj)	गरम	garam
bitter (adj)	कड़वा	karava
tasty (adj)	स्वादिष्ट	svādisht
to cook in boiling water	उबलते पानी में पकाना	ubalate pānī men pakāna
to cook (dinner)	खाना बनाना	khāna banāna
to fry (vt)	भूनना	bhūnana

to heat up (food)	गरम करना	garam karana
to salt (vt)	नमक डालना	namak dālana
to pepper (vt)	मिर्च डालना	mirch dālana
to grate (vt)	कद्दूकश करना	kaddūkash karana
peel (n)	छिलका (f)	chhilaka
to peel (vt)	छिलका निकलना	chhilaka nikalana

50. Spices

salt	नमक (m)	namak
salty (adj)	नमकीन	namakīn
to salt (vt)	नमक डालना	namak dālana
black pepper	काली मिर्च (f)	kālī mirch
red pepper (milled ~)	लाल मिर्च (m)	lāl mirch
mustard	सरसों (m)	sarason
horseradish	अरब मूली (f)	arab mūlī
condiment	मसाला (m)	masāla
spice	मसाला (m)	masāla
sauce	चटनी (f)	chatanī
vinegar	सिरका (m)	siraka
anise	सौंफ़ (f)	saumf
basil	तुलसी (f)	tulasī
cloves	लौंग (f)	laung
ginger	अदरक (m)	adarak
coriander	धनिया (m)	dhaniya
cinnamon	दालचीनी (f)	dālachīnī
sesame	तिल (m)	til
bay leaf	तेजपत्ता (m)	tejapatta
paprika	लाल शिमला मिर्च पाऊडर (m)	lāl shimala mirch paudar
caraway	ज़ीरा (m)	zīra
saffron	ज़ाफ़रान (m)	zāfarān

51. Meals

food	खाना (m)	khāna
to eat (vi, vt)	खाना खाना	khāna khāna
breakfast	नाश्ता (m)	nāshta
to have breakfast	नाश्ता करना	nāshta karana
lunch	दोपहर का भोजन (m)	dopahar ka bhojan
to have lunch	दोपहर का भोजन करना	dopahar ka bhojan karana
dinner	रात्रिभोज (m)	rātribhoj
to have dinner	रात्रिभोज करना	rātribhoj karana

appetite	भूख (f)	bhūkh
Enjoy your meal!	अपने भोजन का आनंद उठाएं!	apane bhojan ka ānand uthaen!
to open (~ a bottle)	खोलना	kholana
to spill (liquid)	गिराना	girāna
to spill out (vi)	गिराना	girāna
to boil (vi)	उबालना	ubālana
to boil (vt)	उबालना	ubālana
boiled (~ water)	उबला हुआ	ubala hua
to chill, cool down (vt)	ठंडा करना	thanda karana
to chill (vi)	ठंडा करना	thanda karana
taste, flavor	स्वाद (m)	svād
aftertaste	स्वाद (m)	svād
to slim down (lose weight)	वज़न घटाना	vazan ghatāna
diet	डाइट (m)	dait
vitamin	विटामिन (m)	vitāmin
calorie	कैलोरी (f)	kailorī
vegetarian (n)	शाकाहारी (m)	shākāhārī
vegetarian (adj)	शाकाहारी	shākāhārī
fats (nutrient)	वसा (m pl)	vasa
proteins	प्रोटीन (m pl)	protīn
carbohydrates	काबोहाइड्रेट (m)	kārbohaidret
slice (of lemon, ham)	टुकड़ा (m)	tukara
piece (of cake, pie)	टुकड़ा (m)	tukara
crumb (of bread, cake, etc.)	टुकड़ा (m)	tukara

52. Table setting

spoon	चम्मच (m)	chammach
knife	छुरी (f)	chhurī
fork	कांटा (m)	kānta
cup (e.g., coffee ~)	प्याला (m)	pyāla
plate (dinner ~)	तश्तरी (f)	tashtarī
saucer	सॉसर (m)	sosar
napkin (on table)	नैपकीन (m)	naipakīn
toothpick	टूथपिक (m)	tūthapik

53. Restaurant

restaurant	रेस्टराँ (m)	restarān
coffee house	कॉफ़ी हाउस (m)	kofī haus

pub, bar	बार (m)	bār
tearoom	चायख़ाना (m)	chāyakhāna
waiter	बैरा (m)	baira
waitress	बैरी (f)	bairī
bartender	बारमैन (m)	bāramain
menu	मेनू (m)	menū
wine list	वाइन सूची (f)	vain sūchī
to book a table	मेज़ बुक करना	mez buk karana
course, dish	पकवान (m)	pakavān
to order (meal)	आर्डर देना	ārdar dena
to make an order	आर्डर देना	ārdar dena
aperitif	एपेरेतीफ़ (m)	eperetīf
appetizer	एपेटाइज़र (m)	epetaizar
dessert	मीठा (m)	mītha
check	बिल (m)	bil
to pay the check	बील का भुगतान करना	bīl ka bhugatān karana
to give change	खुले पैसे देना	khule paise dena
tip	टिप (f)	tip

Family, relatives and friends

54. Personal information. Forms

name (first name)	पहला नाम (m)	pahala nām
surname (last name)	उपनाम (m)	upanām
date of birth	जन्म-दिवस (m)	janm-divas
place of birth	मातृभूमि (f)	mātrbhūmi
nationality	नागरिकता (f)	nāgarikata
place of residence	निवास स्थान (m)	nivās sthān
country	देश (m)	desh
profession (occupation)	पेशा (m)	pesha
gender, sex	लिंग (m)	ling
height	क़द (m)	qad
weight	वज़न (m)	vazan

55. Family members. Relatives

mother	माँ (f)	mān
father	पिता (m)	pita
son	बेटा (m)	beta
daughter	बेटी (f)	betī
younger daughter	छोटी बेटी (f)	chhotī betī
younger son	छोटा बेटा (m)	chhota beta
eldest daughter	बड़ी बेटी (f)	barī betī
eldest son	बड़ा बेटा (m)	bara beta
brother	भाई (m)	bhaī
sister	बहन (f)	bahan
cousin (masc.)	चचेरा भाई (m)	chachera bhaī
cousin (fem.)	चचेरी बहन (f)	chacherī bahan
mom, mommy	अम्मा (f)	amma
dad, daddy	पापा (m)	pāpa
parents	माँ-बाप (m pl)	mān-bāp
child	बच्चा (m)	bachcha
children	बच्चे (m pl)	bachche
grandmother	दादी (f)	dādī
grandfather	दादा (m)	dāda
grandson	पोता (m)	pota

granddaughter	पोती (f)	potī
grandchildren	पोते (m)	pote
uncle	चाचा (m)	chācha
aunt	चाची (f)	chāchī
nephew	भतीजा (m)	bhatīja
niece	भतीजी (f)	bhatījī
mother-in-law (wife's mother)	सास (f)	sās
father-in-law (husband's father)	ससुर (m)	sasur
son-in-law (daughter's husband)	दामाद (m)	dāmād
stepmother	सौतेली माँ (f)	sautelī mān
stepfather	सौतेले पिता (m)	sautele pita
infant	दूधमुँहा बच्चा (m)	dudhamunha bachcha
baby (infant)	शिशु (f)	shishu
little boy, kid	छोटा बच्चा (m)	chhota bachcha
wife	पत्नी (f)	patnī
husband	पति (m)	pati
spouse (husband)	पति (m)	pati
spouse (wife)	पत्नी (f)	patnī
married (masc.)	शादीशुदा	shādīshuda
married (fem.)	शादीशुदा	shādīshuda
single (unmarried)	अविवाहित	avivāhit
bachelor	कुँआरा (m)	kunāra
divorced (masc.)	तलाक़शुदा	talāqashuda
widow	विधवा (f)	vidhava
widower	विधुर (m)	vidhur
relative	रिश्तेदार (m)	rishtedār
close relative	सम्बंधी (m)	sambandhī
distant relative	दूर का रिश्तेदार (m)	dūr ka rishtedār
relatives	रिश्तेदार (m pl)	rishtedār
orphan (boy or girl)	अनाथ (m)	anāth
guardian (of a minor)	अभिभावक (m)	abhibhāvak
to adopt (a boy)	लड़का गोद लेना	laraka god lena
to adopt (a girl)	लड़की गोद लेना	larakī god lena

56. Friends. Coworkers

friend (masc.)	दोस्त (m)	dost
friend (fem.)	सहेली (f)	sahelī
friendship	दोस्ती (f)	dostī
to be friends	दोस्त होना	dost hona

buddy (masc.)	मित्र (m)	mitr
buddy (fem.)	सहेली (f)	sahelī
partner	पार्टनर (m)	pārtanar

chief (boss)	चीफ़ (m)	chīf
superior (n)	अधीक्षक (m)	adhīkshak
subordinate (n)	अधीनस्थ (m)	adhīnasth
colleague	सहकर्मी (m)	sahakarmī

acquaintance (person)	परिचित आदमी (m)	parichit ādamī
fellow traveler	सहगामी (m)	sahagāmī
classmate	सहपाठी (m)	sahapāthī

neighbor (masc.)	पड़ोसी (m)	parosī
neighbor (fem.)	पड़ोसन (f)	parosan
neighbors	पड़ोसी (m pl)	parosī

57. Man. Woman

woman	औरत (f)	aurat
girl (young woman)	लड़की (f)	larakī
bride	दुल्हन (f)	dulhan

beautiful (adj)	सुंदर	sundar
tall (adj)	लम्बा	lamba
slender (adj)	सुडौल	sudaul
short (adj)	छोटे क़द का	chhote qad ka

| blonde (n) | हल्के रंगे के बालोंवाली औरत (f) | halke range ke bālonvālī aurat |
| brunette (n) | काले बालोंवाली औरत (f) | kāle bālonvālī aurat |

ladies' (adj)	महिलाओं का	mahilaon ka
virgin (girl)	कुमारिनी (f)	kumārinī
pregnant (adj)	गर्भवती	garbhavatī

man (adult male)	आदमी (m)	ādamī
blond (n)	हल्के रंगे के बालोंवाला आदमी (m)	halke range ke bālonvāla ādamī
brunet (n)	काले बालोंवाला (m)	kāle bālonvāla
tall (adj)	लम्बा	lamba
short (adj)	छोटे क़द का	chhote qad ka

rude (rough)	अभद्र	abhadr
stocky (adj)	हष्ट-पुष्ट	hrasht-pusht
robust (adj)	तगड़ा	tagara
strong (adj)	ताक़तवर	tākatavar
strength	ताक़त (f)	tāqat
stout, fat (adj)	मोटा	mota
swarthy (adj)	साँवला	sānvala

| slender (well-built) | सुडौल | sudaul |
| elegant (adj) | सजिला | sajila |

58. Age

age	उम्र (f)	umr
youth (young age)	युवा (f)	yuva
young (adj)	जवान	javān

| younger (adj) | कनिष्ठ | kanishth |
| older (adj) | बड़ा | bara |

young man	युवक (m)	yuvak
teenager	किशोर (m)	kishor
guy, fellow	लड़का (m)	laraka

| old man | बूढ़ा आदमी (m) | būrha ādamī |
| old woman | बूढ़ी औरत (f) | būrhī aurat |

adult (adj)	व्यस्क	vyask
middle-aged (adj)	अधेड़	adhed
elderly (adj)	बुजुर्ग	buzurg
old (adj)	साल	sāl

retirement	सेवा-निवृत्ति (f)	seva-nivrtti
to retire (from job)	सेवा-निवृत्त होना	seva-nivrtt hona
retiree	सेवा-निवृत्त (m)	seva-nivrtt

59. Children

child	बच्चा (m)	bachcha
children	बच्चे (m pl)	bachche
twins	जुड़वाँ (m pl)	juravān

cradle	पालना (m)	pālana
rattle	झुनझुना (m)	jhunajhuna
diaper	डायपर (m)	dāyapar

pacifier	चुसनी (f)	chusanī
baby carriage	बच्चा गाड़ी (f)	bachcha gārī
kindergarten	बालवाड़ी (f)	bālavārī
babysitter	दाई (f)	daī

childhood	बचपन (m)	bachapan
doll	गुड़िया (f)	guriya
toy	खिलौना (m)	khilauna
construction set (toy)	निर्माण सेट खिलौना (m)	nirmān set khilauna
well-bred (adj)	तमीज़दार	tamīzadār

| ill-bred (adj) | बदतमीज़ | badatamīz |
| spoiled (adj) | सिरचढ़ा | siracharha |

to be naughty	शरारत करना	sharārat karana
mischievous (adj)	नटखट	natakhat
mischievousness	नटखटपन (m)	natakhatapan
mischievous child	नटखट बच्चा (m)	natakhat bachcha

| obedient (adj) | आज्ञाकारी | āgyākārī |
| disobedient (adj) | अनुज्ञाकारी | anugyākārī |

docile (adj)	विनम्र	vinamr
clever (smart)	बुद्धिमान	buddhimān
child prodigy	अद्भुत बच्चा (m)	adbhut bachcha

60. Married couples. Family life

to kiss (vt)	चुम्बन करना	chumban karana
to kiss (vi)	चुम्बन करना	chumban karana
family (n)	परिवार (m)	parivār
family (as adj)	परिवारिक	parivārik
couple	दंपति (m)	dampatti
marriage (state)	शादी (f)	shādī
hearth (home)	गृह-चूल्हा (m)	grh-chūlha
dynasty	वंश (f)	vansh

| date | मुलाक़ात (f) | mulāqāt |
| kiss | चुम्बन (m) | chumban |

love (for sb)	प्रेम (m)	prem
to love (sb)	प्यार करना	pyār karana
beloved	प्यारा	pyāra

tenderness	स्नेह (f)	sneh
tender (affectionate)	स्नेही	snehī
faithfulness	वफ़ादारी (f)	vafādārī
faithful (adj)	वफ़ादार	vafādār
care (attention)	देखभाल (f)	dekhabhāl
caring (~ father)	परवाह करने वाला	paravāh karane vāla

newlyweds	नवविवाहित (m pl)	navavivāhit
honeymoon	हनीमून (m)	hanīmūn
to get married (ab. woman)	शादी करना	shādī karana
to get married (ab. man)	शादी करना	shādī karana

wedding	शादी (f)	shādī
golden wedding	विवाह की पचासवीं वर्षगांठ (m)	vivāh kī pachāsavīn varshagānth
anniversary	वर्षगांठ (m)	varshagānth

lover (masc.)	प्रेमी (m)	premī
mistress (lover)	प्रेमिका (f)	premika
adultery	व्यभिचार (m)	vyabhichār
to cheat on ... (commit adultery)	संबंधों में धोखा देना	sambandhon men dhokha dena
jealous (adj)	ईष्यालु	īshyālu
to be jealous	ईष्या करना	īshya karana
divorce	तलाक़ (m)	talāq
to divorce (vi)	तलाक़ देना	talāq dena
to quarrel (vi)	झगड़ना	jhagarana
to be reconciled (after an argument)	सुलह करना	sulah karana
together (adv)	साथ	sāth
sex	यौन-क्रिया (f)	yaun-kriya
happiness	खुशी (f)	khushī
happy (adj)	खुश	khush
misfortune (accident)	दुर्घटना (f)	durghatana
unhappy (adj)	नाखुश	nākhush

Character. Feelings. Emotions

61. Feelings. Emotions

feeling (emotion)	भावना (f)	bhāvana
feelings	भावनाएं (f)	bhāvanaen
to feel (vt)	महसूस करना	mahasūs karana
hunger	भूख (f)	bhūkh
to be hungry	भूख लगना	bhūkh lagana
thirst	प्यास (f)	pyās
to be thirsty	प्यास लगना	pyās lagana
sleepiness	उनींदापन (f)	unīndāpan
to feel sleepy	नींद आना	nīnd āna
tiredness	थकान (f)	thakān
tired (adj)	थका हुआ	thaka hua
to get tired	थक जाना	thak jāna
mood (humor)	मन (m)	man
boredom	ऊब (m)	ūb
to be bored	ऊब जाना	ūb jāna
seclusion	अकेलापन (m)	akelāpan
to seclude oneself	एकांत में रहना	ekānt men rahana
to worry (make anxious)	चिन्ता करना	chinta karana
to be worried	फ़िक्रमंद होना	fikramand hona
worrying (n)	फ़िक्र (f)	fikr
anxiety	चिन्ता (f)	chinta
preoccupied (adj)	चिंताकुल	chintākul
to be nervous	घबराना	ghabarāna
to panic (vi)	घबरा जाना	ghabara jāna
hope	आशा (f)	āsha
to hope (vi, vt)	आशा रखना	āsha rakhana
certainty	विश्वास (m)	vishvās
certain, sure (adj)	विश्वास होना	vishvās hona
uncertainty	अविश्वास (m)	avishvās
uncertain (adj)	विश्वास न होना	vishvās na hona
drunk (adj)	मदहोश	madahosh
sober (adj)	बिना नशे के	bina nashe ke
weak (adj)	कमज़ोर	kamazor
happy (adj)	ख़ुश	khush
to scare (vt)	डराना	darāna

fury (madness)	रोष (m)	rosh
rage (fury)	रोष (m)	rosh
depression	उदासी (f)	udāsī
discomfort (unease)	असुविधा (f)	asuvidha
comfort	सुविधा (f)	suvidha
to regret (be sorry)	अफ़सोस करना	afasos karana
regret	अफ़सोस (m)	afasos
bad luck	दुर्भाग्य (f)	durbhāgy
sadness	दुख (m)	dukh
shame (remorse)	शर्म (m)	sharm
gladness	प्रसन्नता (f)	prasannata
enthusiasm, zeal	उत्साह (m)	utsāh
enthusiast	उत्साही (m)	utsāhī
to show enthusiasm	उत्साह दिखाना	utsāh dikhāna

62. Character. Personality

character	चरित्र (m)	charitr
character flaw	चरित्र दोष (m)	charitr dosh
mind	अक़्ल (m)	aql
reason	तर्क करने की क्षमता (f)	tark karane kī kshamata
conscience	अन्तरात्मा (f)	antarātma
habit (custom)	आदत (f)	ādat
ability (talent)	क्षमता (f)	kshamata
can (e.g., ~ swim)	कर सकना	kar sakana
patient (adj)	धैर्यशील	dhairyashīl
impatient (adj)	बेसब्र	besabr
curious (inquisitive)	उत्सुक	utsuk
curiosity	उत्सुकता (f)	utsukata
modesty	लज्जा (f)	lajja
modest (adj)	विनम्र	vinamr
immodest (adj)	अविनम्र	avinamr
laziness	आलस्य (m)	ālasy
lazy (adj)	आलसी	ālasī
lazy person (masc.)	सुस्त आदमी (m)	sust ādamī
cunning (n)	चालाक (m)	chālāk
cunning (as adj)	चालाकी	chālākī
distrust	अविश्वास (m)	avishvās
distrustful (adj)	अविश्वासपूर्ण	avishvāsapūrn
generosity	उदारता (f)	udārata
generous (adj)	उदार	udār
talented (adj)	प्रतिभाशाली	pratibhāshālī

talent	प्रतिभा (m)	pratibha
courageous (adj)	साहसी	sāhasī
courage	साहस (m)	sāhas
honest (adj)	ईमानदार	īmānadār
honesty	ईमानदारी (f)	īmānadārī

careful (cautious)	सावधान	sāvadhān
brave (courageous)	बहादुर	bahādur
serious (adj)	गम्भीर	gambhīr
strict (severe, stern)	सख्त	sakht

decisive (adj)	निर्णयात्मक	nirnayātmak
indecisive (adj)	अनिर्णयक	anirnāyak
shy, timid (adj)	शर्मीला	sharmīla
shyness, timidity	संकोच (m)	sankoch

confidence (trust)	यक़ीन (m)	yaqīn
to believe (trust)	यक़ीन करना	yaqīn karana
trusting (credulous)	भरोसा	bharosa

sincerely (adv)	हार्दिक	hārdik
sincere (adj)	हार्दिक	hārdik
sincerity	निष्ठा (f)	nishtha
open (person)	अनावृत	anāvrt

calm (adj)	शांत	shānt
frank (sincere)	स्पष्ट	spasht
naïve (adj)	भोला	bhola
absent-minded (adj)	भुलक्कड़	bhulakkar
funny (odd)	अजीब	ajīb

greed	लालच (m)	lālach
greedy (adj)	लालची	lālachī
stingy (adj)	कंजूस	kanjūs
evil (adj)	दुष्ट	dusht
stubborn (adj)	ज़िद्दी	ziddī
unpleasant (adj)	अप्रिय	apriy

selfish person (masc.)	स्वार्थी (m)	svārthī
selfish (adj)	स्वार्थ	svārth
coward	कायर (m)	kāyar
cowardly (adj)	कायरता	kāyarata

63. Sleep. Dreams

to sleep (vi)	सोना	sona
sleep, sleeping	सोना (m)	sona
dream	सपना (f)	sapana
to dream (in sleep)	सपना देखना	sapana dekhana
sleepy (adj)	ऊनिंदा	uninda

bed	पलंग (m)	palang
mattress	गद्दा (m)	gadda
blanket (comforter)	कम्बल (m)	kambal
pillow	तकिया (m)	takiya
sheet	चादर (f)	chādar

insomnia	अनिद्रा (m)	anidra
sleepless (adj)	अनिद्र	anidr
sleeping pill	नींद की गोली (f)	nīnd kī golī
to take a sleeping pill	नींद की गोली लेना	nīnd kī golī lena

to feel sleepy	नींद आना	nīnd āna
to yawn (vi)	जँभाई लेना	janbhaī lena
to go to bed	सोने जाना	sone jāna
to make up the bed	बिस्तर बिछाना	bistar bichhāna
to fall asleep	सो जाना	so jāna

nightmare	डरावना सपना (m)	darāvana sapana
snore, snoring	खर्राटे (m)	kharrāte
to snore (vi)	खर्राटे लेना	kharrāte lena

alarm clock	अलार्म घड़ी (f)	alārm gharī
to wake (vt)	जगाना	jagāna
to wake up	जगना	jagana
to get up (vi)	उठना	uthana
to wash up (wash face)	हाथ-मुँह धोना	hāth-munh dhona

64. Humour. Laughter. Gladness

humor (wit, fun)	हास्य (m)	hāsy
sense of humor	मज़ाक करने की आदत (m)	mazāk karane kī ādat
to enjoy oneself	आनंद उठाना	ānand uthāna
cheerful (merry)	हँसमुख	hansamukh
merriment (gaiety)	उत्सव (m)	utsav

smile	मुस्कान (f)	muskān
to smile (vi)	मुस्कुराना	muskurāna
to start laughing	हँसना शुरू करना	hansana shurū karana
to laugh (vi)	हँसना	hansana
laugh, laughter	हँसी (f)	hansī

anecdote	चुटकुला (f)	chutakula
funny (anecdote, etc.)	मज़ाकीय	mazākīy
funny (odd)	हास्यास्प्रद	hāsyāsprad

to joke (vi)	मज़ाक करना	mazāk karana
joke (verbal)	लतीफ़ा (f)	latīfa
joy (emotion)	ख़ुशी (f)	khushī
to rejoice (vi)	ख़ुश होना	khush hona
joyful (adj)	ख़ुश	khush

65. Discussion, conversation. Part 1

communication	संवाद (m)	sanvād
to communicate	संवाद करना	sanvād karana
conversation	बातचीत (f)	bātachīt
dialog	बातचीत (f)	bātachīt
discussion (discourse)	चर्चा (f)	charcha
dispute (debate)	बहस (f)	bahas
to dispute	बहस करना	bahas karana
interlocutor	वार्तीकार (m)	vārtākār
topic (theme)	विषय (m)	vishay
point of view	दृष्टिकोण (m)	drshtikon
opinion (point of view)	राय (f)	rāy
speech (talk)	भाषण (m)	bhāshan
discussion (of report, etc.)	चर्चा (f)	charcha
to discuss (vt)	चर्चा करना	charcha karana
talk (conversation)	बातचीत (f)	bātachīt
to talk (to chat)	बात करना	bāt karana
meeting	भेंट (f)	bhent
to meet (vi, vt)	मिलना	milana
proverb	लोकोक्ति (f)	lokokti
saying	कहावत (f)	kahāvat
riddle (poser)	पहेली (f)	pahelī
to pose a riddle	पहेली पूछना	pahelī pūchhana
password	पासवर्ड (m)	pāsavard
secret	भेद (m)	bhed
oath (vow)	शपथ (f)	shapath
to swear (an oath)	शपथ लेना	shapath lena
promise	वचन (m)	vachan
to promise (vt)	वचन देना	vachan dena
advice (counsel)	सलाह (f)	salāh
to advise (vt)	सलाह देना	salāh dena
to listen to ... (obey)	कहना मानना	kahana mānana
news	समाचार (m)	samāchār
sensation (news)	सनसनी (f)	sanasanī
information (data)	सूचना (f)	sūchana
conclusion (decision)	निष्कर्ष (m)	nishkarsh
voice	आवाज़ (f)	āvāz
compliment	प्रशंसा (m)	prashansa
kind (nice)	दयालु	dayālu
word	शब्द (m)	shabd
phrase	जुमला (m)	jumala
answer	जवाब (m)	javāb

truth	सच (f)	sach
lie	झूठ (f)	jhūth
thought	ख्याल (f)	khyāl
idea (inspiration)	विचार (f)	vichār
fantasy	कल्पना (f)	kalpana

66. Discussion, conversation. Part 2

respected (adj)	आदरणीय	ādaranīy
to respect (vt)	आदर करना	ādar karana
respect	इज्ज़त (m)	izzat
Dear … (letter)	माननीय	mānanīy
to introduce (sb to sb)	परिचय देना	parichay dena
intention	इरादा (m)	irāda
to intend (have in mind)	इरादा करना	irāda karana
wish	इच्छा (f)	ichchha
to wish (~ good luck)	इच्छा करना	ichchha karana
surprise (astonishment)	हैरानी (f)	hairānī
to surprise (amaze)	हैरान करना	hairān karana
to be surprised	हैरान होना	hairān hona
to give (vt)	देना	dena
to take (get hold of)	लेना	lena
to give back	वापस देना	vāpas dena
to return (give back)	वापस करना	vāpas karana
to apologize (vi)	माफ़ी मांगना	māfī māngana
apology	माफ़ी (f)	māfī
to forgive (vt)	क्षमा करना	kshama karana
to talk (speak)	बात करना	bāt karana
to listen (vi)	सुनना	sunana
to hear out	सुन लेना	sun lena
to understand (vt)	समझना	samajhana
to show (to display)	दिखाना	dikhāna
to look at …	देखना	dekhana
to call (yell for sb)	बुलाना	bulāna
to disturb (vt)	परेशान करना	pareshān karana
to pass (to hand sth)	भिजवाना	bhijavāna
demand (request)	प्रार्थना (f)	prārthana
to request (ask)	अनुरोध करना	anurodh karana
demand (firm request)	मांग (f)	māng
to demand (request firmly)	माँगना	māngana
to tease (call names)	चिढ़ाना	chirhāna
to mock (make fun of)	मज़ाक उड़ाना	mazāk urāna

| mockery, derision | मज़ाक (m) | mazāk |
| nickname | मुंह बोला नाम (m) | munh bola nām |

insinuation	इशारा (m)	ishāra
to insinuate (imply)	इशारा करना	ishāra karana
to mean (vt)	मतलब होना	matalab hona

description	वर्णन (m)	varnan
to describe (vt)	वर्णन करना	varnan karana
praise (compliments)	प्रशंसा (m)	prashansa
to praise (vt)	प्रशंसा करना	prashansa karana

disappointment	निराशा (m)	nirāsha
to disappoint (vt)	निराश करना	nirāsh karana
to be disappointed	निराश होना	nirāsh hona

supposition	अंदाज़ा (m)	andāza
to suppose (assume)	अंदाज़ा करना	andāza karana
warning (caution)	चेतावनी (f)	chetāvanī
to warn (vt)	चेतावनी देना	chetāvanī dena

67. Discussion, conversation. Part 3

| to talk into (convince) | मना लेना | mana lena |
| to calm down (vt) | शांत करना | shānt karana |

silence (~ is golden)	ख़ामोशी (f)	khāmoshī
to be silent (not speaking)	चुप रहना	chup rahana
to whisper (vi, vt)	फुसफुसाना	fusafusāna
whisper	फुसफुस (m)	fusafus

| frankly, sincerely (adv) | साफ़ साफ़ | sāf sāf |
| in my opinion ... | मेरे ख्याल में ... | mere khyāl men ... |

detail (of the story)	विस्तार (m)	vistār
detailed (adj)	विस्तृत	vistrt
in detail (adv)	विस्तार से	vistār se

| hint, clue | सुराग़ (m) | surāg |
| to give a hint | सुराग़ देना | surāg dena |

look (glance)	नज़र (m)	nazar
to have a look	देखना	dekhana
fixed (look)	स्थिर	sthir
to blink (vi)	झपकना	jhapakana
to wink (vi)	आँख मारना	ānkh mārana
to nod (in assent)	सिर हिलाना	sir hilāna

| sigh | आह (f) | āh |
| to sigh (vi) | आह भरना | āh bharana |

to shudder (vi)	काँपना	kānpana
gesture	इशारा (m)	ishāra
to touch (one's arm, etc.)	छूना	chhūa
to seize	पकड़ना	pakarana
(e.g., ~ by the arm)		
to tap (on the shoulder)	थपथपाना	thapathapāna
Look out!	खबरदार!	khabaradār!
Really?	सचमुच?	sachamuch?
Are you sure?	क्या तुम्हें यक़ीन है?	kya tumhen yaqīn hai?
Good luck!	सफल हो!	safal ho!
I see!	समझ आया!	samajh āya!
What a pity!	अफ़सोस की बात है!	afasos kī bāt hai!

68. Agreement. Refusal

consent	सहमति (f)	sahamati
to consent (vi)	राज़ी होना	rāzī hona
approval	स्वीकृति (f)	svīkrti
to approve (vt)	स्वीकार करना	svīkār karana
refusal	इन्कार (m)	inkār
to refuse (vi, vt)	इन्कार करना	inkār karana
Great!	बहुत बढ़िया!	bahut barhiya!
All right!	अच्छा है!	achchha hai!
Okay! (I agree)	ठीक!	thīk!
forbidden (adj)	वर्जित	varjit
it's forbidden	मना है	mana hai
it's impossible	सम्भव नहीं	sambhav nahin
incorrect (adj)	ग़लत	galat
to reject (~ a demand)	अस्वीकार करना	asvīkār karana
to support (cause, idea)	समर्थन करना	samarthan karana
to accept (~ an apology)	स्वीकार करना	svīkār karana
to confirm (vt)	पुष्टि करना	pushti karana
confirmation	पुष्टि (f)	pushti
permission	अनुमति (f)	anumati
to permit (vt)	अनुमति देना	anumati dena
decision	फ़ैसला (m)	faisala
to say nothing	चुप रहना	chup rahana
(hold one's tongue)		
condition (term)	हालत (m)	hālat
excuse (pretext)	बहाना (m)	bahāna
praise (compliments)	प्रशंसा (m)	prashansa
to praise (vt)	तारीफ़ करना	tārīf karana

69. Success. Good luck. Failure

success	सफलता (f)	safalata
successfully (adv)	सफलतापूर्वक	safalatāpūrvak
successful (adj)	सफल	safal
luck (good luck)	सौभाग्य (m)	saubhāgy
Good luck!	सफल हो!	safal ho!
lucky (e.g., ~ day)	भाग्यशाली	bhāgyashālī
lucky (fortunate)	भाग्यशाली	bhāgyashālī
failure	विफलता (f)	vifalata
misfortune	नाकामयाबी (f)	nākāmayābī
bad luck	दुर्भाग्य (m)	durbhāgy
unsuccessful (adj)	असफल	asafal
catastrophe	दुर्घटना (f)	durghatana
pride	गर्व (m)	garv
proud (adj)	गर्व	garv
to be proud	गर्व करना	garv karana
winner	विजेता (m)	vijeta
to win (vi)	जीतना	jītana
to lose (not win)	हार जाना	hār jāna
try	कोशिश (f)	koshish
to try (vi)	कोशिश करना	koshish karana
chance (opportunity)	मौक़ा (m)	mauqa

70. Quarrels. Negative emotions

shout (scream)	चिल्लाहट (f)	chillāhat
to shout (vi)	चिल्लाना	chillāna
to start to cry out	चीख़ना	chīkhana
quarrel	झगड़ा (m)	jhagara
to quarrel (vi)	झगड़ना	jhagarana
fight (squabble)	झगड़ा (m)	jhagara
to make a scene	झगड़ना	jhagarana
conflict	टकराव (m)	takarāv
misunderstanding	ग़लतफ़हमी (m)	galatafahamī
insult	अपमान (m)	apamān
to insult (vt)	अपमान करना	apamān karana
insulted (adj)	अपमानित	apamānit
resentment	द्वेष (f)	dvesh
to offend (vt)	नाराज़ करना	nārāz karana
to take offense	बुरा मानना	bura mānana
indignation	क्रोध (m)	krodh
to be indignant	ग़ुस्से में आना	gusse men āna

complaint	शिकायत (f)	shikāyat
to complain (vi, vt)	शिकायत करना	shikāyat karana
apology	माफ़ी (f)	māfī
to apologize (vi)	माफ़ी मांगना	māfī māngana
to beg pardon	क्षमा मांगना	kshama māngana
criticism	आलोचना (f)	ālochana
to criticize (vt)	आलोचना करना	ālochana karana
accusation	आरोप (m)	ārop
to accuse (vt)	आरोप लगाना	ārop lagāna
revenge	बदला (m)	badala
to avenge (get revenge)	बदला लेना	badala lena
to pay back	बदला लेना	badala lena
disdain	नफ़रत (m)	nafarat
to despise (vt)	नफ़रत करना	nafarat karana
hatred, hate	नफ़रत (m)	nafarat
to hate (vt)	नफ़रत करना	nafarat karana
nervous (adj)	घबराना	ghabarāna
to be nervous	घबराना	ghabarāna
angry (mad)	नाराज़	nārāz
to make angry	नाराज़ करना	nārāz karana
humiliation	बेइज़्ज़ती (f)	bezzatī
to humiliate (vt)	निरादर करना	nirādar karana
to humiliate oneself	अपमान होना	apamān hona
shock	हैरानी (f)	hairānī
to shock (vt)	हैरान होना	hairān hona
trouble (e.g., serious ~)	परेशानियाँ (f)	pareshāniyān
unpleasant (adj)	अप्रिय	apriy
fear (dread)	डर (f)	dar
terrible (storm, heat)	भयानक	bhayānak
scary (e.g., ~ story)	भयंकर	bhayankar
horror	दहशत (f)	dahashat
awful (crime, news)	भयानक	bhayānak
to cry (weep)	रोना	rona
to start crying	रोने लगना	rone lagana
tear	आँसु (f)	ānsu
fault	ग़लती (f)	galatī
guilt (feeling)	दोष का एहसास (m)	dosh ka ehasās
dishonor (disgrace)	बदनामी (f)	badanāmī
protest	विरोध (m)	virodh
stress	तनाव (m)	tanāv
to disturb (vt)	परेशान करना	pareshān karana

to be furious	गुस्सा करना	gussa karana
mad, angry (adj)	क्रोधित	krodhit
to end (~ a relationship)	ख़त्म करना	khatm karana
to swear (at sb)	कसम खाना	kasam khāna

to scare (become afraid)	डराना	darāna
to hit (strike with hand)	मारना	mārana
to fight (street fight, etc.)	झगड़ना	jhagarana

to settle (a conflict)	सुलझाना	sulajhāna
discontented (adj)	असंतुष्ट	asantusht
furious (adj)	गुस्सा	gussa

| It's not good! | यह ठीक नहीं। | yah thīk nahin! |
| It's bad! | यह बुरा है। | yah bura hai! |

Medicine

71. Diseases

sickness	बीमारी (f)	bīmārī
to be sick	बीमार होना	bīmār hona
health	सेहत (f)	sehat
runny nose (coryza)	नज़ला (m)	nazala
tonsillitis	टॉन्सिल (m)	tonsil
cold (illness)	ज़ुकाम (f)	zukām
to catch a cold	ज़ुकाम हो जाना	zukām ho jāna
bronchitis	ब्रॉन्काइटिस (m)	bronkaitis
pneumonia	निमोनिया (f)	nimoniya
flu, influenza	फ़्लू (m)	flū
nearsighted (adj)	कमबीन	kamabīn
farsighted (adj)	कमज़ोर दूरदृष्टि	kamazor dūradrshti
strabismus (crossed eyes)	तिरछी नज़र (m)	tirachhī nazar
cross-eyed (adj)	तिरछी नज़रवाला	tirachhī nazaravāla
cataract	मोतिया बिंद (m)	motiya bind
glaucoma	काला मोतिया (m)	kāla motiya
stroke	स्ट्रोक (m)	strok
heart attack	दिल का दौरा (m)	dil ka daura
myocardial infarction	मायोकार्डियल इन्फ़ार्क्शन (m)	māyokārdiyal infārkshan
paralysis	लकवा (m)	lakava
to paralyze (vt)	लक़वा मारना	laqava mārana
allergy	एलर्जी (f)	elarjī
asthma	दमा (f)	dama
diabetes	शूगर (f)	shūgar
toothache	दाँत दर्द (m)	dānt dard
caries	दाँत में कीड़ा (m)	dānt men kīra
diarrhea	दस्त (m)	dast
constipation	कब्ज़ (m)	kabz
stomach upset	पेट ख़राब (m)	pet kharāb
food poisoning	ख़राबू खाने से हुई बीमारी (f)	kharāb khāne se huī bīmārī
to get food poisoning	ख़राब खाने से बीमार पड़ना	kharāb khāne se bīmār parana
arthritis	गठिया (m)	gathiya

rickets	बालवक्र (m)	bālavakr
rheumatism	आमवात (m)	āmavāt
atherosclerosis	धमनीकलाकाठिन्य (m)	dhamanīkalākāṭhiny
gastritis	जठर-शोथ (m)	jathar-shoth
appendicitis	उण्डुक-शोथ (m)	unduk-shoth
cholecystitis	पित्ताशय (m)	pittāshay
ulcer	अल्सर (m)	alsar
measles	मीज़ल्स (m)	mīzals
rubella (German measles)	जर्मन मीज़ल्स (m)	jarman mīzals
jaundice	पीलिया (m)	pīliya
hepatitis	हेपेटाइटिस (m)	hepetaitis
schizophrenia	शीज़ोफ्रेनीय (f)	shīzofrenīy
rabies (hydrophobia)	रेबीज़ (m)	rebīz
neurosis	न्यूरोसिस (m)	nyūrosis
concussion	आघात (m)	āghāt
cancer	कर्क रोग (m)	kark rog
sclerosis	काठिन्य (m)	kāṭhiny
multiple sclerosis	मल्टीपल स्क्लेरोसिस (m)	maltīpal sklerosis
alcoholism	शराबीपन (m)	sharābīpan
alcoholic (n)	शराबी (m)	sharābī
syphilis	सीफ़ीलिस (m)	sīfīlis
AIDS	ऐड्स (m)	aids
tumor	ट्यूमर (m)	tyūmar
malignant (adj)	घातक	ghātak
benign (adj)	अर्बुद	arbud
fever	बुख़ार (m)	bukhār
malaria	मलेरिया (f)	maleriya
gangrene	गैन्ग्रीन (m)	gaingrīn
seasickness	जहाज़ी मतली (f)	jahāzī matalī
epilepsy	मिरगी (f)	miragī
epidemic	महामारी (f)	mahāmārī
typhus	टाइफ़रस (m)	taifas
tuberculosis	टीबी (m)	tībī
cholera	हैज़ा (f)	haiza
plague (bubonic ~)	प्लेग (f)	pleg

72. Symptoms. Treatments. Part 1

symptom	लक्षण (m)	lakshan
temperature	तापमान (m)	tāpamān
high temperature (fever)	बुख़ार (f)	bukhār
pulse	नब्ज़ (f)	nabz

dizziness (vertigo)	सिर का चक्कर (m)	sir ka chakkar
hot (adj)	गरम	garam
shivering	कंपकंपी (f)	kampakampī
pale (e.g., ~ face)	पीला	pīla
cough	खाँसी (f)	khānsī
to cough (vi)	खाँसना	khānsana
to sneeze (vi)	छींकना	chhīnkana
faint	बेहोशी (f)	behoshī
to faint (vi)	बेहोश होना	behosh hona
bruise (hématome)	नील (m)	nīl
bump (lump)	गुमड़ा (m)	gumara
to bang (bump)	चोट लगना	chot lagana
contusion (bruise)	चोट (f)	chot
to get a bruise	घाव लगना	ghāv lagana
to limp (vi)	लँगड़ाना	langarāna
dislocation	हड्डी खिसकना (f)	haddī khisakana
to dislocate (vt)	हड्डी खिसकना	haddī khisakana
fracture	हड्डी टूट जाना (f)	haddī tūt jāna
to have a fracture	हड्डी टूट जाना	haddī tūt jāna
cut (e.g., paper ~)	कट जाना (m)	kat jāna
to cut oneself	ख़ुद को काट लेना	khud ko kāt lena
bleeding	रक्त-स्राव (m)	rakt-srāv
burn (injury)	जला होना	jala hona
to get burned	जल जाना	jal jāna
to prick (vt)	चुभाना	chubhāna
to prick oneself	ख़ुद को चुभाना	khud ko chubhāna
to injure (vt)	घायल करना	ghāyal karana
injury	चोट (f)	chot
wound	घाव (m)	ghāv
trauma	चोट (f)	chot
to be delirious	बेहोशी में बड़बड़ाना	behoshī men barabadāna
to stutter (vi)	हकलाना	hakalāna
sunstroke	धूप आघात (m)	dhūp āghāt

73. Symptoms. Treatments. Part 2

pain, ache	दर्द (f)	dard
splinter (in foot, etc.)	चुभ जाना (m)	chubh jāna
sweat (perspiration)	पसीना (f)	pasīna
to sweat (perspire)	पसीना निकलना	pasīna nikalana
vomiting	वमन (m)	vaman
convulsions	दौरा (m)	daura

pregnant (adj)	गर्भवती	garbhavatī
to be born	जन्म लेना	janm lena
delivery, labor	पैदा करना (m)	paida karana
to deliver (~ a baby)	पैदा करना	paida karana
abortion	गर्भपात (m)	garbhapāt

breathing, respiration	साँस (f)	sāns
in-breath (inhalation)	साँस अंदर खींचना (f)	sāns andar khīnchana
out-breath (exhalation)	साँस बाहर छोड़ना (f)	sāns bāhar chhorana
to exhale (breathe out)	साँस बाहर छोड़ना	sāns bāhar chhorana
to inhale (vi)	साँस अंदर खींचना	sāns andar khīnchana

disabled person	अपाहिज (m)	apāhij
cripple	लूला (m)	lūla
drug addict	नशेबाज़ (m)	nashebāz

deaf (adj)	बहरा	bahara
mute (adj)	गूँगा	gūnga
deaf mute (adj)	बहरा और गूँगा	bahara aur gūnga

mad, insane (adj)	पागल	pāgal
madman (demented person)	पगला (m)	pagala
madwoman	पगली (f)	pagalī
to go insane	पागल हो जाना	pāgal ho jāna

gene	वंशाणु (m)	vanshānu
immunity	रोग प्रतिरोधक शक्ति (f)	rog pratirodhak shakti
hereditary (adj)	जन्मजात	janmajāt
congenital (adj)	पैदाइशी	paidaishī

virus	विषाणु (m)	vishānu
microbe	कीटाणु (m)	kītānu
bacterium	जीवाणु (m)	jīvānu
infection	संक्रमण (m)	sankraman

74. Symptoms. Treatments. Part 3

| hospital | अस्पताल (m) | aspatāl |
| patient | मरीज़ (m) | marīz |

diagnosis	रोग-निर्णय (m)	rog-nirnay
cure	इलाज (m)	ilāj
medical treatment	चिकित्सीय उपचार (m)	chikitsīy upachār
to get treatment	इलाज कराना	ilāj karāna
to treat (~ a patient)	इलाज करना	ilāj karana
to nurse (look after)	देखभाल करना	dekhabhāl karana
care (nursing ~)	देखभाल (f)	dekhabhāl
operation, surgery	ऑपरेशन (m)	opareshan
to bandage (head, limb)	पट्टी बाँधना	pattī bāndhana

bandaging	पट्टी (f)	pattī
vaccination	टीका (m)	tīka
to vaccinate (vt)	टीका लगाना	tīka lagāna
injection, shot	इंजेक्शन (m)	injekshan
to give an injection	इंजेक्शन लगाना	injekshan lagāna

amputation	अंगविच्छेद (f)	angavichchhed
to amputate (vt)	अंगविच्छेद करना	angavichchhed karana
coma	कोमा (m)	koma
to be in a coma	कोमा में चले जाना	koma men chale jāna
intensive care	गहन चिकित्सा (f)	gahan chikitsa

to recover (~ from flu)	ठीक हो जाना	thīk ho jāna
condition (patient's ~)	हालत (m)	hālat
consciousness	होश (m)	hosh
memory (faculty)	याददाश्त (f)	yādadāsht

to pull out (tooth)	दाँत निकालना	dānt nikālana
filling	भराव (m)	bharāv
to fill (a tooth)	दाँत को भरना	dānt ko bharana

hypnosis	हिप्नोसिस (m)	hipanosis
to hypnotize (vt)	हिप्नोटाइज़ करना	hipanotaiz karana

75. Doctors

doctor	डॉक्टर (m)	doktar
nurse	नर्स (m)	nars
personal doctor	निजी डॉक्टर (m)	nijī doktar

dentist	दंत-चिकित्सक (m)	dant-chikitsak
eye doctor	आँखों का डॉक्टर (m)	ānkhon ka doktar
internist	चिकित्सक (m)	chikitsak
surgeon	शल्य-चिकित्सक (m)	shaly-chikitsak

psychiatrist	मनोरोग चिकित्सक (m)	manorog chikitsak
pediatrician	बाल-चिकित्सक (m)	bāl-chikitsak
psychologist	मनोवैज्ञानिक (m)	manovaigyānik
gynecologist	प्रसूतिशास्री (f)	prasūtishāsrī
cardiologist	हृदय रोग विशेषज्ञ (m)	hrday rog visheshagy

76. Medicine. Drugs. Accessories

medicine, drug	दवा (f)	dava
remedy	दवाई (f)	davaī
to prescribe (vt)	नुसखा लिखना	nusakha likhana
prescription	नुसखा (m)	nusakha
tablet, pill	गोली (f)	golī

ointment	मरहम (m)	maraham
ampule	एम्प्यूल (m)	empyūl
mixture	सिरप (m)	sirap
syrup	शरबत (m)	sharabat
pill	गोली (f)	golī
powder	चूरन (m)	chūran

gauze bandage	पट्टी (f)	pattī
cotton wool	रूई का गोला (m)	rūī ka gola
iodine	आयोडीन (m)	āyodīn

Band-Aid	बैंड-एड (m)	baind-ed
eyedropper	आई-ड्रॉपर (m)	āī-dropar
thermometer	थरमामीटर (m)	tharamāmītar
syringe	इंजेक्शन (m)	injekshan

| wheelchair | व्हीलचेयर (f) | vhīlacheyar |
| crutches | बैसाखी (m pl) | baisākhī |

painkiller	दर्द-निवारक (f)	dard-nivārak
laxative	जुलाब की गोली (f)	julāb kī golī
spirits (ethanol)	स्पिरिट (m)	spirit
medicinal herbs	जड़ी-बूटी (f)	jarī-būtī
herbal (~ tea)	जड़ी-बूटियों से बना	jarī-būtiyon se bana

77. Smoking. Tobacco products

tobacco	तम्बाकू (m)	tambākū
cigarette	सिगरेट (m)	sigaret
cigar	सिगार (m)	sigār
pipe	पाइप (f)	paip
pack (of cigarettes)	पैक (m)	paik

matches	माचिस (f pl)	māchis
matchbox	माचिस का डिब्बा (m)	māchis ka dibba
lighter	लाइटर (f)	laitar
ashtray	राखदानी (f)	rākhadānī
cigarette case	सिगरेट केस (m)	sigaret kes
cigarette holder	सिगरेट होलडर (m)	sigaret holadar
filter (cigarette tip)	फ़िल्टर (m)	filtar

to smoke (vi, vt)	धूम्रपान करना	dhumrapān karana
to light a cigarette	सिगरेट जलाना	sigaret jalāna
smoking	धूम्रपान (m)	dhumrapān
smoker	धूम्रपान करने वाला (m)	dhūmrapān karane vāla

stub, butt (of cigarette)	सिगरेट का बचा हुआ टुकड़ा (m)	sigaret ka bacha hua tukara
smoke, fumes	सिगरेट का धुँआ (m)	sigaret ka dhuna
ash	राख (f)	rākh

HUMAN HABITAT

City

city, town	नगर (m)	nagar
capital city	राजधानी (f)	rājadhānī
village	गांव (m)	gānv
city map	नगर का नक्शा (m)	nagar ka naksha
downtown	नगर का केन्द्र (m)	nagar ka kendr
suburb	उपनगर (m)	upanagar
suburban (adj)	उपनगरिक	upanagarik
outskirts	बाहरी इलाका (m)	bāharī ilāka
environs (suburbs)	इर्दगिर्द के इलाके (m pl)	irdagird ke ilāke
city block	सेक्टर (m)	sektar
residential block (area)	मुहल्ला (m)	muhalla
traffic	यातायात (f)	yātāyāt
traffic lights	यातायात सिग्नल (m)	yātāyāt signal
public transportation	जन परिवहन (m)	jan parivahan
intersection	चौराहा (m)	chaurāha
crosswalk	ज़ेबरा क्रॉसिंग (f)	zebara krosing
pedestrian underpass	पैदल यात्रियों के लिए अंडरपास (f)	paidal yātriyon ke lie andarapās
to cross (~ the street)	सड़क पार करना	sarak pār karana
pedestrian	पैदल-यात्री (m)	paidal-yātrī
sidewalk	फुटपाथ (m)	futapāth
bridge	पुल (m)	pul
embankment (river walk)	तट (m)	tat
fountain	फौवारा (m)	fauvāra
allée (garden walkway)	छायापथ (f)	chhāyāpath
park	पार्क (m)	pārk
boulevard	चौड़ी सड़क (m)	chaurī sarak
square	मैदान (m)	maidān
avenue (wide street)	मार्ग (m)	mārg
street	सड़क (f)	sarak
side street	गली (f)	galī
dead end	बंद गली (f)	band galī
house	मकान (m)	makān

| building | इमारत (f) | imārat |
| skyscraper | गगनचुंबी भवन (f) | gaganachumbī bhavan |

facade	अगवाड़ा (m)	agavāra
roof	छत (f)	chhat
window	खिड़की (f)	khirakī
arch	मेहराब (m)	meharāb
column	स्तंभ (m)	stambh
corner	कोना (m)	kona

store window	दुकान का शो-केस (m)	dukān ka sho-kes
signboard (store sign, etc.)	साईनबोर्ड (m)	saīnabord
poster	पोस्टर (m)	postar
advertising poster	विज्ञापन पोस्टर (m)	vigyāpan postar
billboard	बिलबोर्ड (m)	bilabord

garbage, trash	कूड़ा (m)	kūra
trashcan (public ~)	कूड़े का डिब्बा (m)	kūre ka dibba
to litter (vi)	कूड़ा-कर्कट डालना	kūra-karkat dālana
garbage dump	डम्पिंग ग्राउंड (m)	damping graund

phone booth	फ़ोन बूथ (m)	fon būth
lamppost	बिजली का खंभा (m)	bijalī ka khambha
bench (park ~)	पार्क-बेंच (f)	pārk-bench

police officer	पुलिसवाला (m)	pulisavāla
police	पुलिस (m)	pulis
beggar	भिखारी (m)	bhikhārī
homeless (n)	बेघर (m)	beghar

79. Urban institutions

store	दुकान (f)	dukān
drugstore, pharmacy	दवाख़ाना (m)	davākhāna
eyeglass store	चश्मे की दुकान (f)	chashme kī dukān
shopping mall	शॉपिंग मॉल (m)	shoping mol
supermarket	सुपर बाज़ार (m)	supar bāzār

bakery	बेकरी (f)	bekarī
baker	बेकर (m)	bekar
pastry shop	टॉफ़ी की दुकान (f)	tofī kī dukān
grocery store	परचून की दुकान (f)	parachūn kī dukān
butcher shop	गोश्त की दुकान (f)	gosht kī dukān

| produce store | सब्ज़ियों की दुकान (f) | sabziyon kī dukān |
| market | बाज़ार (m) | bāzār |

coffee house	काफ़ी हाउस (m)	kāfī haus
restaurant	रेस्टराँ (m)	restarān
pub, bar	शराबख़ाना (m)	sharābakhāna

pizzeria	पिट्ज़ा की दुकान (f)	pitza kī dukān
hair salon	नाई की दुकान (f)	naī kī dukān
post office	डाकघर (m)	dākaghar
dry cleaners	ड्राइक्लीनर (m)	draiklīnar
photo studio	फ़ोटो की दुकान (f)	foto kī dukān
shoe store	जूते की दुकान (f)	jūte kī dukān
bookstore	किताबों की दुकान (f)	kitābon kī dukān
sporting goods store	खेलकूद की दुकान (f)	khelakūd kī dukān
clothes repair shop	कपड़ों की मरम्मत की दुकान (f)	kaparon kī marammat kī dukān
formal wear rental	कपड़ों को किराए पर देने की दुकान (f)	kaparon ko kirae par dene kī dukān
video rental store	वीडियो रेन्टल दुकान (f)	vīdiyo rental dukān
circus	सर्कस (m)	sarkas
zoo	चिड़ियाघर (m)	chiriyāghar
movie theater	सिनेमाघर (m)	sinemāghar
museum	संग्रहालय (m)	sangrahālay
library	पुस्तकालय (m)	pustakālay
theater	रंगमंच (m)	rangamanch
opera (opera house)	ओपेरा (m)	opera
nightclub	नाईट क्लब (m)	naīt klab
casino	केसिनो (m)	kesino
mosque	मस्जिद (m)	masjid
synagogue	सीनागोग (m)	sīnāgog
cathedral	गिरजाघर (m)	girajāghar
temple	मंदिर (m)	mandir
church	गिरजाघर (m)	girajāghar
college	कॉलेज (m)	kolej
university	विश्वविद्यालय (m)	vishvavidyālay
school	विद्यालय (m)	vidyālay
prefecture	प्रशासक प्रान्त (m)	prashāsak prānt
city hall	सिटी हॉल (m)	sitī hol
hotel	होटल (f)	hotal
bank	बैंक (m)	baink
embassy	दूतावस (m)	dūtāvas
travel agency	पर्यटन आफ़िस (m)	paryatan āfis
information office	पूछताछ कार्यालय (m)	pūchhatāchh kāryālay
currency exchange	मुद्रालय (m)	mudrālay
subway	मेट्रो (m)	metro
hospital	अस्पताल (m)	aspatāl
gas station	पेट्रोल पम्प (f)	petrol pamp
parking lot	पार्किंग (f)	pārking

80. Signs

signboard (store sign, etc.)	साईनबोर्ड (m)	saīnabord
notice (door sign, etc.)	दुकान का साईन (m)	dukān ka saīn
poster	पोस्टर (m)	postar
direction sign	दिशा संकेतक (m)	disha sanketak
arrow (sign)	तीर दिशा संकेतक (m)	tīr disha sanketak
caution	चेतावनी (f)	chetāvanī
warning sign	चेतावनी संकेतक (m)	chetāvanī sanketak
to warn (vt)	चेतावनी देना	chetāvanī dena
rest day (weekly ~)	छुट्टी का दिन (m)	chhuttī ka din
timetable (schedule)	समय सारणी (f)	samay sāranī
opening hours	खुलने का समय (m)	khulane ka samay
WELCOME!	आपका स्वागत है!	āpaka svāgat hai!
ENTRANCE	प्रवेश	pravesh
EXIT	निकास	nikās
PUSH	धक्का दें	dhakka den
PULL	खींचे	khīnche
OPEN	खुला	khula
CLOSED	बंद	band
WOMEN	औरतों के लिये	auraton ke liye
MEN	आदमियों के लिये	ādamiyon ke liye
DISCOUNTS	डिस्काउन्ट	diskaunt
SALE	सेल	sel
NEW!	नया!	naya!
FREE	मुफ्त	muft
ATTENTION!	ध्यान दें!	dhyān den!
NO VACANCIES	कोई जगह खाली नहीं है	koī jagah khālī nahin hai
RESERVED	रिज़र्वड	rizarvad
ADMINISTRATION	प्रशासन	prashāsan
STAFF ONLY	केवल कर्मचारियों के लिए	keval karmachāriyon ke lie
BEWARE OF THE DOG!	कुत्ते से सावधान!	kutte se sāvadhān!
NO SMOKING	धुम्रपान निषेध!	dhumrapān nishedh!
DO NOT TOUCH!	छूना मना!	chhūna mana!
DANGEROUS	खतरा	khatara
DANGER	खतरा	khatara
HIGH VOLTAGE	उच्च वोल्टेज	uchch voltej
NO SWIMMING!	तैरना मना!	tairana mana!
OUT OF ORDER	ख़राब	kharāb
FLAMMABLE	ज्वलनशील	jvalanashīl
FORBIDDEN	निषिद्ध	nishiddh

| NO TRESPASSING! | प्रवेश निषेध! | pravesh nishedh! |
| WET PAINT | गीला पेंट | gīla pent |

81. Urban transportation

bus	बस (f)	bas
streetcar	ट्रैम (m)	traim
trolley bus	ट्रॉलीबस (f)	trolības
route (of bus, etc.)	मार्ग (m)	mārg
number (e.g., bus ~)	नम्बर (m)	nambar

to go by ...	के माध्यम से जाना	ke mādhyam se jāna
to get on (~ the bus)	सवार होना	savār hona
to get off ...	उतरना	utarana

stop (e.g., bus ~)	बस स्टॉप (m)	bas stop
next stop	अगला स्टॉप (m)	agala stop
terminus	अंतिम स्टेशन (m)	antim steshan
schedule	समय सारणी (f)	samay sāranī
to wait (vt)	इतज़ार करना	intazār karana

ticket	टिकट (m)	tikat
fare	टिकट का किराया (m)	tikat ka kirāya
cashier (ticket seller)	कैशियर (m)	kaishiyar
ticket inspection	टिकट जाँच (f)	tikat jānch
ticket inspector	कंडक्टर (m)	kandaktar

to be late (for ...)	देर हो जाना	der ho jāna
to miss (~ the train, etc.)	छूट जाना	chhūt jāna
to be in a hurry	जल्दी में रहना	jaldī men rahana

taxi, cab	टैक्सी (m)	taiksī
taxi driver	टैक्सीवाला (m)	taiksīvāla
by taxi	टैक्सी से (m)	taiksī se
taxi stand	टैक्सी स्टैंड (m)	taiksī staind
to call a taxi	टैक्सी बुलाना	taiksī bulāna
to take a taxi	टैक्सी लेना	taiksī lena

traffic	यातायात (f)	yātāyāt
traffic jam	ट्रैफ़िक जाम (m)	traifik jām
rush hour	भीड़ का समय (m)	bhīr ka samay
to park (vi)	पार्क करना	pārk karana
to park (vt)	पार्क करना	pārk karana
parking lot	पार्किंग (f)	pārking

subway	मेट्रो (m)	metro
station	स्टेशन (m)	steshan
to take the subway	मेट्रो लेना	metro lena
train	रेलगाड़ी, ट्रेन (f)	relagārī, tren
train station	स्टेशन (m)	steshan

82. Sightseeing

monument	स्मारक (m)	smārak
fortress	किला (m)	kila
palace	भवन (m)	bhavan
castle	महल (m)	mahal
tower	मीनार (m)	mīnār
mausoleum	समाधि (f)	samādhi
architecture	वस्तुशाला (m)	vastushāla
medieval (adj)	मध्ययुगीय	madhayayugīy
ancient (adj)	प्राचीन	prāchīn
national (adj)	राष्ट्रीय	rāshtrīy
famous (monument, etc.)	मशहूर	mashhūr
tourist	पर्यटक (m)	paryatak
guide (person)	गाइड (m)	gaid
excursion, sightseeing tour	पर्यटन यात्रा (m)	paryatan yātra
to show (vt)	दिखाना	dikhāna
to tell (vt)	बताना	batāna
to find (vt)	ढूँढना	dhūnrhana
to get lost (lose one's way)	खो जाना	kho jāna
map (e.g., subway ~)	नक्शा (m)	naksha
map (e.g., city ~)	नक्शा (m)	naksha
souvenir, gift	यादगार (m)	yādagār
gift shop	गिफ्ट शॉप (f)	gift shop
to take pictures	फोटो खींचना	foto khīnchana
to have one's picture taken	अपना फ़ोटो खिंचवाना	apana foto khinchavāna

83. Shopping

to buy (purchase)	खरीदना	kharīdana
purchase	खरीदारी (f)	kharīdārī
to go shopping	खरीदारी करने जाना	kharīdārī karane jāna
shopping	खरीदारी (f)	kharīdārī
to be open (ab. store)	खुला होना	khula hona
to be closed	बन्द होना	band hona
footwear, shoes	जूता (m)	jūta
clothes, clothing	पोशाक (m)	poshāk
cosmetics	श्रृंगार-सामग्री (f)	shrrngār-sāmagrī
food products	खाने-पीने की चीज़ें (f pl)	khāne-pīne kī chīzen
gift, present	उपहार (m)	upahār
salesman	बेचनेवाला (m)	bechanevāla
saleswoman	बेचनेवाली (f)	bechanevālī

check out, cash desk	कैश-काउन्टर (m)	kaish-kauntar
mirror	आईना (m)	āīna
counter (store ~)	काउन्टर (m)	kauntar
fitting room	ट्राई करने का कमरा (m)	traī karane ka kamara
to try on	ट्राई करना	traī karana
to fit (ab. dress, etc.)	फिटिंग करना	fiting karana
to like (I like …)	पसंद करना	pasand karana
price	दाम (m)	dām
price tag	प्राइस टैग (m)	prais taig
to cost (vt)	दाम होना	dām hona
How much?	कितना?	kitana?
discount	डिस्काउन्ट (m)	diskaunt
inexpensive (adj)	सस्ता	sasta
cheap (adj)	सस्ता	sasta
expensive (adj)	महंगा	mahanga
It's expensive	यह महंगा है	yah mahanga hai
rental (n)	रेन्टल (m)	rental
to rent (~ a tuxedo)	किराए पर लेना	kirae par lena
credit (trade credit)	क्रेडिट (m)	kredit
on credit (adv)	क्रेडिट पर	kredit par

84. Money

money	पैसा (m pl)	paisa
currency exchange	मुद्रा विनिमय (m)	mudra vinimay
exchange rate	विनिमय दर (m)	vinimay dar
ATM	एटीएम (m)	etīem
coin	सिक्का (m)	sikka
dollar	डॉलर (m)	dolar
euro	यूरो (m)	yūro
lira	लीरा (f)	līra
Deutschmark	डचमार्क (m)	dachamārk
franc	फ़्रांक (m)	fränk
pound sterling	पाउन्ड स्टरलिंग (m)	paund staraling
yen	येन (m)	yen
debt	क़र्ज़ (m)	karz
debtor	क़र्ज़दार (m)	qarzadār
to lend (money)	क़र्ज़ देना	karz dena
to borrow (vi, vt)	क़र्ज़ लेना	karz lena
bank	बैंक (m)	baink
account	बैंक खाता (m)	baink khāta
to deposit into the account	बैंक खाते में जमा करना	baink khāte men jama karana

to withdraw (vt)	खाते से पैसे निकालना	khāte se paise nikālana
credit card	क्रेडिट कार्ड (m)	kredit kārd
cash	कैश (m pl)	kaish
check	चेक (m)	chek
to write a check	चेक लिखना	chek likhana
checkbook	चेकबुक (f)	chekabuk
wallet	बटुआ (m)	batua
change purse	बटुआ (m)	batua
safe	लॉकर (m)	lokar
heir	उत्तराधिकारी (m)	uttarādhikārī
inheritance	उत्तराधिकार (m)	uttarādhikār
fortune (wealth)	संपत्ति (f)	sampatti
lease	किराये पर देना (m)	kirāye par dena
rent (money)	किराया (m)	kirāya
to rent (sth from sb)	किराए पर लेना	kirae par lena
price	दाम (m)	dām
cost	कीमत (f)	kīmat
sum	रक़म (m)	raqam
to spend (vt)	खर्च करना	kharch karana
expenses	खर्च (m pl)	kharch
to economize (vi, vt)	बचत करना	bachat karana
economical	किफ़ायती	kifāyatī
to pay (vi, vt)	दाम चुकाना	dām chukāna
payment	भुगतान (m)	bhugatān
change (give the ~)	चिल्लर (m)	chillar
tax	टैक्स (m)	taiks
fine	जुर्माना (m)	jurmāna
to fine (vt)	जुर्माना लगाना	jurmāna lagāna

85. Post. Postal service

post office	डाकघर (m)	dākaghar
mail (letters, etc.)	डाक (m)	dāk
mailman	डाकिया (m)	dākiya
opening hours	खुलने का समय (m)	khulane ka samay
letter	पत्र (m)	patr
registered letter	रजिस्टरी पत्र (m)	rajistarī patr
postcard	पोस्ट कार्ड (m)	post kārd
telegram	तार (m)	tār
package (parcel)	पार्सल (f)	pārsal
money transfer	मनी ट्रांसफर (m)	manī trānsafar
to receive (vt)	पाना	pāna

| to send (vt) | भेजना | bhejana |
| sending | भेज (m) | bhej |

address	पता (m)	pata
ZIP code	पिन कोड (m)	pin kod
sender	भेजनेवाला (m)	bhejanevāla
receiver	पानेवाला (m)	pānevāla

| name (first name) | पहला नाम (m) | pahala nām |
| surname (last name) | उपनाम (m) | upanām |

postage rate	डाक दर (m)	dāk dar
standard (adj)	मानक	mānak
economical (adj)	किफ़ायती	kifāyatī

weight	वज़न (m)	vazan
to weigh (~ letters)	तोलना	tolana
envelope	लिफ़ाफ़ा (m)	lifāfa
postage stamp	डाक टिकट (m)	dāk tikat
to stamp an envelope	डाक टिकट लगाना	dāk tikat lagāna

Dwelling. House. Home

86. House. Dwelling

house	मकान (m)	makān
at home (adv)	घर पर	ghar par
yard	आंगन (m)	āngan
fence (iron ~)	बाड़ (f)	bār
brick (n)	ईंट (f)	īnt
brick (as adj)	ईंट का	īnt ka
stone (n)	पत्थर (m)	patthar
stone (as adj)	पत्थरीला	pattharīla
concrete (n)	कंक्रीट (m)	kankrīt
concrete (as adj)	कंक्रीट का	kankrīt ka
new (new-built)	नया	naya
old (adj)	पुराना	purāna
decrepit (house)	टूटा-फूटा	tūta-fūta
modern (adj)	आधुनिक	ādhunik
multistory (adj)	बहुमंज़िला	bahumanzila
tall (~ building)	ऊंचा	ūncha
floor, story	मंज़िल (f)	manzil
single-story (adj)	एकमंज़िला	ekamanzila
1st floor	पहली मंज़िल (f)	pahalī manzil
top floor	ऊपरी मंज़िल (f)	ūparī manzil
roof	छत (f)	chhat
chimney	चिमनी (f)	chimanī
roof tiles	खपड़ा (m)	khapara
tiled (adj)	टाइल का बना	tail ka bana
attic (storage place)	अटारी (f)	atārī
window	खिड़की (f)	khirakī
glass	कांच (f)	kānch
window ledge	विन्डो सिल (m)	vindo sil
shutters	शट्टर (m)	shattar
wall	दीवार (f)	dīvār
balcony	बाल्कनी (f)	bālkanī
downspout	जल निकास पाइप (f)	jal nikās paip
upstairs (to be ~)	ऊपर	ūpar
to go upstairs	ऊपर जाना	ūpar jāna
to come down (the stairs)	नीचे उतरना	nīche utarana
to move (to new premises)	घर बदलना	ghar badalana

87. House. Entrance. Lift

entrance	प्रवेश-द्वार (m)	pravesh-dvār
stairs (stairway)	सीढ़ी (f)	sīrhī
steps	सीढ़ी (f)	sīrhī
banister	रेलिंग (f pl)	reling
lobby (hotel ~)	हॉल (m)	hol
mailbox	लेटर बॉक्स (m)	letar boks
garbage can	कचरे का डब्बा (m)	kachare ka dabba
trash chute	कचरे का श्यूट (m)	kachare ka shyūt
elevator	लिफ़्ट (m)	lift
freight elevator	लिफ़्ट (m)	lift
elevator cage	लिफ़्ट (f)	lift
to take the elevator	लिफ़्ट से जाना	lift se jāna
apartment	फ़्लैट (f)	flait
residents (~ of a building)	निवासी (m)	nivāsī
neighbor (masc.)	पड़ोसी (m)	parosī
neighbor (fem.)	पड़ोसन (f)	parosan
neighbors	पड़ोसी (m pl)	parosī

88. House. Electricity

electricity	बिजली (f)	bijalī
light bulb	बल्ब (m)	balb
switch	स्विच (m)	svich
fuse (plug fuse)	फ्यूज़ बटन (m)	fyūz batan
cable, wire (electric ~)	तार (m)	tār
wiring	तार (m)	tār
electricity meter	बिजली का मीटर (m)	bijalī ka mītar
readings	मीटर रीडिंग (f)	mītar rīding

89. House. Doors. Locks

door	दरवाज़ा (m)	daravāza
gate (vehicle ~)	फाटक (m)	fātak
handle, doorknob	हत्था (m)	hattha
to unlock (unbolt)	खोलना	kholana
to open (vt)	खोलना	kholana
to close (vt)	बंद करना	band karana
key	चाबी (f)	chābī
bunch (of keys)	चाबियों का गुच्छा (m)	chābiyon ka guchchha
to creak (door, etc.)	चरमराना	charamarāna

creak	चरमराने की आवाज़ (m)	charamarāne kī āvāz
hinge (door ~)	क़ब्ज़ा (m)	qabza
doormat	पायदान (m)	pāyadān

door lock	ताला (m)	tāla
keyhole	ताला (m)	tāla
crossbar (sliding bar)	अर्गला (f)	argala
door latch	अर्गला (f)	argala
padlock	ताला (m)	tāla

to ring (~ the door bell)	बजाना	bajāna
ringing (sound)	घंटी (f)	ghantī
doorbell	घंटी (f)	ghantī
doorbell button	घंटी (f)	ghantī
knock (at the door)	खटखट (f)	khatakhat
to knock (vi)	खटखटाना	khatakhatāna

code	कोड (m)	kod
combination lock	कॉम्बिनेशन लॉक (m)	kombineshan lok
intercom	इंटरकॉम (m)	intarakom
number (on the door)	मकान नम्बर (m)	makān nambar
doorplate	नेम प्लेट (f)	nem plet
peephole	पीप होल (m)	pīp hol

90. Country house

village	गांव (m)	gānv
vegetable garden	सब्ज़ियों का बगीचा (m)	sabziyon ka bagīcha
fence	बाड़ा (m)	bāra

| picket fence | बाड़ (f) | bār |
| wicket gate | छोटा फाटक (m) | chhota fātak |

| granary | अनाज का गोदाम (m) | anāj ka godām |
| root cellar | सब्ज़ियों का गोदाम (m) | sabziyon ka godām |

| shed (garden ~) | शेड (m) | shed |
| well (water) | कुआँ (m) | kuān |

| stove (wood-fired ~) | चूल्हा (m) | chūlha |
| to stoke the stove | चूल्हा जलाना | chūlaha jalāna |

| firewood | लकड़ियां (f pl) | lakariyān |
| log (firewood) | लकड़ी (f) | lakarī |

| veranda | बराम्दा (f) | barāmda |
| deck (terrace) | छत (f) | chhat |

| stoop (front steps) | पोर्च (m) | porch |
| swing (hanging seat) | झूले वाली कुर्सी (f) | jhūle vālī kursī |

91. Villa. Mansion

country house	गाँव का मकान (m)	gānv ka makān
villa (seaside ~)	बंगला (m)	bangala
wing (~ of a building)	खंड (m)	khand
garden	बाग़ (m)	bāg
park	पार्क (m)	pārk
tropical greenhouse	ग्रीनहाउस (m)	grīnahaus
to look after (garden, etc.)	देखभाल करना	dekhabhāl karana
swimming pool	तरण-ताल (m)	taran-tāl
gym (home gym)	व्यायाम कक्ष (m)	vyāyām kaksh
tennis court	टेनिस-कोर्ट (m)	tenis-kort
home theater (room)	सिनेमाघर (m)	sinemāghar
garage	गराज (m)	garāj
private property	नीजी सम्पत्ति (f)	nījī sampatti
private land	नीजी ज़मीन (f)	nījī zamīn
warning (caution)	चेतावनी (f)	chetāvanī
warning sign	चेतावनी संकेत (m)	chetāvanī sanket
security	सुरक्षा (f)	suraksha
security guard	पहरेदार (m)	paharedār
burglar alarm	चोर घंटी (f)	chor ghantī

92. Castle. Palace

castle	महल (m)	mahal
palace	भवन (m)	bhavan
fortress	किला (m)	kila
wall (round castle)	दीवार (f)	dīvār
tower	मीनार (m)	mīnār
keep, donjon	केन्द्रीय मीनार (m)	kendrīy mīnār
portcullis	आरोहण द्वार (m)	ārohan dvār
underground passage	भूमिगत सुरंग (m)	bhūmigat surang
moat	खाई (f)	khaī
chain	जंजीर (f)	janjīr
arrow loop	ऐरो लूप (m)	airo lūp
magnificent (adj)	शानदार	shānadār
majestic (adj)	महिमामय	mahimāmay
impregnable (adj)	अभेध	abhedy
medieval (adj)	मध्ययुगीय	madhayayugīy

93. Apartment

apartment	फ़्लैट (f)	flait
room	कमरा (m)	kamara
bedroom	सोने का कमरा (m)	sone ka kamara
dining room	खाने का कमरा (m)	khāne ka kamara
living room	बैठक (f)	baithak
study (home office)	घरेलू कार्यालय (m)	gharelū kāryālay
entry room	प्रवेश कक्ष (m)	pravesh kaksh
bathroom (room with a bath or shower)	स्नानघर (m)	snānaghar
half bath	शौचालय (m)	shauchālay
ceiling	छत (f)	chhat
floor	फ़र्श (m)	farsh
corner	कोना (m)	kona

94. Apartment. Cleaning

to clean (vi, vt)	साफ़ करना	sāf karana
to put away (to stow)	रख देना	rakh dena
dust	धूल (m)	dhūl
dusty (adj)	धूसर	dhūsar
to dust (vt)	धूल पोंछना	dhūl ponchhana
vacuum cleaner	वैक्युम क्लीनर (m)	vaikyum klīnar
to vacuum (vt)	वैक्यूम करना	vaikyūm karana
to sweep (vi, vt)	झाड़ू लगाना	jhārū lagāna
sweepings	कूड़ा (m)	kūra
order	तरतीब (m)	taratīb
disorder, mess	बेतरतीब (f)	betaratīb
mop	पोंछा (m)	ponchha
dust cloth	डस्टर (m)	dastar
short broom	झाड़ू (m)	jhārū
dustpan	कूड़ा उठाने का तसला (m)	kūra uthāne ka tasala

95. Furniture. Interior

furniture	फ़र्निचर (m)	farnichar
table	मेज़ (f)	mez
chair	कुर्सी (f)	kursī
bed	पलंग (m)	palang
couch, sofa	सोफ़ा (m)	sofa
armchair	हत्थे वाली कुर्सी (f)	hatthe vālī kursī
bookcase	किताबों की अलमारी (f)	kitābon kī alamārī

shelf	शेल्फ़ (f)	shelf
wardrobe	कपड़ों की अलमारी (f)	kaparon kī alamārī
coat rack (wall-mounted ~)	खूँटी (f)	khūntī
coat stand	खूँटी (f)	khūntī
bureau, dresser	कपड़ों की अलमारी (f)	kaparon kī alamārī
coffee table	कॉफ़ी की मेज़ (f)	kofī kī mez
mirror	आईना (m)	āīna
carpet	कालीन (m)	kālīn
rug, small carpet	दरी (f)	darī
fireplace	चिमनी (f)	chimanī
candle	मोमबत्ती (f)	momabattī
candlestick	मोमबत्तीदान (m)	momabattīdān
drapes	परदे (m pl)	parade
wallpaper	वॉल पेपर (m)	vol pepar
blinds (jalousie)	जेलुज़ी (f pl)	jeluzī
table lamp	मेज़ का लैम्प (m)	mez ka laimp
wall lamp (sconce)	दिवार का लैम्प (m)	divār ka laimp
floor lamp	फ़र्श का लैम्प (m)	farsh ka laimp
chandelier	झूमर (m)	jhūmar
leg (of chair, table)	पाँव (m)	pānv
armrest	कुर्सी का हत्था (m)	kursī ka hattha
back (backrest)	कुर्सी की पीठ (f)	kursī kī pīth
drawer	दराज़ (m)	darāz

96. Bedding

bedclothes	बिस्तर के कपड़े (m)	bistar ke kapare
pillow	तकिया (m)	takiya
pillowcase	ग़िलाफ़ (m)	gilāf
duvet, comforter	रज़ाई (f)	razaī
sheet	चादर (f)	chādar
bedspread	चादर (f)	chādar

97. Kitchen

kitchen	रसोईघर (m)	rasoīghar
gas	गैस (m)	gais
gas stove (range)	गैस का चूल्हा (m)	gais ka chūlha
electric stove	बिजली का चूल्हा (m)	bijalī ka chūlha
oven	ओवन (m)	ovan
microwave oven	माइक्रोवेव ओवन (m)	maikrovev ovan
refrigerator	फ़्रिज (m)	frij

freezer	फ़्रीजर (m)	frījar
dishwasher	डिशवॉशर (m)	dishavoshar
meat grinder	कीमा बनाने की मशीन (f)	kīma banāne kī mashīn
juicer	जूसर (m)	jūsar
toaster	टोस्टर (m)	tostar
mixer	मिक्सर (m)	miksar
coffee machine	कॉफ़ी मशीन (f)	kofī mashīn
coffee pot	कॉफ़ी पॉट (m)	kofī pot
coffee grinder	कॉफ़ी पीसने की मशीन (f)	kofī pīsane kī mashīn
kettle	केतली (f)	ketalī
teapot	चायदानी (f)	chāyadānī
lid	ढक्कन (m)	dhakkan
tea strainer	छलनी (f)	chhalanī
spoon	चम्मच (m)	chammach
teaspoon	चम्मच (m)	chammach
soup spoon	चम्मच (m)	chammach
fork	काँटा (m)	kānta
knife	छुरी (f)	chhurī
tableware (dishes)	बरतन (m)	baratan
plate (dinner ~)	तश्तरी (f)	tashtarī
saucer	तश्तरी (f)	tashtarī
shot glass	जाम (m)	jām
glass (tumbler)	गिलास (m)	gilās
cup	प्याला (m)	pyāla
sugar bowl	चीनीदानी (f)	chīnīdānī
salt shaker	नमकदानी (m)	namakadānī
pepper shaker	मिर्चदानी (f)	mirchadānī
butter dish	मक्खनदानी (f)	makkhanadānī
stock pot (soup pot)	सॉसपैन (m)	sosapain
frying pan (skillet)	फ़्राइ पैन (f)	frai pain
ladle	डोई (f)	doī
colander	कालेन्डर (m)	kālendar
tray (serving ~)	थाली (m)	thālī
bottle	बोतल (f)	botal
jar (glass)	शीशी (f)	shīshī
can	डिब्बा (m)	dibba
bottle opener	बोतल ओपनर (m)	botal opanar
can opener	ओपनर (m)	opanar
corkscrew	पेंचकस (m)	penchakas
filter	फ़िल्टर (m)	filtar
to filter (vt)	फ़िल्टर करना	filtar karana
trash, garbage (food waste, etc.)	कूड़ा (m)	kūra
trash can (kitchen ~)	कूड़े की बाल्टी (f)	kūre kī bāltī

98. Bathroom

bathroom	स्नानघर (m)	snānaghar
water	पानी (m)	pānī
faucet	नल (m)	nal
hot water	गरम पानी (m)	garam pānī
cold water	ठंडा पानी (m)	thanda pānī
toothpaste	टूथपेस्ट (m)	tūthapest
to brush one's teeth	दाँत ब्रश करना	dānt brash karana
to shave (vi)	शेव करना	shev karana
shaving foam	शेविंग फ़ोम (m)	sheving fom
razor	रेज़र (f)	rezar
to wash (one's hands, etc.)	धोना	dhona
to take a bath	नहाना	nahāna
shower	शावर (m)	shāvar
to take a shower	शावर लेना	shāvar lena
bathtub	बाथटब (m)	bāthatab
toilet (toilet bowl)	संडास (m)	sandās
sink (washbasin)	सिंक (m)	sink
soap	साबुन (m)	sābun
soap dish	साबुनदानी (f)	sābunadānī
sponge	स्पंज (f)	spanj
shampoo	शैम्पू (m)	shaimpū
towel	तौलिया (f)	tauliya
bathrobe	चोगा (m)	choga
laundry (process)	धुलाई (f)	dhulaī
washing machine	वॉशिंग मशीन (f)	voshing mashīn
to do the laundry	कपड़े धोना	kapare dhona
laundry detergent	कपड़े धोने का पाउडर (m)	kapare dhone ka paudar

99. Household appliances

TV set	टीबी सेट (m)	tīvī set
tape recorder	टेप रिकार्डर (m)	tep rikārdar
VCR (video recorder)	वीडियो टेप रिकार्डर (m)	vīdiyo tep rikārdar
radio	रेडियो (m)	rediyo
player (CD, MP3, etc.)	प्लेयर (m)	pleyar
video projector	वीडियो प्रोजेक्टर (m)	vīdiyo projektar
home movie theater	होम थीएटर (m)	hom thīetar
DVD player	डीवीडी प्लेयर (m)	dīvīdī pleyar
amplifier	ध्वनि-विस्तारक (m)	dhvani-vistārak

video game console	वीडियो गेम कन्सोल (m)	vīdiyo gem kansol
video camera	वीडियो कैमरा (m)	vīdiyo kaimara
camera (photo)	कैमरा (m)	kaimara
digital camera	डीजिटल कैमरा (m)	dījital kaimara
vacuum cleaner	वैक्यूम क्लीनर (m)	vaikyūm klīnar
iron (e.g., steam ~)	इस्तरी (f)	istarī
ironing board	इस्तरी तख्ता (m)	istarī takhta
telephone	टेलीफ़ोन (m)	telīfon
cell phone	मोबाइल फ़ोन (m)	mobail fon
typewriter	टाइपराइटर (m)	taiparaitar
sewing machine	सिलाई मशीन (f)	silaī mashīn
microphone	माइक्रोफ़ोन (m)	maikrofon
headphones	हैडफ़ोन (m pl)	hairafon
remote control (TV)	रिमोट (m)	rimot
CD, compact disc	सीडी (m)	sīdī
cassette, tape	कैसेट (f)	kaiset
vinyl record	रिकार्ड (m)	rikārd

100. Repairs. Renovation

renovations	नवीकरण (m)	navīkaran
to renovate (vt)	नवीकरण करना	navīkaran karana
to repair, to fix (vt)	मरम्मत करना	marammat karana
to put in order	ठीक करना	thīk karana
to redo (do again)	फिर से करना	fir se karana
paint	रंग (m)	rang
to paint (~ a wall)	रंगना	rangana
house painter	रोग़न करनेवाला (m)	rogan karanevāla
paintbrush	सफ़ेदी का ब्रश (m)	safedī ka brash
whitewash	सफ़ेदी (f)	safedī
to whitewash (vt)	सफ़ेदी करना	safedī karana
wallpaper	वॉल-पैपर (m pl)	vol-paipar
to wallpaper (vt)	वाल-पैपर लगाना	vāl-paipar lagāna
varnish	पॉलिश (f)	polish
to varnish (vt)	पॉलिश करना	polish karana

101. Plumbing

water	पानी (m)	pānī
hot water	गरम पानी (m)	garam pānī
cold water	ठंडा पानी (m)	thanda pānī

faucet	टोंटी (f)	tontī
drop (of water)	बूँद (m)	būnd
to drip (vi)	टपकना	tapakana
to leak (ab. pipe)	बहना	bahana
leak (pipe ~)	लीक (m)	līk
puddle	डबरा (m)	dabara
pipe	पाइप (f)	paip
valve (e.g., ball ~)	वॉल्व (m)	volv
to be clogged up	भर जाना	bhar jāna
tools	औज़ार (m pl)	auzār
adjustable wrench	रिंच (m)	rinch
to unscrew (lid, filter, etc.)	खोलना	kholana
to screw (tighten)	बंद करना	band karana
to unclog (vt)	सफ़ाई करना	safaī karana
plumber	प्लम्बर (m)	plambar
basement	तहख़ाना (m)	tahakhāna
sewerage (system)	मलप्रवाह-पद्धति (f)	malapravāh-paddhati

102. Fire. Conflagration

fire (accident)	आग (f)	āg
flame	आग की लपटें (f)	āg kī lapaten
spark	चिंगारी (f)	chingārī
smoke (from fire)	धुँआ (m)	dhuna
torch (flaming stick)	मशाल (m)	mashāl
campfire	कैम्प फ़ायर (m)	kaimp fāyar
gas, gasoline	पेट्रोल (m)	petrol
kerosene (type of fuel)	केरोसीन (m)	kerosīn
flammable (adj)	ज्वलनशील	jvalanashīl
explosive (adj)	विस्फोटक	visfotak
NO SMOKING	धूम्रपान निषेध!	dhumrapān nishedh!
safety	सुरक्षा (f)	suraksha
danger	ख़तरा (f)	khatara
dangerous (adj)	ख़तरनाक	khataranāk
to catch fire	आग लग जाना	āg lag jāna
explosion	विस्फोट (m)	visfot
to set fire	आग लगाना	āg lagāna
arsonist	आग लगानेवाला (m)	āg lagānevāla
arson	आगज़नी (f)	āgazanī
to blaze (vi)	दहकना	dahakana
to burn (be on fire)	जलना	jalana
to burn down	जल जाना	jal jāna
firefighter, fireman	दमकल कर्मचारी (m)	damakal karmachārī

fire truck	दमकल (m)	damakal
fire department	फ़ायरब्रिगेड (m)	fâyarabriged
fire truck ladder	फ़ायर ट्रक सीढ़ी (f)	fâyar trak sīrhī
fire hose	आग बुझाने का पाइप (m)	āg bujhāne ka paip
fire extinguisher	अग्निशामक (m)	agnishāmak
helmet	हेलमेट (f)	helamet
siren	साइरन (m)	sairan
to cry (for help)	चिल्लाना	chillāna
to call for help	मदद के लिए बुलाना	madad ke lie bulāna
rescuer	बचानेवाला (m)	bachānevāla
to rescue (vt)	बचाना	bachāna
to arrive (vi)	पहुँचना	pahunchana
to extinguish (vt)	आग बुझाना	āg bujhāna
water	पानी (m)	pānī
sand	रेत (f)	ret
ruins (destruction)	खंडहर (m pl)	khandahar
to collapse (building, etc.)	गिर जाना	gir jāna
to fall down (vi)	टूटकर गिरना	tūtakar girana
to cave in (ceiling, floor)	ढहना	dhahana
piece of debris	मलबे का टुकड़ा (m)	malabe ka tukara
ash	राख (m)	rākh
to suffocate (die)	दम घुटना	dam ghutana
to be killed (perish)	मर जाना	mar jāna

HUMAN ACTIVITIES

Job. Business. Part 1

103. Office. Working in the office

office (company ~)	कार्यालय (m)	kāryālay
office (of director, etc.)	कार्यालय (m)	kāryālay
reception desk	रिसेप्शन (m)	risepshan
secretary (fem.)	सेक्रटरी (f)	sekratarī
director	निदेशक (m)	nideshak
manager	मैनेजर (m)	mainejar
accountant	लेखापाल (m)	lekhāpāl
employee	कर्मचारी (m)	karmachārī
furniture	फ़र्निचर (m)	farnichar
desk	मेज़ (f)	mez
desk chair	कुर्सी (f)	kursī
drawer unit	साइड टेबल (f)	said tebal
coat stand	खूँटी (f)	khūntī
computer	कंप्यूटर (m)	kampyūtar
printer	प्रिन्टर (m)	printar
fax machine	फ़ैक्स मशीन (f)	faiks mashīn
photocopier	ज़ीरोक्स (m)	zīroks
paper	काग़ज़ (m)	kāgaz
office supplies	स्टेशनरी (m pl)	steshanarī
mouse pad	माउस पैड (m)	maus paid
sheet (of paper)	पन्ना (m)	panna
binder	बाइन्डर (m)	baindar
catalog	कैटेलॉग (m)	kaitelog
phone directory	डाइरेक्टरी (f)	dairektarī
documentation	दस्तावेज़ (m)	dastāvez
brochure (e.g., 12 pages ~)	पुस्तिका (f)	pustika
leaflet (promotional ~)	पर्चा (m)	parcha
sample	नमूना (m)	namūna
training meeting	प्रशिक्षण बैठक (f)	prashikshan baithak
meeting (of managers)	बैठक (f)	baithak
lunch time	मध्यान्तर (m)	madhyāntar
to make a copy	कॉपी करना	kopī karana

to make multiple copies	ज़िरोक्स करना	zīroks karana
to receive a fax	फ़ैक्स मिलना	faiks milana
to send a fax	फ़ैक्स भेजना	faiks bhejana
to call (by phone)	फ़ोन करना	fon karana
to answer (vt)	जवाब देना	javāb dena
to put through	फ़ोन ट्रांस्फर करना	fon trānsfar karana
to arrange, to set up	व्यवस्थित करना	vyavasthit karana
to demonstrate (vt)	प्रदर्शित करना	pradarshit karana
to be absent	अनुपस्थित होना	anupasthit hona
absence	अनुपस्थिती (f)	anupasthitī

104. Business processes. Part 1

occupation	पेशा (m)	pesha
firm	कम्पनी (f)	kampanī
company	कम्पनी (f)	kampanī
corporation	निगम (m)	nigam
enterprise	उद्योग (m)	udyog
agency	एजेंसी (f)	ejensī
agreement (contract)	समझौता (f)	samajhauta
contract	ठेका (m)	theka
deal	सौदा (f)	sauda
order (to place an ~)	आर्डर (m)	ārdar
terms (of the contract)	शर्तें (f)	sharten
wholesale (adv)	थोक	thok
wholesale (adj)	थोक	thok
wholesale (n)	थोक (m)	thok
retail (adj)	खुदरा	khudara
retail (n)	खुदरा (m)	khudara
competitor	प्रतियोगी (m)	pratiyogī
competition	प्रतियोगिता (f)	pratiyogita
to compete (vi)	प्रतियोगिता करना	pratiyogita karana
partner (associate)	सहयोगी (f)	sahayogī
partnership	साझेदारी (f)	sājhedārī
crisis	संकट (m)	sankat
bankruptcy	दिवाला (m)	divāla
to go bankrupt	दिवालिया हो जाना	divāliya ho jāna
difficulty	कठिनाई (f)	kathinaī
problem	समस्या (f)	samasya
catastrophe	दुर्घटना (f)	durghatana
economy	अर्थशास्त्र (f)	arthashāstr
economic (~ growth)	आर्थिक	ārthik

economic recession	अार्थिक गिरावट (f)	arthik girāvat
goal (aim)	लक्ष्य (m)	lakshy
task	कार्य (m)	kāry
to trade (vi)	व्यापार करना	vyāpār karana
network (distribution ~)	जाल (m)	jāl
inventory (stock)	गोदाम (m)	godām
range (assortment)	किस्म (m)	kism
leader (leading company)	लीडर (m)	līdar
large (~ company)	विशाल	vishāl
monopoly	एकाधिकार (m)	ekādhikār
theory	सिद्धांत (f)	siddhānt
practice	व्यवहार (f)	vyavahār
experience (in my ~)	अनुभव (m)	anubhav
trend (tendency)	प्रवृत्ति (f)	pravrtti
development	विकास (m)	vikās

105. Business processes. Part 2

profit (foregone ~)	लाभ (f)	lābh
profitable (~ deal)	फ़ायदेमन्द	fāyademand
delegation (group)	प्रतिनिधिमंडल (f)	pratinidhimandal
salary	आय (m)	āy
to correct (an error)	ठीक करना	thīk karana
business trip	व्यापारिक यात्रा (f)	vyāpārik yātra
commission	आयोग (f)	āyog
to control (vt)	जांचना	jānchana
conference	सम्मेलन (m)	sammelan
license	अनुज्ञप्ति (f)	anugyapti
reliable (~ partner)	विश्वसनीय	vishvasanīy
initiative (undertaking)	पहल (f)	pahal
norm (standard)	मानक (m)	mānak
circumstance	परिस्थिति (f)	paristhiti
duty (of employee)	कर्तव्य (m)	kartavy
organization (company)	संगठन (f)	sangathan
organization (process)	आयोजन (m)	āyojan
organized (adj)	आयोजित	āyojit
cancellation	निरस्तीकरण (m)	nirastīkaran
to cancel (call off)	रद्द करना	radd karana
report (official ~)	रिपोर्ट (m)	riport
patent	पेटेंट (m)	petent
to patent (obtain patent)	पेटेंट करना	petent karana
to plan (vt)	योजना बनाना	yojana banāna

bonus (money)	बोनस (m)	bonas
professional (adj)	पेशेवर	peshevar
procedure	प्रक्रिया (f)	prakriya
to examine (contract, etc.)	विचार करना	vichār karana
calculation	हिसाब (m)	hisāb
reputation	प्रतिष्ठा (f)	pratishtha
risk	जोखिम (m)	jokhim
to manage, to run	प्रबंध करना	prabandh karana
information	सूचना (f)	sūchana
property	जायदाद (f)	jāyadād
union	संघ (m)	sangh
life insurance	जीवन-बीमा (m)	jīvan-bīma
to insure (vt)	बीमा करना	bīma karana
insurance	बीमा (m)	bīma
auction (~ sale)	नीलामी (m pl)	nīlāmī
to notify (inform)	जानकारी देना	jānakārī dena
management (process)	प्रबंधन (m)	prabandhan
service (~ industry)	सेवा (f)	seva
forum	मंच (m)	manch
to function (vi)	कार्य करना	kāry karana
stage (phase)	चरण (m)	charan
legal (~ services)	कानूनी	kānūnī
lawyer (legal advisor)	वकील (m)	vakīl

106. Production. Works

plant	कारख़ाना (m)	kārakhāna
factory	कारख़ाना (m)	kārakhāna
workshop	वर्कशाप (m)	varkashāp
works, production site	उत्पादन स्थल (m)	utpādan sthal
industry (manufacturing)	उद्योग (m)	udyog
industrial (adj)	औद्योगिक	audyogik
heavy industry	भारी उद्योग (m)	bhārī udyog
light industry	हल्का उद्योग (m)	halka udyog
products	उत्पाद (m)	utpād
to produce (vt)	उत्पादन करना	utpādan karana
raw materials	कच्चा माल (m)	kachcha māl
foreman (construction ~)	फ़ोरमैन (m)	foramain
workers team (crew)	मज़दूर दल (m)	mazadūr dal
worker	मज़दूर (m)	mazadūr
working day	कार्यदिवस (m)	kāryadivas
pause (rest break)	अंतराल (m)	antarāl

meeting	बैठक (f)	baithak
to discuss (vt)	चर्चा करना	charcha karana
plan	योजना (f)	yojana
to fulfill the plan	योजना बनाना	yojana banāna
rate of output	उत्पादन दर (f)	utpādan dar
quality	गुणवत्ता (m)	gunavatta
control (checking)	जाँच (f)	jānch
quality control	गुणवत्ता जाँच (f)	gunavatta jānch
workplace safety	कार्यस्थल सुरक्षा (f)	kāryasthal suraksha
discipline	अनुशासन (m)	anushāsan
violation (of safety rules, etc.)	उल्लंघन (m)	ullanghan
to violate (rules)	उल्लंघन करना	ullanghan karana
strike	हड़ताल (f)	haratāl
striker	हड़तालकारी (m)	haratālakārī
to be on strike	हड़ताल करना	haratāl karana
labor union	ट्रेड-यूनियन (m)	tred-yūniyan
to invent (machine, etc.)	आविष्कार करना	āvishkār karana
invention	आविष्कार (m)	āvishkār
research	अनुसंधान (f)	anusandhān
to improve (make better)	सुधारना	sudhārana
technology	प्रौद्योगिकी (f)	praudyogikī
technical drawing	तकनीकी चित्रकारी (f)	takanīkī chitrakārī
load, cargo	भार (m)	bhār
loader (person)	कुली (m)	kulī
to load (vehicle, etc.)	लादना	lādana
loading (process)	लादना (m)	lādana
to unload (vi, vt)	सामान उतारना	sāmān utārana
unloading	उतारना	utārana
transportation	परिवहन (m)	parivahan
transportation company	परिवहन कम्पनी (f)	parivahan kampanī
to transport (vt)	अपवाहन करना	apavāhan karana
freight car	माल गाड़ी (f)	māl gārī
tank (e.g., oil ~)	टैंकर (m)	tainkar
truck	ट्रक (m)	trak
machine tool	मशीनी उपकरण (m)	mashīnī upakaran
mechanism	यंत्र (m)	yantr
industrial waste	औद्योगिक अवशेष (m)	audyogik avashesh
packing (process)	पैकिंग (f)	paiking
to pack (vt)	पैक करना	paik karana

107. Contract. Agreement

contract	ठेका (m)	theka
agreement	समझौता (f)	samajhauta
addendum	परिशिष्ट (f)	parishisht
to sign a contract	अनुबंध पर हस्ताक्षर करना	anubandh par hastākshar karana
signature	हस्ताक्षर (m)	hastākshar
to sign (vt)	हस्ताक्षर करना	hastākshar karana
seal (stamp)	सील (m)	sīl
subject of contract	अनुबंध की विषय-वस्तु (f)	anubandh kī vishay-vastu
clause	धारा (f)	dhāra
parties (in contract)	पार्टी (f)	pārtī
legal address	कानूनी पता (m)	kānūnī pata
to violate the contract	अनुबंध का उल्लंघन करना	anubandh ka ullanghan karana
commitment (obligation)	प्रतिबद्धता (f)	pratibaddhta
responsibility	ज़िम्मेदारी (f)	zimmedārī
force majeure	अप्रत्याशित घटना (f)	apratyāshit ghatana
dispute	विवाद (m)	vivād
penalties	जुर्माना (m)	jurmāna

108. Import & Export

import	आयात (m)	āyāt
importer	आयातकर्ता (m)	āyātakarta
to import (vt)	आयात करना	āyāt karana
import (as adj.)	आयातित	āyātit
exporter	निर्यातकर्ता (m)	niryātakarta
to export (vi, vt)	निर्यात करना	niryāt karana
goods (merchandise)	माल (m)	māl
consignment, lot	प्रेषित माल (m)	preshit māl
weight	वज़न (m)	vazan
volume	आयतन (m)	āyatan
cubic meter	घन मीटर (m)	ghan mītar
manufacturer	उत्पादक (m)	utpādak
transportation company	वाहन कम्पनी (f)	vāhan kampanī
container	डिब्बा (m)	dibba
border	सीमा (f)	sīma
customs	सीमाशुल्क कार्यालय (f)	sīmāshulk kāryālay
customs duty	सीमाशुल्क (m)	sīmāshulk

customs officer	सीमाशुल्क अधिकारी (m)	sīmāshulk adhikārī
smuggling	तस्करी (f)	taskarī
contraband (smuggled goods)	तस्करी का माल (m)	taskarī ka māl

109. Finances

stock (share)	शेयर (f)	sheyar
bond (certificate)	बॉंड (m)	bānd
promissory note	विनिमय पत्र (m)	vinimay patr

| stock exchange | स्टॉक मार्केट (m) | stok mārket |
| stock price | शेयर का मूल्य (m) | sheyar ka mūly |

| to go down (become cheaper) | मूल्य कम होना | mūly kam hona |
| to go up (become more expensive) | मूल्य बढ़ जाना | mūly barh jāna |

controlling interest	नियंत्रण हित (f)	niyantran hit
investment	निवेश (f)	nivesh
to invest (vt)	निवेश करना	nivesh karana
percent	प्रतिशत (f)	pratishat
interest (on investment)	ब्याज (m pl)	byāj

profit	नफ़ा (m)	nafa
profitable (adj)	लाभदायक	lābhadāyak
tax	कर (f)	kar

currency (foreign ~)	मुद्रा (m)	mudra
national (adj)	राष्ट्रीय	rāshtrīy
exchange (currency ~)	विनिमय (m)	vinimay

| accountant | लेखापाल (m) | lekhāpāl |
| accounting | लेखा विभाग (m) | lekha vibhāg |

bankruptcy	दिवाला (m)	divāla
collapse, crash	वित्तीय पतन (m)	vittīy pattan
ruin	बरबादी (m)	barabādī
to be ruined (financially)	आर्थिक रूप से बरबादी	ārthik rūp se barabādī

| inflation | मुद्रास्फीति (f) | mudrāsfīti |
| devaluation | अवमूल्यन (m) | avamūlyan |

capital	पूँजी (f)	pūnjī
income	आय (f)	āy
turnover	कुल बिक्री (f)	kul bikrī
resources	वित्तीय संसाधन (m)	vittīy sansādhan
monetary resources	मुद्रागत संसाधन (m)	mudrāgat sansādhan
to reduce (expenses)	कम करना	kam karana

110. Marketing

marketing	विपणन (m)	vipanan
market	मंडी (f)	mandī
market segment	बाज़ार क्षेत्र (m)	bāzār kshetr
product	उत्पाद (m)	utpād
goods (merchandise)	माल (m)	māl
trademark	ट्रेड मार्क (m)	tred mārk
logotype	लोगोटाइप (m)	logotaip
logo	लोगो (m)	logo
demand	मांग (f)	māng
supply	आपूर्ति (f)	āpūrti
need	ज़रूरत (f)	zarūrat
consumer	उपभोक्ता (m)	upabhokta
analysis	विश्लेषण (m)	vishleshan
to analyze (vt)	विश्लेषण करना	vishleshan karana
positioning	स्थिति-निर्धारण (f)	sthiti-nirdhāran
to position (vt)	स्थिति-निर्धारण करना	sthiti-nirdhāran karana
price	दाम (m)	dām
pricing policy	मूल्य निर्धारण नीति (f)	mūly nirdhāran nīti
price formation	मूल्य स्थापना (f)	mūly sthāpana

111. Advertising

advertising	विज्ञापन (m)	vigyāpan
to advertise (vt)	विज्ञापन देना	vigyāpan dena
budget	बजट (m)	bajat
ad, advertisement	विज्ञापन (m)	vigyāpan
TV advertising	टीवी विज्ञापन (m)	tīvī vigyāpan
radio advertising	रेडियो विज्ञापन (m)	rediyo vigyāpan
outdoor advertising	बिलबोर्ड विज्ञापन (m)	bilabord vigyāpan
mass media	जनसंपर्क माध्यम (m)	janasampark mādhyam
periodical (n)	पत्रिका (f)	patrika
image (public appearance)	सार्वजनिक छवि (f)	sārvajanik chhavi
slogan	नारा (m)	nāra
motto (maxim)	नारा (m)	nāra
campaign	अभियान (m)	abhiyān
advertising campaign	विज्ञापन प्रचार (m)	vigyāpan prachār
target group	श्रोतागण (f)	shrotāgan
business card	बिज़नेस कार्ड (m)	bizanes kārd
leaflet (promotional ~)	पर्चा (f)	parcha

brochure (e.g., 12 pages ~)	ब्रोशर (m)	broshar
pamphlet	पर्चा (f)	parcha
newsletter	सूचनापत्र (m)	sūchanāpatr
signboard (store sign, etc.)	नेमप्लेट (m)	nemaplet
poster	पोस्टर (m)	postar
billboard	इश्तहार (m)	ishtahār

112. Banking

bank	बैंक (m)	baink
branch (of bank, etc.)	शाखा (f)	shākha
bank clerk, consultant	क्लर्क (m)	klark
manager (director)	मैनेजर (m)	mainejar
bank account	बैंक खाता (m)	baink khāta
account number	खाते का नम्बर (m)	khāte ka nambar
checking account	चालू खाता (m)	chālū khāta
savings account	बचत खाता (m)	bachat khāta
to open an account	खाता खोलना	khāta kholana
to close the account	खाता बंद करना	khāta band karana
to deposit into the account	खाते में जमा करना	khāte men jama karana
to withdraw (vt)	खाते से पैसा निकालना	khāte se paisa nikālana
deposit	जमा (m)	jama
to make a deposit	जमा करना	jama karana
wire transfer	तार स्थानांतरण (m)	tār sthānāntaran
to wire, to transfer	पैसे स्थानांतरित करना	paise sthānāntarit karana
sum	रक़म (m)	raqam
How much?	कितना?	kitana?
signature	हस्ताक्षर (f)	hastākshar
to sign (vt)	हस्ताक्षर करना	hastākshar karana
credit card	क्रेडिट कार्ड (m)	kredit kārd
code (PIN code)	पिन कोड (m)	pin kod
credit card number	क्रेडिट कार्ड संख्या (f)	kredit kārd sankhya
ATM	एटीएम (m)	etīem
check	चेक (m)	chek
to write a check	चेक लिखना	chek likhana
checkbook	चेकबुक (f)	chekabuk
loan (bank ~)	उधार (m)	uthār
to apply for a loan	उधार के लिए आवेदन करना	udhār ke lie āvedan karana

to get a loan	उधार लेना	uthār lena
to give a loan	उधार देना	uthār dena
guarantee	गारन्टी (f)	gāranti

113. Telephone. Phone conversation

telephone	फ़ोन (m)	fon
cell phone	मोबाइल फ़ोन (m)	mobail fon
answering machine	जवाबी मशीन (f)	javābī mashīn

| to call (by phone) | फ़ोन करना | fon karana |
| phone call | कॉल (m) | kol |

to dial a number	नम्बर लगाना	nambar lagāna
Hello!	हेलो!	helo!
to ask (vt)	पूछना	pūchhana
to answer (vi, vt)	जवाब देना	javāb dena

to hear (vt)	सुनना	sunana
well (adv)	ठीक	thīk
not well (adv)	ठीक नहीं	thīk nahin
noises (interference)	आवाज़ें (f)	āvāzen

receiver	रिसीवर (m)	risīvar
to pick up (~ the phone)	फ़ोन उठाना	fon uthāna
to hang up (~ the phone)	फ़ोन रखना	fon rakhana

busy (engaged)	बिज़ी	bizī
to ring (ab. phone)	फ़ोन बजना	fon bajana
telephone book	टेलीफ़ोन बुक (m)	telīfon buk
local (adj)	लोकल	lokal
long distance (~ call)	लंबी दूरी की कॉल	lambī dūrī kī kol
international (adj)	अंतर्राष्ट्रीय	antarrāshtrīy

114. Cell phone

cell phone	मोबाइल फ़ोन (m)	mobail fon
display	डिस्प्ले (m)	disple
button	बटन (m)	batan
SIM card	सिम कार्ड (m)	sim kārd

battery	बैटरी (f)	baitarī
to be dead (battery)	बैटरी डेड हो जाना	baitarī ded ho jāna
charger	चार्जर (m)	chārjar

menu	मीनू (m)	mīnū
settings	सेटिंग्स (f)	setings
tune (melody)	कॉलर ट्यून (m)	kolar tyūn

to select (vt)	चुनना	chunana
calculator	कैल्कुलेटर (m)	kailkulaitar
voice mail	वॉयस मेल (f)	voyas mel
alarm clock	अलार्म घड़ी (f)	alārm gharī
contacts	संपर्क (m)	sampark
SMS (text message)	एसएमएस (m)	esemes
subscriber	सदस्य (m)	sadasy

115. Stationery

ballpoint pen	बॉल पेन (m)	bol pen
fountain pen	फाउन्टेन पेन (m)	faunten pen
pencil	पेंसिल (f)	pensil
highlighter	हाइलाइटर (m)	hailaitar
felt-tip pen	फ़ेल्ट टिप पेन (m)	felt tip pen
notepad	नोटबुक (m)	notabuk
agenda (diary)	डायरी (f)	dāyarī
ruler	स्केल (m)	skel
calculator	कैल्कुलेटर (m)	kailkuletar
eraser	रबड़ (f)	rabar
thumbtack	थंबटैक (m)	thanrbataik
paper clip	पेपर क्लिप (m)	pepar klip
glue	गोंद (f)	gond
stapler	स्टेप्लर (m)	steplar
hole punch	होल पंचर (m)	hol panchar
pencil sharpener	शार्पनर (m)	shārpanar

116. Various kinds of documents

account (report)	रिपोर्ट (m)	riport
agreement	समझौता (f)	samajhauta
application form	आवेदन प्रपत्र (m)	āvedan prapatr
authentic (adj)	असल	asal
badge (identity tag)	बैज (f)	baij
business card	बिज़नेस कार्ड (m)	bizanes kārd
certificate (~ of quality)	प्रमाणपत्र (m)	pramānapatr
check (e.g., draw a ~)	चेक (m)	chek
check (in restaurant)	बिल (m)	bil
constitution	संविधान (m)	sanvidhān
contract (agreement)	अनुबंध (m)	anubandh
copy	कॉपी (f)	kopī

copy (of contract, etc.)	प्रति (f)	prati
customs declaration	सीमाशुल्क घोषणा (f)	sīmāshulk ghoshana
document	दस्तावेज़ (m)	dastāvez
driver's license	ड्राइवर-लाइसेंस (m)	draivar-laisens
addendum	परिशिष्ट (f)	parishisht
form	प्रपत्र (m)	prapatr
ID card (e.g., FBI ~)	पहचान पत्र (m)	pahachān patr
inquiry (request)	पूछताछ (f)	pūchhatāchh
invitation card	निमंत्रण-पत्र (m)	nimantran-patr
invoice	इन्वॉएस (m)	invoes
law	कानून (m)	kānūn
letter (mail)	पत्र (m)	patr
letterhead	लेटरहेड (m)	letarahed
list (of names, etc.)	सूची (f)	sūchī
manuscript	हस्तलेख (m)	hastalekh
newsletter	संवादपत्र (m)	sanvādapatr
note (short letter)	नोट (m)	not
pass (for worker, visitor)	पास (m)	pās
passport	पासपोर्ट (m)	pāsaport
permit	अनुमति (f)	anumati
résumé	रेज्यूम (m)	rijyūm
debt note, IOU	ऋण नोट (m)	ririn not
receipt (for purchase)	रसीद (f)	rasīd
sales slip, receipt	बिक्री रसीद (f)	bikrī rasīd
report (mil.)	रिपोर्ट (m)	riport
to show (ID, etc.)	दिखाना	dikhāna
to sign (vt)	हस्ताक्षर करना	hastākshar karana
signature	हस्ताक्षर (f)	hastākshar
seal (stamp)	सील (m)	sīl
text	पाठ (m)	pāth
ticket (for entry)	प्रवेश टिकट (m)	pravesh tikat
to cross out	रेखा खींचकर काटना	rekha khīnchakar kātana
to fill out (~ a form)	भरना	bharana
waybill (shipping invoice)	रसीद (f)	rasīd
will (testament)	वसीयत (m)	vasīyat

117. Kinds of business

accounting services	लेखा सेवा (f)	lekha seva
advertising	विज्ञापन (m)	vigyāpan
advertising agency	विज्ञापन एजन्सी (f)	vigyāpan ejansī
air-conditioners	वातानुकूलक सेवा (f)	vātānukūlak seva
airline	हवाई कम्पनी (f)	havaī kampanī
alcoholic beverages	मद्य पदार्थ (m)	mady padārth

antiques (antique dealers)	पुरानी चीज़ें (f)	purānī chīzen
art gallery (contemporary ~)	चित्रशाला (f)	chitrashāla
audit services	लेखापरीक्षा सेवा (f)	lekhāparīksha seva
banking industry	बैंक (m)	baink
bar	बार (m)	bār
beauty parlor	ब्यूटी पार्लर (m)	byūtī pārlar
bookstore	किताबों की दुकान (f)	kitābon kī dukān
brewery	शराब की भठ्ठी (f)	sharāb kī bhaththī
business center	व्यापार केन्द्र (m)	vyāpār kendr
business school	व्यापार विद्यालय (m)	vyāpār vidyālay
casino	केसिनो (m)	kesino
construction	निर्माण (m)	nirmān
consulting	परामर्श सेवा (f)	parāmarsh seva
dental clinic	दंतचिकित्सा क्लिनिक (f)	dantachikitsa klinik
design	डिज़ाइन (m)	dizain
drugstore, pharmacy	दवाख़ाना (m)	davākhāna
dry cleaners	ड्राइक्लीनिंग (f)	draiklīning
employment agency	रोज़गार एजेंसी (f)	rozagār ejensī
financial services	वित्त सेवा (f)	vitt seva
food products	खाद्य पदार्थ (m)	khādy padārth
funeral home	शमशान घाट (m)	shamashān ghāt
furniture (e.g., house ~)	फ़र्निचर (m)	farnichar
clothing, garment	पोशाक (m)	poshāk
hotel	होटल (m)	hotal
ice-cream	आईसक्रीम (f)	āīsakrīm
industry (manufacturing)	उद्योग (m)	udyog
insurance	बीमा (m)	bīma
Internet	इन्टरनेट (m)	intaranet
investments (finance)	निवेश (f)	nivesh
jeweler	सुनार (m)	sunār
jewelry	आभूषण (m)	ābhūshan
laundry (shop)	धोबीघर (m)	dhobīghar
legal advisor	कानूनी सलाह (f)	kānūnī salāh
light industry	हल्का उद्योग (m)	halka udyog
magazine	पत्रिका (f)	patrika
mail-order selling	मेल-ऑर्डर विक्रय (m)	mel-ordar vikray
medicine	औषधि (f)	aushadhi
movie theater	सिनेमाघर (m)	sinemāghar
museum	संग्रहालय (m)	sangrahālay
news agency	सूचना केन्द्र (m)	sūchana kendr
newspaper	अख़बार (m)	akhabār
nightclub	नाइट क्लब (m)	nait klab
oil (petroleum)	पेट्रोलियम (m)	petroliyam

courier services	कुरियर सेवा (f)	kuriyar seva
pharmaceutics	औषधि (f)	aushadhi
printing (industry)	छपाई (m)	chhapaī
publishing house	प्रकाशन गृह (m)	prakāshan grh
radio (~ station)	रेडियो (m)	rediyo
real estate	अचल संपत्ति (f)	achal sampatti
restaurant	रेस्टराँ (m)	restarān
security company	सुरक्षा एजेंसी (f)	suraksha ejensī
sports	क्रीड़ा (f)	krīra
stock exchange	स्टॉक मार्केट (m)	stok mārket
store	दुकान (f)	dukān
supermarket	सुपर बाज़ार (m)	supar bāzār
swimming pool (public ~)	तरण-ताल (m)	taran-tāl
tailor shop	दर्ज़ी (m)	darzī
television	टीवी (m)	tīvī
theater	रंगमंच (m)	rangamanch
trade (commerce)	व्यापार (m)	vyāpār
transportation	परिवहन (m)	parivahan
travel	पर्यटन (m)	paryatan
veterinarian	पशुचिकित्सक (m)	pashuchikitsak
warehouse	भंडार (m)	bhandār
waste collection	कूड़ा उठाने की सेवा (f)	kūra uthāne kī seva

Job. Business. Part 2

118. Show. Exhibition

exhibition, show	प्रदर्शनी (f)	pradarshanī
trade show	व्यापारिक प्रदर्शनी (f)	vyāpārik pradarshanī
participation	शिरकत (f)	shirakat
to participate (vi)	भाग लेना	bhāg lena
participant (exhibitor)	प्रतिभागी (m)	pratibhāgī
director	निदेशक (m)	nideshak
organizers' office	आयोजकों का कार्यालिय (m)	āyojakon ka kāryālay
organizer	आयोजक (m)	āyojak
to organize (vt)	आयोजित करना	āyojit karana
participation form	प्रतिभागी प्रपत्र (m)	pratibhāgī prapatr
to fill out (vt)	भरना	bharana
details	विवरण (m)	vivaran
information	जानकारी (f)	jānakārī
price (cost, rate)	दाम (m)	dām
including	सहित	sahit
to include (vt)	शामिल करना	shāmil karana
to pay (vi, vt)	दाम चुकाना	dām chukāna
registration fee	पंजीकरण शुल्क (f)	panjīkaran shulk
entrance	प्रवेश (m)	pravesh
pavilion, hall	हॉल (m)	hol
to register (vt)	पंजीकरण करवाना	panjīkaran karavāna
badge (identity tag)	बैज (f)	baij
booth, stand	स्टेंड (m)	stend
to reserve, to book	बुक करना	buk karana
display case	प्रदर्शन खिड़की (f)	pradarshan khirakī
spotlight	स्पॉटलाइट (f)	spotalait
design	डिज़ाइन (m)	dizain
to place (put, set)	रखना	rakhana
distributor	वितरक (m)	vitarak
supplier	आपूर्तिकर्ता (m)	āpūrtikarta
country	देश (m)	desh
foreign (adj)	विदेश	videsh
product	उत्पाद (m)	utpād

association	संस्था (f)	sanstha
conference hall	सम्मेलन भवन (m)	sammelan bhavan
congress	सम्मेलन (m)	sammelan
contest (competition)	प्रतियोगिता (f)	pratiyogita

visitor (attendee)	सहभागी (m)	sahabhāgī
to visit (attend)	भाग लेना	bhāg lena
customer	ग्राहक (m)	grāhak

119. Mass Media

newspaper	अख़बार (m)	akhabār
magazine	पत्रिका (f)	patrika
press (printed media)	प्रेस (m)	pres
radio	रेडियो (m)	rediyo
radio station	रेडियो स्टेशन (m)	rediyo steshan
television	टीवी (m)	tīvī

presenter, host	प्रस्तुतकर्ता (m)	prastutakarta
newscaster	उद्घोषक (m)	udghoshak
commentator	टिप्पणीकार (m)	tippanīkār

journalist	पत्रकार (m)	patrakār
correspondent (reporter)	पत्रकार (m)	patrakār
press photographer	फ़ोटो पत्रकार (m)	foto patrakār
reporter	पत्रकार (m)	patrakār

| editor | संपादक (m) | sampādak |
| editor-in-chief | मूख्य संपादक (m) | mūkhy sampādak |

to subscribe (to …)	सदस्य बनना	sadasy banana
subscription	सदस्यता शुल्क (f)	sadasyata shulk
subscriber	सदस्य (m)	sadasy
to read (vi, vt)	पढ़ना	parhana
reader	पाठक (m)	pāthak

circulation (of newspaper)	प्रतियों की संख्या (f)	pratiyon kī sankhya
monthly (adj)	मासिक	māsik
weekly (adj)	सप्ताहिक	saptāhik
issue (edition)	संस्करण संख्या (f)	sanskaran sankhya
new (~ issue)	ताज़ा	tāza

headline	हेडलाइन (f)	hedalain
short article	लघु लेख (m)	laghu lekh
column (regular article)	कॉलम (m)	kolam
article	लेख (m)	lekh
page	पृष्ठ (m)	prshth

| reportage, report | रिपोर्ट (f) | riport |
| event (happening) | घटना (f) | ghatana |

sensation (news)	सनसनी (f)	sanasanī
scandal	कांड (m)	kānd
scandalous (adj)	चौंका देने वाला	chaunka dene vāla
great (~ scandal)	बड़ा	bara
show (e.g., cooking ~)	प्रसारण (m)	prasāran
interview	साक्षात्कार (m)	sākshātkār
live broadcast	सीधा प्रसारण (m)	sīdha prasāran
channel	चैनल (m)	chainal

120. Agriculture

agriculture	खेती (f)	khetī
peasant (masc.)	किसान (m)	kisān
peasant (fem.)	किसान (f)	kisān
farmer	किसान (m)	kisān
tractor (farm ~)	ट्रैक्टर (m)	traiktar
combine, harvester	फ़सल काटने की मशीन (f)	fasal kātane kī mashīn
plow	हल (m)	hal
to plow (vi, vt)	जोतना	jotana
plowland	जोत भूमि (f)	jot bhūmi
furrow (in field)	जोती गई भूमि (f)	jotī gaī bhūmi
to sow (vi, vt)	बोना	bona
seeder	बोने की मशीन (f)	bone kī mashīn
sowing (process)	बोवाई (f)	bovaī
scythe	हँसिया (m)	hansiya
to mow, to scythe	काटना	kātana
spade (tool)	कुदाल (m)	kudāl
to till (vt)	खोदना	khodana
hoe	फावड़ा (m)	fāvara
to hoe, to weed	निराना	nirāna
weed (plant)	जंगली घास	jangalī ghās
watering can	सींचाई कनस्तर (m)	sīnchaī kanastar
to water (plants)	सींचना	sīnchana
watering (act)	सींचाई (f)	sīnchaī
pitchfork	पंजा (m)	panja
rake	जेली (f)	jelī
fertilizer	खाद (f)	khād
to fertilize (vt)	खाद डालना	khād dālana
manure (fertilizer)	गोबर (m)	gobar
field	खेत (f)	khet

meadow	केदार (m)	kedār
vegetable garden	सब्जियों का बगीचा (m)	sabziyon ka bagīcha
orchard (e.g., apple ~)	बाग़ (m)	bāg
to graze (vt)	चराना	charāna
herder (herdsman)	चरवाहा (m)	charavāha
pasture	चरागाह (f)	charāgāh
cattle breeding	पशुपालन (m)	pashupālan
sheep farming	भेड़पालन (m)	bherapālan
plantation	बागान (m)	bāgān
row (garden bed ~s)	क्यारी (f)	kyārī
hothouse	पौधाघर (m)	paudhāghar
drought (lack of rain)	सूखा (f)	sūkha
dry (~ summer)	सूखा	sūkha
cereal crops	अनाज (m pl)	anāj
to harvest, to gather	फ़सल काटना	fasal kātana
miller (person)	चक्कीवाला (m)	chakkīvāla
mill (e.g., gristmill)	चक्की (f)	chakkī
to grind (grain)	पीसना	pīsana
flour	आटा (m)	āta
straw	फूस (m)	fūs

121. Building. Building process

construction site	निर्माण स्थल (m)	nirmān sthal
to build (vt)	निर्माण करना	nirmān karana
construction worker	मज़दूर (m)	mazadūr
project	परियोजना (m)	pariyojana
architect	वास्तुकार (m)	vāstukār
worker	मज़दूर (m)	mazadūr
foundation (of a building)	आधार (m)	ādhār
roof	छत (f)	chhat
foundation pile	नींव (m)	nīnv
wall	दीवार (f)	dīvār
reinforcing bars	मज़बूत सलाखें (m)	mazabūt salākhen
scaffolding	मचान (m)	machān
concrete	कंक्रीट (m)	kankrīt
granite	ग्रेनाइट (m)	grenait
stone	पत्थर (m)	patthar
brick	ईंट (f)	īnt
sand	रेत (f)	ret

cement	सीमेन्ट (m)	sīment
plaster (for walls)	प्लस्तर (m)	plastar
to plaster (vt)	प्लस्तर लगाना	plastar lagāna
paint	रंग (m)	rang
to paint (~ a wall)	रंगना	rangana
barrel	पीपा (m)	pīpa
crane	क्रेन (m)	kren
to lift, to hoist (vt)	उठाना	uthāna
to lower (vt)	नीचे उतारना	nīche utārana
bulldozer	बुल्डोज़र (m)	buldozar
excavator	उत्खनक (m)	utkhanak
scoop, bucket	उत्खनक बाल्टी (m)	utkhanak bāltī
to dig (excavate)	खोदना	khodana
hard hat	हेलमेट (f)	helamet

122. Science. Research. Scientists

science	विज्ञान (m)	vigyān
scientific (adj)	वैज्ञानिक	vaigyānik
scientist	वैज्ञानिक (m)	vaigyānik
theory	सिद्धांत (f)	siddhānt
axiom	सिद्ध प्रमाण (m)	siddh pramān
analysis	विश्लेषण (m)	vishleshan
to analyze (vt)	विश्लेषण करना	vishleshan karana
argument (strong ~)	तथ्य (m)	tathy
substance (matter)	पदार्थ (m)	padārth
hypothesis	परिकल्पना (f)	parikalpana
dilemma	दुविधा (m)	duvidha
dissertation	शोधनिबंध (m)	shodhanibandh
dogma	हठधर्मिता (f)	hathadharmita
doctrine	सिद्धांत (m)	siddhānt
research	शोध (m)	shodh
to research (vt)	शोध करना	shodh karana
tests (laboratory ~)	जांच (f)	jānch
laboratory	प्रयोगशाला (f)	prayogashāla
method	वीधि (f)	vīdhi
molecule	अणु (m)	anu
monitoring	निगरानी (f)	nigarānī
discovery (act, event)	आविष्कार (m)	āvishkār
postulate	स्वसिद्ध (m)	svasiddh
principle	सिद्धांत (m)	siddhānt
forecast	पूर्वानुमान (m)	pūrvānumān
to forecast (vt)	पूर्वानुमान करना	pūrvānumān karana

synthesis	संश्लेषण (m)	sanshleshan
trend (tendency)	प्रवृत्ति (f)	pravrtti
theorem	प्रमेय (m)	pramey

teachings	शिक्षा (f)	shiksha
fact	तथ्य (m)	tathy
expedition	अभियान (m)	abhiyān
experiment	प्रयोग (m)	prayog

academician	अकदमीशियन (m)	akadamīshiyan
bachelor (e.g., ~ of Arts)	स्नातक (m)	snātak
doctor (PhD)	डॉक्टर (m)	doktar
Associate Professor	सह - प्राध्यापक (m)	sah - prādhyāpak
Master (e.g., ~ of Arts)	स्नातकोत्तर (m)	snātakottar
professor	प्रोफ़ेसर (m)	profesar

Professions and occupations

123. Job search. Dismissal

job	नौकरी (f)	naukarī
personnel	कर्मचारी (m)	karmachārī
career	व्यवसाय (m)	vyavasāy
prospects (chances)	संभावना (f)	sambhāvana
skills (mastery)	हुनर (m)	hunar
selection (screening)	चुनाव (m)	chunāv
employment agency	रोज़गार केन्द्र (m)	rozagār kendr
résumé	रेज़्यूम (m)	rijyūm
job interview	नौकरी के लिए साक्षात्कार (m)	naukarī ke lie sākshātkār
vacancy, opening	रिक्ति (f)	rikti
salary, pay	वेतन (m)	vetan
fixed salary	वेतन (m)	vetan
pay, compensation	भुगतान (m)	bhugatān
position (job)	पद (m)	pad
duty (of employee)	कर्तव्य (m)	kartavy
range of duties	कार्य-क्षेत्र (m)	kāry-kshetr
busy (I'm ~)	व्यस्त	vyast
to fire (dismiss)	बरख़ास्त करना	barakhāst karana
dismissal	बरख़ास्तगी (f)	barakhāstagī
unemployment	बेरोज़गारी (f)	berozagārī
unemployed (n)	बेरोज़गार (m)	berozagār
retirement	सेवा-निवृत्ति (f)	seva-nivrtti
to retire (from job)	सेवा-निवृत्त होना	seva-nivrtt hona

124. Business people

director	निदेशक (m)	nideshak
manager (director)	प्रबंधक (m)	prabandhak
boss	मालिक (m)	mālik
superior	वरिष्ठ अधिकारी (m)	varishth adhikārī
superiors	वरिष्ठ अधिकारी (m)	varishth adhikārī
president	अध्यक्ष (m)	adhyaksh

chairman	सभाध्यक्ष (m)	sabhādhyaksh
deputy (substitute)	उपाध्यक्ष (m)	upādhyaksh
assistant	सहायक (m)	sahāyak
secretary	सेक्रटरी (f)	sekratarī
personal assistant	निजी सहायक (m)	nijī sahāyak

businessman	व्यापारी (m)	vyāpārī
entrepreneur	उद्यमी (m)	udyamī
founder	संस्थापक (m)	sansthāpak
to found (vt)	स्थापित करना	sthāpit karana

incorporator	स्थापक (m)	sthāpak
partner	पार्टनर (m)	pārtanar
stockholder	शेयर होलडर (m)	sheyar holadar

millionaire	लखपति (m)	lakhapati
billionaire	करोड़पति (m)	karorapati
owner, proprietor	मालिक (m)	mālik
landowner	ज़मीनदार (m)	zamīnadār

client	ग्राहक (m)	grāhak
regular client	खरीदार (m)	kharīdār
buyer (customer)	ग्राहक (m)	grāhak
visitor	आगंतुक (m)	āgantuk

professional (n)	पेशेवर (m)	peshevar
expert	विशेषज्ञ (m)	visheshagy
specialist	विशेषज्ञ (m)	visheshagy

| banker | बैंकर (m) | bainkar |
| broker | ब्रोकर (m) | brokar |

cashier, teller	कैशियर (m)	kaishiyar
accountant	लेखापाल (m)	lekhāpāl
security guard	पहरेदार (m)	paharedār

investor	निवेशक (m)	niveshak
debtor	क़र्ज़दार (m)	qarzadār
creditor	लेनदार (m)	lenadār
borrower	कर्ज़दार (m)	karzadār

| importer | आयातकर्ता (m) | āyātakartta |
| exporter | निर्यातकर्ता (m) | niryātakartta |

manufacturer	उत्पादक (m)	utpādak
distributor	वितरक (m)	vitarak
middleman	बिचौलिया (m)	bichauliya

consultant	सलाहकार (m)	salāhakār
sales representative	बिक्री प्रतिनिधि (m)	bikrī pratinidhi
agent	एजेंट (m)	ejent
insurance agent	बीमा एजन्ट (m)	bīma ejant

125. Service professions

cook	बावरची (m)	bāvarachī
chef (kitchen chef)	मुख्य बावरची (m)	mukhy bāvarachī
baker	बेकर (m)	bekar
bartender	बारेटेन्डर (m)	bāretendar
waiter	बैरा (m)	baira
waitress	बैरा (f)	baira
lawyer, attorney	वकील (m)	vakīl
lawyer (legal expert)	वकील (m)	vakīl
notary	नोटरी (m)	notarī
electrician	बिजलीवाला (m)	bijalīvāla
plumber	प्लम्बर (m)	plambar
carpenter	बढ़ई (m)	barhī
masseur	मालिशिया (m)	mālishiya
masseuse	मालिशिया (m)	mālishiya
doctor	चिकित्सक (m)	chikitsak
taxi driver	टैक्सीवाला (m)	taiksīvāla
driver	ड्राइवर (m)	draivar
delivery man	कूरियर (m)	kūriyar
chambermaid	चैम्बरमेड (f)	chaimbaramed
security guard	पहरेदार (m)	paharedār
flight attendant (fem.)	एयर होस्टेस (f)	eyar hostes
schoolteacher	शिक्षक (m)	shikshak
librarian	पुस्तकाध्यक्ष (m)	pustakādhyaksh
translator	अनुवादक (m)	anuvādak
interpreter	दुभाषिया (m)	dubhāshiya
guide	गाइड (m)	gaid
hairdresser	नाई (m)	naī
mailman	डाकिया (m)	dākiya
salesman (store staff)	विक्रेता (m)	vikreta
gardener	माली (m)	mālī
domestic servant	नौकर (m)	naukar
maid (female servant)	नौकरानी (f)	naukarānī
cleaner (cleaning lady)	सफ़ाईवाली (f)	safaīvālī

126. Military professions and ranks

private	सैनिक (m)	sainik
sergeant	सार्जेंट (m)	sārjent

lieutenant	लेफ्टिनेंट (m)	leftinent
captain	कैप्टन (m)	kaiptan
major	मेजर (m)	mejar
colonel	कर्नल (m)	karnal
general	जनरल (m)	janaral
marshal	मार्शल (m)	mārshal
admiral	एडमिरल (m)	edamiral
military (n)	सैनिक (m)	sainik
soldier	सिपाही (m)	sipāhī
officer	अफ्सर (m)	afsar
commander	कमांडर (m)	kamāndar
border guard	सीमा रक्षक (m)	sīma rakshak
radio operator	रेडियो ऑपरेटर (m)	rediyo oparetar
scout (searcher)	गुप्तचर (m)	guptachar
pioneer (sapper)	युद्ध इंजीनियर (m)	yuddh injīniyar
marksman	तीरंदाज़ (m)	tīrandāz
navigator	नैवीगेटर (m)	naivīgetar

127. Officials. Priests

king	बादशाह (m)	bādashāh
queen	महारानी (f)	mahārānī
prince	राजकुमार (m)	rājakumār
princess	राजकुमारी (f)	rājakumārī
czar	राजा (m)	rāja
czarina	रानी (f)	rānī
president	राष्ट्रपति (m)	rāshtrapati
Secretary (minister)	मंत्री (m)	mantrī
prime minister	प्रधान मंत्री (m)	pradhān mantrī
senator	सांसद (m)	sānsad
diplomat	राजनयिक (m)	rājanayik
consul	राजनयिक (m)	rājanayik
ambassador	राजदूत (m)	rājadūt
counsilor (diplomatic officer)	राजनयिक परामर्शदाता (m)	rājanayik parāmarshadāta
official, functionary (civil servant)	अधिकारी (m)	adhikārī
prefect	अधिकारी (m)	adhikārī
mayor	मेयर (m)	meyar
judge	न्यायाधीश (m)	nyāyādhīsh
prosecutor (e.g., district attorney)	अभियोक्ता (m)	abhiyokta

missionary	पादरी (m)	pādarī
monk	मठवासी (m)	mathavāsī
abbot	मठाधीश (m)	mathādhīsh
rabbi	रब्बी (m)	rabbī

vizier	वज़ीर (m)	vazīr
shah	शाह (m)	shāh
sheikh	शेख़ (m)	shekh

128. Agricultural professions

beekeeper	मधुमक्खी-पालक (m)	madhumakkhī-pālak
herder, shepherd	चरवाहा (m)	charavāha
agronomist	कृषिविज्ञानी (m)	krshivigyānī
cattle breeder	पशुपालक (m)	pashupālak
veterinarian	पशुचिकित्सक (m)	pashuchikitsak

farmer	किसान (m)	kisān
winemaker	मदिराकारी (m)	madirākārī
zoologist	जीव विज्ञानी (m)	jīv vigyānī
cowboy	चरवाहा (m)	charavāha

129. Art professions

actor	अभिनेता (m)	abhineta
actress	अभिनेत्री (f)	abhinetrī

singer (masc.)	गायक (m)	gāyak
singer (fem.)	गायिका (f)	gāyika

dancer (masc.)	नर्तक (m)	nartak
dancer (fem.)	नर्तकी (f)	nartakī

performer (masc.)	अदाकार (m)	adākār
performer (fem.)	अदाकारा (f)	adākāra

musician	साज़िन्दा (m)	sāzinda
pianist	पियानो वादक (m)	piyāno vādak
guitar player	गिटार वादक (m)	gitār vādak

conductor (orchestra ~)	बैंड कंडक्टर (m)	baind kandaktar
composer	संगीतकार (m)	sangītakār
impresario	इम्प्रेसारियो (m)	impresāriyo

film director	निर्देशक (m)	nirdeshak
producer	प्रोड्यूसर (m)	prodyūsar
scriptwriter	लेखक (m)	lekhak
critic	आलोचक (m)	ālochak

writer	लेखक (m)	lekhak
poet	कवि (m)	kavi
sculptor	मूर्तिकार (m)	mūrtikār
artist (painter)	चित्रकार (m)	chitrakār

juggler	बाज़ीगर (m)	bāzīgar
clown	जोकर (m)	jokar
acrobat	कलाबाज़ (m)	kalābāz
magician	जादूगर (m)	jādūgar

130. Various professions

doctor	चिकित्सक (m)	chikitsak
nurse	नर्स (m)	nars
psychiatrist	मनोचिकित्सक (m)	manochikitsak
dentist	दंतचिकित्सक (m)	dantachikitsak
surgeon	शल्य-चिकित्सक (m)	shaly-chikitsak

astronaut	अंतरिक्षयात्री (m)	antarikshayātrī
astronomer	खगोल-विज्ञानी (m)	khagol-vigyānī
pilot	पाइलट (m)	pailat

driver (of taxi, etc.)	ड्राइवर (m)	draivar
engineer (train driver)	इंजन ड्राइवर (m)	injan draivar
mechanic	मैकेनिक (m)	maikenik

miner	खनिक (m)	khanik
worker	मज़दूर (m)	mazadūr
locksmith	ताला बनानेवाला (m)	tāla banānevāla
joiner (carpenter)	बढ़ई (m)	barhī
turner (lathe machine operator)	खरादी (m)	kharādī

| construction worker | मज़दूर (m) | mazūdar |
| welder | वेल्डर (m) | veldar |

professor (title)	प्रोफ़ेसर (m)	profesar
architect	वास्तुकार (m)	vāstukār
historian	इतिहासकार (m)	itihāsakār
scientist	वैज्ञानिक (m)	vaigyānik
physicist	भौतिक विज्ञानी (m)	bhautik vigyānī
chemist (scientist)	रसायनविज्ञानी (m)	rasāyanavigyānī

archeologist	पुरातत्वविद (m)	purātatvavid
geologist	भूविज्ञानी (m)	bhūvigyānī
researcher (scientist)	शोधकर्ता (m)	shodhakarta

babysitter	दाई (f)	daī
teacher, educator	शिक्षक (m)	shikshak
editor	संपादक (m)	sampādak
editor-in-chief	मुख्य संपादक (m)	mūkhy sampādak

correspondent	पत्रकार (m)	patrakār
typist (fem.)	टाइपिस्ट (f)	taipist
designer	डिज़ाइनर (m)	dizainar
computer expert	कंप्यूटर विशेषज्ञ (m)	kampyūtar visheshagy
programmer	प्रोग्रामर (m)	progrāmar
engineer (designer)	इंजीनियर (m)	injīniyar
sailor	मल्लाह (m)	mallāh
seaman	मल्लाह (m)	mallāh
rescuer	बचानेवाला (m)	bachānevāla
fireman	दमकल कर्मचारी (m)	damakal karmachārī
police officer	पुलिसवाला (m)	pulisavāla
watchman	पहरेदार (m)	paharedār
detective	जासूस (m)	jāsūs
customs officer	सीमाशुल्क अधिकारी (m)	sīmāshulk adhikārī
bodyguard	अंगरक्षक (m)	angarakshak
prison guard	जेल का पहरेदार (m)	jel ka paharedār
inspector	अधीक्षक (m)	adhīkshak
sportsman	खिलाड़ी (m)	khilārī
trainer, coach	प्रशिक्षक (m)	prashikshak
butcher	कसाई (m)	kasaī
cobbler (shoe repairer)	मोची (m)	mochī
merchant	व्यापारी (m)	vyāpārī
loader (person)	कुली (m)	kulī
fashion designer	फैशन डिज़ाइनर (m)	faishan dizainar
model (fem.)	मॉडल (m)	modal

131. Occupations. Social status

schoolboy	छात्र (m)	chhātr
student (college ~)	विद्यार्थी (m)	vidyārthī
philosopher	दर्शनशास्त्री (m)	darshanashāstrī
economist	अर्थशास्त्री (m)	arthashāstrī
inventor	आविष्कारक (m)	āvishkārak
unemployed (n)	बेरोज़गार (m)	berozagār
retiree	सेवा-निवृत्त (m)	seva-nivrtt
spy, secret agent	गुप्तचर (m)	guptachar
prisoner	क़ैदी (m)	qaidī
striker	हड़तालकारी (m)	haratālakārī
bureaucrat	अफ़सरशाह (m)	afasarashāh
traveler (globetrotter)	यात्री (m)	yātrī
gay, homosexual (n)	समलैंगिक (m)	samalaingik

hacker	हैकर (m)	haikar
bandit	डाकू (m)	dākū
hit man, killer	हत्यारा (m)	hatyāra
drug addict	नशेबाज़ (m)	nashebāz
drug dealer	नशीली दवाओं का विक्रेता (m)	nashīlī davaon ka vikreta
prostitute (fem.)	वैश्या (f)	vaishya
pimp	दलाल (m)	dalāl
sorcerer	जादूगर (m)	jādūgar
sorceress (evil ~)	डायन (f)	dāyan
pirate	समुद्री लूटेरा (m)	samudrī lūtera
slave	दास (m)	dās
samurai	सामुराई (m)	sāmuraī
savage (primitive)	जंगली (m)	jangalī

Sports

132. Kinds of sports. Sportspersons

sportsman	खिलाड़ी (m)	khilārī
kind of sports	खेल (m)	khel
basketball	बास्केटबॉल (f)	bāsketabol
basketball player	बास्केटबॉल खिलाड़ी (m)	bāsketabol khilārī
baseball	बेसबॉल (f)	besabol
baseball player	बेसबॉल खिलाड़ी (m)	besabol khilārī
soccer	फुटबॉल (f)	futabol
soccer player	फुटबॉल खिलाड़ी (m)	futabol khilārī
goalkeeper	गोलची (m)	golachī
hockey	हॉकी (f)	hokī
hockey player	हॉकी खिलाड़ी (m)	hokī khilārī
volleyball	वॉलीबॉल (f)	volībol
volleyball player	वॉलीबॉल खिलाड़ी (m)	volībol khilārī
boxing	मुक्केबाज़ी (f)	mukkebāzī
boxer	मुक्केबाज़ (m)	mukkebāz
wrestling	कुश्ती (m)	kushtī
wrestler	पहलवान (m)	pahalavān
karate	कराटे (m)	karāte
karate fighter	कराटेबाज़ (m)	karātebāz
judo	जूडो (m)	jūdo
judo athlete	जूडोबाज़ (m)	jūdobāz
tennis	टेनिस (m)	tenis
tennis player	टेनिस खिलाड़ी (m)	tenis khilārī
swimming	तैराकी (m)	tairākī
swimmer	तैराक (m)	tairāk
fencing	तलवारबाज़ी (f)	talavārabāzī
fencer	तलवारबाज़ (m)	talavārabāz
chess	शतरंज (m)	shataranj
chess player	शतंरजबाज़ (m)	shatanrajabāz

| alpinism | पर्वतारोहण (m) | parvatārohan |
| alpinist | पर्वतारोही (m) | parvatārohī |

| running | दौड़ (f) | daur |
| runner | धावक (m) | dhāvak |

| athletics | एथलेटिक्स (f) | ethaletiks |
| athlete | एथलीट (m) | ethalīt |

| horseback riding | घुड़सवारी (f) | ghurasavārī |
| horse rider | घुड़सवार (m) | ghurasavār |

figure skating	फ़ीगर स्केटिन्ग (m)	fīgar sketing
figure skater (masc.)	फ़ीगर स्केटर (m)	fīgar sketar
figure skater (fem.)	फ़ीगर स्केटर (f)	fīgar sketar

powerlifting	पॉवरलिफ़्टिंग (m)	povaralifting
car racing	कार रेस (f)	kār res
racing driver	रेस ड्राइवर (m)	res draivar

| cycling | साइकिलिंग (f) | saikiling |
| cyclist | साइकिल चालक (m) | saikil chālak |

broad jump	लांग जम्प (m)	lāng jamp
pole vault	बांस कूद (m)	bāns kūd
jumper	जम्पर (m)	jampar

133. Kinds of sports. Miscellaneous

football	फ़ुटबाल (m)	futabāl
badminton	बैडमिंटन (m)	baidamintan
biathlon	बायएथलॉन (m)	bāyethalon
billiards	बिलियड्स (m)	biliyards

bobsled	बोबस्लेड (m)	bobasled
bodybuilding	बॉडीबिल्डिंग (m)	bodībilding
water polo	वॉटर-पोलो (m)	votar-polo
handball	हैन्डबॉल (f)	haindabol
golf	गोल्फ़ (m)	golf

rowing, crew	नौकायन (m)	naukāyan
scuba diving	स्कूबा डाइविंग (f)	skūba daiving
cross-country skiing	क्रॉस कंट्री स्कीइंग (f)	kros kantrī skīing
table tennis (ping-pong)	टेबल टेनिस (m)	tebal tenis

sailing	पाल नौकायन (m)	pāl naukāyan
rally racing	रैली रेसिंग (f)	railī resing
rugby	रग्बी (m)	ragbī
snowboarding	स्नोबोर्डिंग (m)	snobording
archery	तीरंदाज़ी (f)	tīrandāzī

134. Gym

barbell	वेट (m)	vet
dumbbells	डाम्बबेल्स (m pl)	dāmbabels
training machine	ट्रेनिंग मशीन (f)	trening mashīn
exercise bicycle	व्यायाम साइकिल (f)	vyāyām saikil
treadmill	ट्रेडमिल (f)	tredamil
horizontal bar	क्षैतिज बार (m)	kshaitij bār
parallel bars	समानांतर बार (m)	samānāntar bār
vault (vaulting horse)	घोड़ा (m)	ghora
mat (exercise ~)	मैट (m)	mait
aerobics	एरोबिक (m)	erobik
yoga	योग (m)	yog

135. Hockey

hockey	हॉकी (f)	hokī
hockey player	हॉकी का खिलाड़ी (m)	hokī ka khilārī
to play hockey	हॉकी खेलना	hokī khelana
ice	बर्फ़ (m)	barf
puck	पक (m)	pak
hockey stick	स्टिक (m)	stik
ice skates	आइस स्केट्स (m)	āis skets
board (ice hockey rink ~)	बोर्ड (m)	bord
shot	शॉट (m)	shot
goaltender	गोलची (m)	golachī
goal (score)	गोल (m)	gol
to score a goal	गोल करना	gol karana
period	अवधि (f)	avadhi
substitutes bench	सब्सचिट्यूट बेंच (f)	sabsachityūt bench

136. Soccer

soccer	फ़ुटबॉल (m)	futabol
soccer player	फ़ुटबॉल का खिलाड़ी (m)	futabol ka khilārī
to play soccer	फ़ुटबॉल खेलना	futabol khelana
major league	मेजर लीग (m)	mejar līg
soccer club	फ़ुटबॉल क्लब (m)	futabol klab
coach	प्रशिक्षक (m)	prashikshak

owner, proprietor	मालिक (m)	mālik
team	दल (m)	dal
team captain	दल का कप्तान (m)	dal ka kaptān
player	खिलाड़ी (m)	khilārī
substitute	रिज़र्व-खिलाड़ी (m)	rizarv-khilārī

forward	फ़ॉर्वर्ड (m)	forvard
center forward	केन्द्रिय फ़ॉर्वर्ड (m)	kendriy forvard
scorer	गोल स्कोरर (m)	gol skorar
defender, back	रक्षक (m)	rakshak
midfielder, halfback	हाफ़बैक (m)	hāfabaik

match	मैच (m)	maich
to meet (vi, vt)	मिलना	milana
final	फ़ाइनल (m)	fainal
semi-final	सेमीफ़ाइनल (m)	semīfainal
championship	चैम्पियनशिप (f)	chaimpiyanaship

period, half	हाफ़ (m)	hāf
first period	पहला हाफ़ (m)	pahala hāf
half-time	अंतराल (m)	antarāl

goal	गोल (m)	gol
goalkeeper	गोलची (m)	golachī
goalpost	गोलपोस्ट (m)	golapost
crossbar	अर्गला (f)	argala
net	जाल (m)	jāl
to concede a goal	गोल देना	gol dena

ball	गेंद (m)	gend
pass	पास (m)	pās
kick	किक (f)	kik
to kick (~ the ball)	किक करना	kik karana
free kick (direct ~)	फ़्री किक (f)	frī kik
corner kick	कॉर्नर किक (f)	kornar kik

attack	आक्रमण (m)	ākraman
counterattack	काउन्टर अटैक (m)	kauntar ataik
combination	कॉम्बिनेशन (m)	kombineshan

referee	रेफ़री (m)	refarī
to blow the whistle	सीटी बजाना	sītī bajāna
whistle (sound)	सीटी (f)	sītī
foul, misconduct	फाउल (m)	faul
to commit a foul	फाउल करना	faul karana
to send off	बाहर निकालना	bāhar nikālana

yellow card	पीला कार्ड (m)	pīla kārd
red card	लाल कार्ड (m)	lāl kārd
disqualification	डिसक्वालिफ़िकेशन (m)	disakvālifikeshan
to disqualify (vt)	डिस्क्वालिफ़ाई करना	diskvālifaī karana
penalty kick	पेनल्टी किक (f)	penaltī kik

wall	दीवार (f)	dīvār
to score (vi, vt)	स्कोर करना	skor karana
goal (score)	गोल (m)	gol
to score a goal	गोल करना	gol karana

substitution	बदलाव (m)	badalāv
to replace (a player)	खिलाड़ी बदलना	khilārī badalana
rules	नियम (m pl)	niyam
tactics	टैक्टिक्स (m)	taiktiks

stadium	स्टेडियम (m)	stediyam
stand (bleachers)	स्टॉल (m)	stol
fan, supporter	फ़ैन (m)	fain
to shout (vi)	चिल्लाना	chillāna

| scoreboard | स्कोरबोर्ड (m) | skorabord |
| score | स्कोर (m) | skor |

defeat	हार (f)	hār
to lose (not win)	हारना	hārana
tie	टाई (m)	taī
to tie (vi)	टाई करना	taī karana

victory	विजय (m)	vijay
to win (vi, vt)	जीतना	jītana
champion	चैम्पियन (m)	chaimpiyan
best (adj)	सर्वोत्तम	sarvottam
to congratulate (vt)	बधाई देना	badhaī dena

commentator	टिप्पणीकार (m)	tippanīkār
to commentate (vt)	टिप्पणी करना	tippanī karana
broadcast	प्रसारण (m)	prasāran

137. Alpine skiing

skis	स्की (m pl)	skī
to ski (vi)	स्की करना	skī karana
mountain-ski resort	माउंटेन स्की कैम्प (m)	maunten skī kaimp
ski lift	स्की लिफ़्ट (m)	skī lift

ski poles	स्की की डंडियाँ (f)	skī kī dandiyān
slope	ढलान (f)	dhalān
slalom	स्लालोम (m)	slālom

138. Tennis. Golf

| golf | गोल्फ़ (m) | golf |
| golf club | गोल्फ़-क्लब (m) | golf-klab |

golfer	गोल्फ़-खिलाड़ी (m)	golf-khilārī
hole	गुच्ची (f)	guchchī
club	डंडा (m)	danda
golf trolley	स्टिकों की गाड़ी (f)	stikon kī gāṛī

tennis	टेनिस (m)	tenis
tennis court	कोर्ट (m)	kort
serve	सर्विस (f)	sarvis
to serve (vt)	सर्विस करना	sarvis karana
racket	रैकेट (m)	raiket
net	नेट (m)	net
ball	गेंद (m)	gend

139. Chess

chess	शतरंज (m)	shataranj
chessmen	शतरंज के मोहरे (m pl)	shataranj ke mohare
chess player	शतरंज का खिलाड़ी (m)	shataranj ka khilārī
chessboard	शतरंज की बिसात (f)	shataranj kī bisāt
chessman	शतरंज का मोहरा (m)	shataranj ka mohara

| White (white pieces) | सफ़ेद (m) | safed |
| Black (black pieces) | काला (m) | kāla |

pawn	प्यादा (f)	pyāda
bishop	ऊँठ (m)	ūnth
knight	घोड़ा (m)	ghora
rook	हाथी (m)	hāthī
queen	रानी (f)	rānī
king	बादशाह (m)	bādashāh

move	चाल (f)	chāl
to move (vi, vt)	चाल चलना	chāl chalana
to sacrifice (vt)	त्याग देना	tyāg dena
castling	कैसलिंग (m)	kaisaling
check	शह (m)	shah
checkmate	शह और मात (m)	shah aur māt

chess tournament	शतरंज की प्रतियोगिता (f)	shataranj kī pratiyogita
Grand Master	ग्रांडमास्टर (m)	grāndamāstar
combination	कॉम्बिनेशन (m)	kombineshan
game (in chess)	बाज़ी (f)	bāzī
checkers	चेकर्स (m)	chekars

140. Boxing

| boxing | मुक्केबाज़ी (f) | mukkebāzī |
| fight (bout) | लड़ाई (f) | laraī |

boxing match	मुक्केबाज़ी का मुक़ाबला (m)	mukkebāzī ka muqābala
round (in boxing)	मुक्केबाज़ी का राउंड (m)	mukkevāzī ka raund
ring	बॉक्सिंग रिंग (f)	boksing ring
gong	घंटा (m)	ghanta
punch	प्रहार (m)	prahār
knockdown	नॉकडाउन (m)	nokadaun
knockout	नॉकआउट (m)	nokaut
to knock out	नॉकआउट करना	nokaut karana
boxing glove	मुक्केबाज़ी के दस्ताने (m)	mukkebāzī ke dastāne
referee	रेफ़री (m)	refarī
lightweight	कम वज़न (m)	kam vazan
middleweight	मध्यम वज़न (m)	madhyam vazan
heavyweight	भारी वज़न (m)	bhārī vazan

141. Sports. Miscellaneous

Olympic Games	ओलिम्पिक खेल (m pl)	olimpik khel
winner	विजेता (m)	vijeta
to be winning	विजय पाना	vijay pāna
to win (vi)	जीतना	jītana
leader	लीडर (m)	līdar
to lead (vi)	लीड करना	līd karana
first place	पहला स्थान (m)	pahala sthān
second place	दूसरा स्थान (m)	dūsara sthān
third place	तीसरा स्थान (m)	tīsara sthān
medal	मेडल (m)	medal
trophy	ट्रॉफ़ी (f)	trofī
prize cup (trophy)	कप (m)	kap
prize (in game)	पुरस्कार (m)	puraskār
main prize	मुख्य पुरस्कार (m)	mukhy puraskār
record	रिकॉर्ड (m)	rikord
to set a record	रिकॉर्ड बनाना	rikord banāna
final	फ़ाइनल (m)	fainal
final (adj)	अंतिम	antim
champion	चेम्पियन (m)	chempiyan
championship	चैम्पियनशिप (f)	chaimpiyanaship
stadium	स्टेडियम (m)	stediyam
stand (bleachers)	सीट (f)	sīt

fan, supporter	फ़ैन (m)	fain
opponent, rival	प्रतिद्वंद्वी (f)	pratidvandvī
start (start line)	स्टार्ट (m)	stārt
finish line	फ़िनिश (f)	finish
defeat	हार (f)	hār
to lose (not win)	हारना	hārana
referee	रेफ़री (m)	refarī
jury (judges)	ज्यूरी (m)	jyūrī
score	स्कोर (m)	skor
tie	टाई (m)	taī
to tie (vi)	खेल टाइ करना	khel tai karana
point	अंक (m)	ank
result (final score)	नतीजा (m)	natīja
period	टाइम (m)	taim
half-time	हाफ़ टाइम (m)	hāf taim
doping	अवैध दवाओं का इस्तेमाल (m)	avaidh davaon ka istemāl
to penalize (vt)	पेनल्टी लगाना	penaltī lagāna
to disqualify (vt)	डिस्क्वेलिफ़ाई करना	diskvelifaī karana
apparatus	खेलकूद का सामान (m)	khelakūd ka sāmān
javelin	भाला (m)	bhāla
shot (metal ball)	गोला (m)	gola
ball (snooker, etc.)	गेंद (m)	gend
aim (target)	निशाना (m)	nishāna
target	निशाना (m)	nishāna
to shoot (vi)	गोली चलाना	golī chalāna
accurate (~ shot)	सटीक	satīk
trainer, coach	प्रशिक्षक (m)	prashikshak
to train (sb)	प्रशिक्षित करना	prashikshit karana
to train (vi)	प्रशिक्षण करना	prashikshan karana
training	प्रशिक्षण (f)	prashikshan
gym	जिम (m)	jim
exercise (physical)	व्यायाम (m)	vyāyām
warm-up (athlete ~)	वार्म-अप (m)	vārm-ap

Education

142. School

school	पाठशाला (m)	pāthashāla
principal (headmaster)	प्रिंसिपल (m)	prinsipal
pupil (boy)	छात्र (m)	chhātr
pupil (girl)	छात्रा (f)	chhātra
schoolboy	छात्र (m)	chhātr
schoolgirl	छात्रा (f)	chhātra
to teach (sb)	पढ़ाना	parhāna
to learn (language, etc.)	पढ़ना	parhana
to learn by heart	याद करना	yād karana
to learn (~ to count, etc.)	सीखना	sīkhana
to be in school	स्कूल में पढ़ना	skūl men parhana
to go to school	स्कूल जाना	skūl jāna
alphabet	वर्णमाला (f)	varnamāla
subject (at school)	विषय (m)	vishay
classroom	कक्षा (f)	kaksha
lesson	पाठ (m)	pāth
recess	अंतराल (m)	antarāl
school bell	स्कूल की घंटी (f)	skūl kī ghantī
school desk	बेंच (f)	bench
chalkboard	चॉकबोर्ड (m)	chokabord
grade	अंक (m)	ank
good grade	अच्छे अंक (m)	achchhe ank
bad grade	कम अंक (m)	kam ank
to give a grade	मार्क्स देना	mārks dena
mistake, error	ग़लती (f)	galatī
to make mistakes	ग़लती करना	galatī karana
to correct (an error)	ठीक करना	thīk karana
cheat sheet	कुंजी (f)	kunjī
homework	गृहकार्य (m)	grhakāry
exercise (in education)	अभ्यास (m)	abhyās
to be present	उपस्थित होना	upasthit hona
to be absent	अनुपस्थित होना	anupasthit hona
to punish (vt)	सज़ा देना	saza dena

punishment	सज़ा (f)	saza
conduct (behavior)	बरताव (m)	baratāv
report card	रिपोर्ट कार्ड (f)	riport kārd
pencil	पेंसिल (f)	pensil
eraser	रबड़ (f)	rabar
chalk	चॉक (m)	chok
pencil case	पेंसिल का डिब्बा (m)	pensil ka dibba
schoolbag	बस्ता (m)	basta
pen	कलम (m)	kalam
school notebook	कॉपी (f)	kopī
textbook	पाठ्यपुस्तक (f)	pāthyapustak
compasses	कंपास (m)	kampās
to make technical drawings	तकनीकी चित्रकारी बनाना	takanīkī chitrakārī banāna
technical drawing	तकनीकी चित्रकारी (f)	takanīkī chitrakārī
poem	कविता (f)	kavita
by heart (adv)	रटकर	ratakar
to learn by heart	याद करना	yād karana
school vacation	छुट्टियाँ (f pl)	chhuttiyān
to be on vacation	छुट्टी पर होना	chhuttī par hona
test (written math ~)	परीक्षा (f)	parīksha
essay (composition)	रचना (f)	rachana
dictation	श्रुतलेख (m)	shrutalekh
exam (examination)	परीक्षा (f)	parīksha
to take an exam	परीक्षा देना	parīksha dena
experiment (e.g., chemistry ~)	परीक्षण (m)	parīkshan

143. College. University

academy	अकादमी (f)	akādamī
university	विश्वविद्यालय (m)	vishvavidyālay
faculty (e.g., ~ of Medicine)	संकाय (f)	sankāy
student (masc.)	छात्र (m)	chhātr
student (fem.)	छात्रा (f)	chhātra
lecturer (teacher)	अध्यापक (m)	adhyāpak
lecture hall, room	व्याख्यान कक्ष (m)	vyākhyān kaksh
graduate	स्नातक (m)	snātak
diploma	डिप्लोमा (m)	diploma
dissertation	शोधनिबंध (m)	shodhanibandh
study (report)	अध्ययन (m)	adhyayan

laboratory	प्रयोगशाला (f)	prayogashāla
lecture	व्याख्यान (f)	vyākhyān
coursemate	सहपाठी (m)	sahapāthī
scholarship	छात्रवृत्ति (f)	chhātravrtti
academic degree	शैक्षणिक डिग्री (f)	shaikshanik digrī

144. Sciences. Disciplines

mathematics	गणितशास्त्र (m)	ganitashāstr
algebra	बीजगणित (m)	bījaganit
geometry	रेखागणित (m)	rekhāganit

astronomy	खगोलवैज्ञान (m)	khagolavaigyān
biology	जीवविज्ञान (m)	jīvavigyān
geography	भूगोल (m)	bhūgol
geology	भूविज्ञान (m)	bhūvigyān
history	इतिहास (m)	itihās

medicine	चिकित्सा (m)	chikitsa
pedagogy	शिक्षाविज्ञान (m)	shikshāvigyān
law	कानून (m)	kānūn

physics	भौतिकविज्ञान (m)	bhautikavigyān
chemistry	रसायन (m)	rasāyan
philosophy	दर्शनशास्त्र (m)	darshanashāstr
psychology	मनोविज्ञान (m)	manovigyān

145. Writing system. Orthography

grammar	व्याकरण (m)	vyākaran
vocabulary	शब्दावली (f)	shabdāvalī
phonetics	स्वरविज्ञान (m)	svaravigyān

noun	संज्ञा (f)	sangya
adjective	विशेषण (m)	visheshan
verb	क्रिया (m)	kriya
adverb	क्रिया विशेषण (f)	kriya visheshan

pronoun	सर्वनाम (m)	sarvanām
interjection	विस्मयादिबोधक (m)	vismayādibodhak
preposition	पूर्वसर्ग (m)	pūrvasarg

root	मूल शब्द (m)	mūl shabd
ending	अन्त्याक्षर (m)	antyākshar
prefix	उपसर्ग (m)	upasarg
syllable	अक्षर (m)	akshar
suffix	प्रत्यय (m)	pratyay
stress mark	बल चिह्न (m)	bal chihn

apostrophe	वर्णलोप चिह्न (m)	varnalop chihn
period, dot	पूर्णविराम (m)	pūrnavirām
comma	उपविराम (m)	upavirām
semicolon	अर्धविराम (m)	ardhavirām

colon	कोलन (m)	kolan
ellipsis	तीन बिन्दु (m)	tīn bindu

question mark	प्रश्न चिह्न (m)	prashn chihn
exclamation point	विस्मयादिबोधक चिह्न (m)	vismayādibodhak chihn

quotation marks	उद्धरण चिह्न (m)	uddharan chihn
in quotation marks	उद्धरण चिह्न में	uddharan chihn men

parenthesis	कोष्ठक (m pl)	koshthak
in parenthesis	कोष्ठक में	koshthak men

hyphen	हाइफन (m)	haifan
dash	डैश (m)	daish
space (between words)	रिक्त स्थान (m)	rikt sthān

letter	अक्षर (m)	akshar
capital letter	बड़ा अक्षर (m)	bara akshar

vowel (n)	स्वर (m)	svar
consonant (n)	समस्वर (m)	samasvar

sentence	वाक्य (m)	vāky
subject	कर्ता (m)	kartta
predicate	विधेय (m)	vidhey

line	पंक्ति (f)	pankti
on a new line	नई पंक्ति पर	naī pankti par
paragraph	अनुच्छेद (m)	anuchchhed

word	शब्द (m)	shabd
group of words	शब्दों का समूह (m)	shabdon ka samūh
expression	अभिव्यक्ति (f)	abhivyakti

synonym	समनार्थक शब्द (m)	samanārthak shabd
antonym	विपरीतार्थी शब्द (m)	viparītārthī shabd

rule	नियम (m)	niyam
exception	अपवाद (m)	apavād
correct (adj)	ठीक	thīk

conjugation	क्रियारूप संयोजन (m)	kriyārūp sanyojan
declension	विभक्ति-रूप (m)	vibhakti-rūp
nominal case	कारक (m)	kārak
question	प्रश्न (m)	prashn
to underline (vt)	रेखांकित करना	rekhānkit karana
dotted line	बिन्दुरेखा (f)	bindurekha

146. Foreign languages

language	भाषा (f)	bhāsha
foreign language	विदेशी भाषा (f)	videshī bhāsha
to study (vt)	पढ़ना	parhana
to learn (language, etc.)	सीखना	sīkhana
to read (vi, vt)	पढ़ना	parhana
to speak (vi, vt)	बोलना	bolana
to understand (vt)	समझना	samajhana
to write (vt)	लिखना	likhana
fast (adv)	तेज़	tez
slowly (adv)	धीरे	dhīre
fluently (adv)	धड़ल्ले से	dharalle se
rules	नियम (m pl)	niyam
grammar	व्याकरण (m)	vyākaran
vocabulary	शब्दावली (f)	shabdāvalī
phonetics	स्वरविज्ञान (m)	svaravigyān
textbook	पाठ्यपुस्तक (f)	pāthyapustak
dictionary	शब्दकोश (m)	shabdakosh
teach-yourself book	स्वयंशिक्षक पुस्तक (m)	svayanshikshak pustak
phrasebook	वार्त्तालाप-पुस्तिका (f)	vārttālāp-pustika
cassette, tape	कैसेट (f)	kaiset
videotape	वीडियो कैसेट (m)	vīdiyo kaiset
CD, compact disc	सीडी (m)	sīdī
DVD	डीवीडी (m)	dīvīdī
alphabet	वर्णमाला (f)	varnamāla
to spell (vt)	हिज्जे करना	hijje karana
pronunciation	उच्चारण (m)	uchchāran
accent	लहज़ा (m)	lahaza
with an accent	लहज़े के साथ	lahaze ke sāth
without an accent	बिना लहज़े	bina lahaze
word	शब्द (m)	shabd
meaning	मतलब (m)	matalab
course (e.g., a French ~)	पाठ्यक्रम (m)	pāthyakram
to sign up	सदस्य बनना	sadasy banana
teacher	शिक्षक (m)	shikshak
translation (process)	तर्जुमा (m)	tarjuma
translation (text, etc.)	अनुवाद (m)	anuvād
translator	अनुवादक (m)	anuvādak
interpreter	दुभाषिया (m)	dubhāshiya
polyglot	बहुभाषी (m)	bahubhāshī
memory	स्मृति (f)	smrti

147. Fairy tale characters

Santa Claus	सांता क्लॉज़ (m)	sānta kloz
mermaid	जलपरी (f)	jalaparī
magician, wizard	जादूगर (m)	jādūgar
fairy	परी (f)	parī
magic (adj)	जादूई	jādūī
magic wand	जादू की छड़ी (f)	jādū kī chharī
fairy tale	परियों की कहानी (f)	pariyon kī kahānī
miracle	करामात (f)	karāmāt
dwarf	बौना (m)	bauna
to turn into ...	... में बदल जाना	... men badal jāna
ghost	भूत (m)	bhūt
phantom	प्रेत (m)	pret
monster	राक्षस (m)	rākshas
dragon	पंखवाला नाग (m)	pankhavāla nāg
giant	भीमकाय (m)	bhīmakāy

148. Zodiac Signs

Aries	मेष (m)	mesh
Taurus	वृषभ (m)	vrshabh
Gemini	मिथुन (m)	mithun
Cancer	कर्क (m)	kark
Leo	सिंह (m)	sinh
Virgo	कन्या (f)	kanya
Libra	तुला (f pl)	tula
Scorpio	वृश्चिक (m)	vrshchik
Sagittarius	धनु (m)	dhanu
Capricorn	मकर (m)	makar
Aquarius	कुंभ (m)	kumbh
Pisces	मीन (m pl)	mīn
character	स्वभाव (m)	svabhāv
character traits	गुण (m pl)	gun
behavior	बरताव (m)	baratāv
to tell fortunes	भविष्यवाणी करना	bhavishyavānī karana
fortune-teller	ज्योतिषी (m)	jyotishī
horoscope	जन्म कुंडली (f)	janm kundalī

Arts

149. Theater

theater	रंगमंच (m)	rangamanch
opera	ओपेरा (m)	opera
operetta	ऑपेराटा (m)	operāta
ballet	बैले (m)	baile

theater poster	रंगमंच इश्तहार (m)	rangamanch ishtahār
troupe (theatrical company)	थियेटर कंपनी (f)	thiyetar kampanī
tour	दौरा (m)	daura
to be on tour	दौरे पर जाना	daure par jāna
to rehearse (vi, vt)	अभ्यास करना	abhyās karana
rehearsal	अभ्यास (m)	abhyās
repertoire	प्रदर्शनों की सूची (f)	pradarshanon kī sūchī

performance	प्रदर्शन (m)	pradarshan
theatrical show	प्रदर्शन (m)	pradarshan
play	नाटक (m)	nātak

ticket	टिकट (m)	tikat
box office (ticket booth)	टिकट घर (m)	tikat ghar
lobby, foyer	हॉल (m)	hol
coat check (cloakroom)	कपड़द्वार (m)	kaparadvār
coat check tag	कपड़द्वार टैग (m)	kaparadvār taig
binoculars	दूरबीन (f)	dūrabīn
usher	कंडक्टर (m)	kandaktar

orchestra seats	सीटें (f)	sīten
balcony	अपर सर्कल (m)	apar sarkal
dress circle	दूसरी मंज़िल (f)	dūsarī manzil
box	बॉक्स (m)	boks
row	कतार (m)	katār
seat	सीट (f)	sīt

audience	दर्शक (m)	darshak
spectator	दर्शक (m)	darshak
to clap (vi, vt)	ताली बजाना	tālī bajāna
applause	तालियाँ (f pl)	tāliyān
ovation	तालियों की गड़गड़ाहट (m)	tāliyon kī garagarāhat

stage	मंच (m)	manch
curtain	पर्दा (m)	parda
scenery	मंच सज्जा (f)	manch sajja

backstage	नेपथ्य (m pl)	nepathy
scene (e.g., the last ~)	दृश्य (m)	drshy
act	एक्ट (m)	ekt
intermission	अंतराल (m)	antarāl

150. Cinema

actor	अभिनेता (m)	abhineta
actress	अभिनेत्री (f)	abhinetrī
movies (industry)	सिनेमा (m)	sinema
movie	फ़िल्म (m)	film
episode	उपकथा (m)	upakatha
detective movie	जासूसी फ़िल्म (f)	jāsūsī film
action movie	एक्शन फ़िल्म (f)	ekshan film
adventure movie	जोखिम भरी फ़िल्म (f)	jokhim bharī film
science fiction movie	कल्पित विज्ञान की फ़िल्म (f)	kalpit vigyān kī film
horror movie	डरावनी फ़िल्म (f)	darāvanī film
comedy movie	मज़ाकिया फ़िल्म (f)	mazākiya film
melodrama	भावुक नाटक (m)	bhāvuk nātak
drama	नाटक (m)	nātak
fictional movie	काल्पनिक फ़िल्म (f)	kālpanik film
documentary	वृत्तचित्र (m)	vrttachitr
cartoon	कार्टून (m)	kārtūn
silent movies	मूक फ़िल्म (f)	mūk film
role (part)	भूमिका (f)	bhūmika
leading role	मुख्य भूमिका (f)	mūkhy bhūmika
to play (vi, vt)	भूमिका निभाना	bhūmika nibhāna
movie star	फ़िल्म स्टार (m)	film stār
well-known (adj)	मशहूर	mashahūr
famous (adj)	मशहूर	mashahūr
popular (adj)	लोकप्रिय	lokapriy
script (screenplay)	पटकथा (f)	patakatha
scriptwriter	पटकथा लेखक (m)	patakatha lekhak
movie director	निर्देशक (m)	nirdeshak
producer	प्रड्यूसर (m)	pradyūsar
assistant	सहायक (m)	sahāyak
cameraman	कैमरामैन (m)	kaimarāmain
stuntman	स्टंटमैन (m)	stantamain
to shoot a movie	फ़िल्म शूट करना	film shūt karana
audition, screen test	स्क्रीन टेस्ट (m)	skrīn test
shooting	शूटिंग (f pl)	shūting

movie crew	शूटिंग दल (m)	shūting dal
movie set	शूटिंग स्थल (m)	shuting sthal
camera	कैमरा (m)	kaimara
movie theater	सिनेमाघर (m)	sinemāghar
screen (e.g., big ~)	स्क्रीन (m)	skrīn
to show a movie	फ़िल्म दिखाना	film dikhāna
soundtrack	साउंडट्रैक (m)	saundatraik
special effects	ख़ास प्रभाव (m pl)	khās prabhāv
subtitles	सबटाइटिल (f)	sabataitil
credits	टाइटिल (m pl)	taitil
translation	अनुवाद (m)	anuvād

151. Painting

art	कला (f)	kala
fine arts	ललित कला (f)	lalit kala
art gallery	चित्रशाला (f)	chitrashāla
art exhibition	चित्रों की प्रदर्शनी (f)	chitron kī pradarshanī
painting (art)	चित्रकला (f)	chitrakala
graphic art	रेखाचित्र कला (f)	rekhāchitr kala
abstract art	अमूर्त चित्रण (m)	amūrtt chitran
impressionism	प्रभाववाद (m)	prabhāvavād
picture (painting)	चित्र (m)	chitr
drawing	रेखाचित्र (f)	rekhāchitr
poster	पोस्टर (m)	postar
illustration (picture)	चित्रण (m)	chitran
miniature	लघु चित्र (m)	laghu chitr
copy (of painting, etc.)	प्रति (f)	prati
reproduction	प्रतिकृत (f)	pratikrt
mosaic	पच्चीकारी (f)	pachchīkārī
stained glass window	रंगीन काँच	rangīn kānch
fresco	लेपचित्र (m)	lepachitr
engraving	एनग्रेविंग (m)	enagreving
bust (sculpture)	बस्ट (m)	bast
sculpture	मूर्तिकला (f)	mūrtikala
statue	मूर्ति (f)	mūrti
plaster of Paris	सिलखड़ी (f)	silakharī
plaster (as adj)	सिलखड़ी से	silakharī se
portrait	रूपचित्र (m)	rūpachitr
self-portrait	स्वचित्र (m)	svachitr
landscape painting	प्रकृति चित्र (m)	prakrti chitr
still life	अचल चित्र (m)	achal chitr

caricature	कार्टून (m)	kārtūn
sketch	रेखाचित्र (f)	rekhāchitr
paint	पेंट (f)	pent
watercolor paint	जलरंग (m)	jalarang
oil (paint)	तेलरंग (m)	telarang
pencil	पेंसिल (f)	pensil
India ink	स्याही (f)	syāhī
charcoal	कोयला (m)	koyala
to draw (vi, vt)	रेखाचित्र बनाना	rekhāchitr banāna
to pose (vi)	पोज़ करना	poz karana
artist's model (masc.)	मॉडल (m)	modal
artist's model (fem.)	मॉडल (m)	modal
artist (painter)	चित्रकार (m)	chitrakār
work of art	कलाकृति (f)	kalākrti
masterpiece	अत्युत्तम कृति (f)	atyuttam krti
studio (artist's workroom)	स्टुडियो (m)	studiyo
canvas (cloth)	चित्रपटी (f)	chitrapatī
easel	चित्राधार (m)	chitrādhār
palette	रंग पट्टिका (f)	rang pattika
frame (picture ~, etc.)	ढांचा (m)	dhāncha
restoration	जीर्णोद्धार (m)	jīrnoddhār
to restore (vt)	मरम्मत करना	marammat karana

152. Literature & Poetry

literature	साहित्य (m)	sāhity
author (writer)	लेखक (m)	lekhak
pseudonym	छद्मनाम (m)	chhadmanām
book	किताब (f)	kitāb
volume	खंड (m)	khand
table of contents	अनुक्रमणिका (f)	anukramanika
page	पृष्ठ (m)	prshth
main character	मुख्य किरदार (m)	mūkhy kiradār
autograph	स्वाक्षर (m)	svākshar
short story	लघु कथा (f)	laghu katha
story (novella)	उपन्यासिका (f)	upanyāsika
novel	उपन्यास (m)	upanyās
work (writing)	रचना (f)	rachana
fable	नीतिकथा (f)	nītikatha
detective novel	जासूसी कहानी (f)	jāsūsī kahānī
poem (verse)	कविता (f)	kavita
poetry	काव्य (m)	kāvy

| poem (epic, ballad) | कविता (f) | kavita |
| poet | कवि (m) | kavi |

fiction	उपन्यास (m)	upanyās
science fiction	विज्ञान कथा (f)	vigyān katha
adventures	रोमांच (m)	romānch
educational literature	शैक्षिक साहित्य (m)	shaikshik sāhity
children's literature	बाल साहित्य (m)	bāl sāhity

153. Circus

circus	सर्कस (m)	sarkas
traveling circus	सर्कस (m)	sarkas
program	प्रोग्रम (m)	program
performance	तमाशा (m)	tamāsha

| act (circus ~) | ऐक्ट (m) | aikt |
| circus ring | सर्कस रिंग (m) | sarkas ring |

| pantomime (act) | मूकाभिनय (m) | mūkābhinay |
| clown | जोकर (m) | jokar |

acrobat	कलाबाज़ (m)	kalābāz
acrobatics	कलाबाज़ी (f)	kalābāzī
gymnast	जिमनैस्ट (m)	jimanaist
gymnastics	जिमनैस्टिक्स (m)	jimanaistiks
somersault	कलैया (m)	kalaiya

athlete (strongman)	एथलीट (m)	ethalīt
tamer (e.g., lion ~)	जानवरों का शिक्षक (m)	jānavaron ka shikshak
rider (circus horse ~)	सवारी (m)	savārī
assistant	सहायक (m)	sahāyak

stunt	कलाबाज़ी (f)	kalābāzī
magic trick	जादू (m)	jādū
conjurer, magician	जादूगर (m)	jādūgar

juggler	बाज़ीगर (m)	bāzīgar
to juggle (vi, vt)	बाज़ीगिरी दिखाना	bāzīgirī dikhāna
animal trainer	जानवरों का प्रशिक्षक (m)	jānavaron ka prashikshak
animal training	पशु प्रशिक्षण (m)	pashu prashikshan
to train (animals)	प्रशिक्षण देना	prashikshan dena

154. Music. Pop music

music	संगीत (m)	sangit
musician	साज़िन्दा (m)	sāzinda
musical instrument	बाजा (m)	bāja

to play ...	... बजाना	... bajāna
guitar	गिटार (m)	gitār
violin	वॉयलिन (m)	voyalin
cello	चैलो (m)	chailo
double bass	डबल बास (m)	dabal bās
harp	हार्प (m)	hārp
piano	पियानो (m)	piyāno
grand piano	ग्रैंड पियानो (m)	graind piyāno
organ	ऑर्गन (m)	organ
wind instruments	सुषिर वाद्य (m)	sushir vādy
oboe	ओबो (m)	obo
saxophone	सैक्सोफ़ोन (m)	saiksofon
clarinet	क्लेरिनेट (m)	klerinet
flute	मुरली (f)	muralī
trumpet	तुरही (m)	turahī
accordion	एकॉर्डियन (m)	ekordiyan
drum	नगाड़ा (m)	nagāra
duo	द्विवाद्य (m)	dvivādy
trio	त्रयी (f)	trayī
quartet	क्वार्टेट (m)	kvārtat
choir	कोरस (m)	koras
orchestra	ऑर्केस्ट्रा (m)	orkestra
pop music	पॉप संगीत (m)	pop sangīt
rock music	रॉक संगीत (m)	rok sangīt
rock group	रोक ग्रूप (m)	rok grūp
jazz	जैज़ (m)	jaiz
idol	आइडल (m)	āidal
admirer, fan	प्रशंसक (m)	prashansak
concert	कंसर्ट (m)	kansart
symphony	वाद्य-वृंद रचना (f)	vādy-vrnd rachana
composition	रचना (f)	rachana
to compose (write)	रचना बनाना	rachana banāna
singing (n)	गाना (m)	gāna
song	गीत (m)	gīt
tune (melody)	संगीत (m)	sangit
rhythm	ताल (m)	tāl
blues	ब्लूज़ (m)	blūz
sheet music	शीट संगीत (m)	shīt sangīt
baton	छड़ी (f)	chharī
bow	गज (m)	gaj
string	तार (m)	tār
case (e.g., guitar ~)	केस (m)	kes

Rest. Entertainment. Travel

155. Trip. Travel

tourism, travel	पर्यटन (m)	paryatan
tourist	पर्यटक (m)	paryatak
trip, voyage	यात्रा (f)	yātra
adventure	जाँबाज़ी (f)	jānbāzī
trip, journey	यात्रा (f)	yātra
vacation	छुट्टी (f)	chhuttī
to be on vacation	छुट्टी पर होना	chhuttī par hona
rest	आराम (m)	ārām
train	रेलगाड़ी, ट्रेन (f)	relagārī, tren
by train	रैलगाड़ी से	railagārī se
airplane	विमान (m)	vimān
by airplane	विमान से	vimān se
by car	कार से	kār se
by ship	जहाज़ पर	jahāz par
luggage	सामान (m)	sāmān
suitcase	सूटकेस (m)	sūtakes
luggage cart	सामान के लिये गाड़ी (f)	sāmān ke liye gārī
passport	पासपोर्ट (m)	pāsaport
visa	वीज़ा (m)	vīza
ticket	टिकट (m)	tikat
air ticket	हवाई टिकट (m)	havaī tikat
guidebook	गाइडबुक (f)	gaidabuk
map (tourist ~)	नक्शा (m)	naksha
area (rural ~)	क्षेत्र (m)	kshetr
place, site	स्थान (m)	sthān
exotica (n)	विचित्र वस्तुएं	vichitr vastuen
exotic (adj)	विचित्र	vichitr
amazing (adj)	अजीब	ajīb
group	समूह (m)	samūh
excursion, sightseeing tour	पर्यटन (f)	paryatan
guide (person)	गाइड (m)	gaid

156. Hotel

hotel	होटल (f)	hotal
motel	मोटल (m)	motal
three-star (~ hotel)	तीन सितारा	tīn sitāra
five-star	पाँच सितारा	pānch sitāra
to stay (in a hotel, etc.)	ठहरना	thaharana
room	कमरा (m)	kamara
single room	एक पलंग का कमरा (m)	ek palang ka kamara
double room	दो पलंगों का कमरा (m)	do palangon ka kamara
to book a room	कमरा बुक करना	kamara buk karana
half board	हाफ़-बोर्ड (m)	hāf-bord
full board	फ़ुल-बोर्ड (m)	ful-bord
with bath	स्नानघर के साथ	snānaghar ke sāth
with shower	शॉवर के साथ	shovar ke sāth
satellite television	सैटेलाइट टेलीविज़न (m)	saitelait telīvizan
air-conditioner	एयर-कंडिशनर (m)	eyar-kandishanar
towel	तौलिया (f)	tauliya
key	चाबी (f)	chābī
administrator	मैनेजर (m)	mainejar
chambermaid	चैमबरमैड (f)	chaimabaramaid
porter, bellboy	कुली (m)	kulī
doorman	दरबान (m)	darabān
restaurant	रेस्टराँ (m)	restarān
pub, bar	बार (m)	bār
breakfast	नाश्ता (m)	nāshta
dinner	रात्रिभोज (m)	rātribhoj
buffet	बुफ़े (m)	bufe
lobby	लॉबी (f)	lobī
elevator	लिफ़्ट (m)	lift
DO NOT DISTURB	परेशान न करें	pareshān na karen
NO SMOKING	धूम्रपान निषेध!	dhumrapān nishedh!

157. Books. Reading

book	किताब (f)	kitāb
author	लेखक (m)	lekhak
writer	लेखक (m)	lekhak
to write (~ a book)	लिखना	likhana
reader	पाठक (m)	pāthak
to read (vi, vt)	पढ़ना	parhana

reading (activity)	पढ़ना (f)	parhana
silently (to oneself)	मन ही मन	man hī man
aloud (adv)	बोलकर	bolakar
to publish (vt)	प्रकाशित करना	prakāshit karana
publishing (process)	प्रकाशन (m)	prakāshan
publisher	प्रकाशक (m)	prakāshak
publishing house	प्रकाशन संस्था (m)	prakāshan sanstha
to come out (be released)	बाज़ार में निकालना (m)	bāzār men nikālana
release (of a book)	बाज़ार में निकालना (m)	bāzār men nikālana
print run	मुद्रण संख्या (f)	mudran sankhya
bookstore	किताबों की दुकान (f)	kitābon kī dukān
library	पुस्तकालय (m)	pustakālay
story (novella)	उपन्यासिका (f)	upanyāsika
short story	लघु कहानी (f)	laghu kahānī
novel	उपन्यास (m)	upanyās
detective novel	जासूसी किताब (m)	jāsūsī kitāb
memoirs	संस्मरण (m pl)	sansmaran
legend	उपाख्यान (m)	upākhyān
myth	पुराणकथा (m)	purānakatha
poetry, poems	कविताएँ (f pl)	kavitaen
autobiography	आत्मकथा (m)	ātmakatha
selected works	चुनिंदा कृतियाँ (f)	chuninda krtiyān
science fiction	कल्पित विज्ञान (m)	kalpit vigyān
title	किताब का नाम (m)	kitāb ka nām
introduction	भूमिका (f)	bhūmika
title page	टाइटिल पृष्ठ (m)	taitil prshth
chapter	अध्याय (m)	adhyāy
extract	अंश (m)	ansh
episode	उपकथा (f)	upakatha
plot (storyline)	कथानक (m)	kathānak
contents	कथा-वस्तु (f)	katha-vastu
table of contents	अनुक्रमणिका (f)	anukramanika
main character	मुख्य किरदार (m)	mūkhy kiradār
volume	खंड (m)	khand
cover	जिल्द (f)	jild
binding	जिल्द (f)	jild
bookmark	बुकमार्क (m)	bukamārk
page	पृष्ठ (m)	prshth
to page through	पन्ने पलटना	panne palatana
margins	हाशिया (m pl)	hāshiya
annotation (marginal note, etc.)	टिप्पणी (f)	tippanī

footnote	टिप्पणी (f)	tippanī
text	पाठ (m)	pāth
type, font	मुद्रलिपि (m)	mudrālipi
misprint, typo	छपाई की भूल (f)	chhapaī kī bhūl
translation	अनुवाद (m)	anuvād
to translate (vt)	अनुवाद करना	anuvād karana
original (n)	मूल पाठ (m)	mūl pāth
famous (adj)	मशहूर	mashahūr
unknown (not famous)	अपरिचित	aparichit
interesting (adj)	दिलचस्प	dilachasp
bestseller	बेस्ट सेलर (m)	best selar
dictionary	शब्दकोश (m)	shabdakosh
textbook	पाठ्यपुस्तक (f)	pāthyapustak
encyclopedia	विश्वकोश (m)	vishvakosh

158. Hunting. Fishing

hunting	शिकार (m)	shikār
to hunt (vi, vt)	शिकार करना	shikār karana
hunter	शिकारी (m)	shikārī
to shoot (vi)	गोली चलाना	golī chalāna
rifle	बंदूक (m)	bandūk
bullet (shell)	कारतूस (m)	kāratūs
shot (lead balls)	कारतूस (m)	kāratūs
steel trap	जाल (m)	jāl
snare (for birds, etc.)	जाल (m)	jāl
to lay a steel trap	जाल बिछाना	jāl bichhāna
poacher	चोर शिकारी (m)	chor shikārī
game (in hunting)	शिकार के पशुपक्षी (f)	shikār ke pashupakshī
hound dog	शिकार का कुत्ता (m)	shikār ka kutta
safari	सफ़ारी (m)	safārī
mounted animal	जानवरों का पुतला (m)	jānavaron ka putala
fisherman, angler	मछुआरा (m)	machhuāra
fishing (angling)	मछली पकड़ना (f)	machhalī pakarana
to fish (vi)	मछली पकड़ना	machhalī pakarana
fishing rod	बंसी (f)	bansī
fishing line	डोरी (f)	dorī
hook	हूक (m)	hūk
float, bobber	फ्लोट (m)	flot
bait	चारा (m)	chāra
to cast a line	बंसी डालना	bansī dālana
to bite (ab. fish)	चुगना	chugana

catch (of fish)	मछलियाँ (f)	machhaliyān
ice-hole	आइस होल (m)	āis hol
fishing net	जाल (m)	jāl
boat	नाव (m)	nāv
to net (to fish with a net)	जाल से पकड़ना	jāl se pakarana
to cast[throw] the net	जाल डालना	jāl dālana
to haul the net in	जाल निकालना	jāl nikālana
whaler (person)	ह्वेलर (m)	hvelar
whaleboat	ह्वेलमार जहाज़ (m)	hvelamār jahāz
harpoon	मत्स्यभाला (m)	matsyabhāla

159. Games. Billiards

billiards	बिलियइर्स (m)	biliyards
billiard room, hall	बिलियइर्स का कमरा (m)	biliyards ka kamara
ball (snooker, etc.)	बिलियइर्स की गेंद (f)	biliyards kī gend
to pocket a ball	गेंद पॉकेट में डालना	gend poket men dālana
cue	बिलियइर्स का क्यू (m)	biliyards ka kyū
pocket	बिलियइर्स की पॉकेट (f)	biliyards kī poket

160. Games. Playing cards

diamonds	ईंट (f pl)	īnt
spades	हुक्म (m pl)	hukm
hearts	पान (m)	pān
clubs	चिड़ी (m)	chirī
ace	इक्का (m)	ikka
king	बादशाह (m)	bādashāh
queen	बेगम (f)	begam
jack, knave	गुलाम (m)	gulām
playing card	ताश का पत्ता (m)	tāsh ka patta
cards	ताश के पत्ते (m pl)	tāsh ke patte
trump	ट्रम्प (m)	tramp
deck of cards	ताश की गड्डी (f)	tāsh kī gaddī
to deal (vi, vt)	ताश बांटना	tāsh bāntana
to shuffle (cards)	पत्ते फेंटना	patte fentana
lead, turn (n)	चाल (f)	chāl
cardsharp	पत्तेबाज़ (m)	pattebāz

161. Casino. Roulette

casino	केसिनो (m)	kesino
roulette (game)	रूले (m)	rūle
bet	दांव (m)	dānv
to place bets	दांव लगाना	dānv lagāna
red	लाल (m)	lāl
black	काला (m)	kāla
to bet on red	लाल पर दांव लगाना	lāl par dānv lagāna
to bet on black	काले पर दांव लगाना	kāle par dānv lagāna
croupier (dealer)	क्रूप्ये (m)	krūpye
to spin the wheel	पहिया घुमाना	pahiya ghumāna
rules (of game)	खेल के नियम (m pl)	khel ke niyam
chip	चिप (m)	chip
to win (vi, vt)	जीतना	jītana
win (winnings)	जीती हुई रकम (f)	jītī huī rakam
to lose (~ 100 dollars)	हार जाना	hār jāna
loss (losses)	हारी हुई रकम (f)	hārī huī rakam
player	खिलाड़ी (m)	khilārī
blackjack (card game)	ब्लैक जैक (m)	blaik jaik
craps (dice game)	पासे का खेल (m)	pāse ka khel
slot machine	स्लॉट मशीन (f)	slot mashīn

162. Rest. Games. Miscellaneous

to stroll (vi, vt)	घुमना	ghūmana
stroll (leisurely walk)	सैर (f)	sair
car ride	सफ़र (m)	safar
adventure	साहसिक कार्य (m)	sāhasik kāry
picnic	पिकनिक (f)	pikanik
game (chess, etc.)	खेल (m)	khel
player	खिलाड़ी (m)	khilārī
game (one ~ of chess)	बाज़ी (f)	bāzī
collector (e.g., philatelist)	संग्राहक (m)	sangrāhak
to collect (stamps, etc.)	संग्राहण करना	sangrāhan karana
collection	संग्रह (m)	sangrah
crossword puzzle	पहेली (f)	pahelī
racetrack	रेसकोर्स (m)	resakors
(horse racing venue)		
disco (discotheque)	डिस्को (m)	disko
sauna	सौना (m)	sauna

lottery	लॉटरी (f)	lotarī
camping trip	कैम्पिंग ट्रिप (f)	kaimping trip
camp	डेरा (m)	dera
tent (for camping)	तंबू (m)	tambū
compass	दिशा सूचक यंत्र (m)	disha sūchak yantr
camper	शिविरार्थी (m)	shivirārthī
to watch (movie, etc.)	देखना	dekhana
viewer	दर्शक (m)	darshak
TV show (TV program)	टीवी प्रसारण (m)	tīvī prasāran

163. Photography

camera (photo)	कैमरा (m)	kaimara
photo, picture	फ़ोटो (m)	foto
photographer	फ़ोटोग्राफ़र (m)	fotogrāfar
photo studio	फ़ोटो स्टूडियो (m)	foto stūdiyo
photo album	फ़ोटो अल्बम (f)	foto albam
camera lens	कैमरे का लेंस (m)	kaimare ka lens
telephoto lens	टेलिफ़ोटो लेन्स (m)	telifoto lens
filter	फ़िल्टर (m)	filtar
lens	लेंस (m)	lens
optics (high-quality ~)	प्रकाशिकी (f)	prakāshikī
diaphragm (aperture)	डायफ़राम (m)	dāyafarām
exposure time (shutter speed)	शटर समय (m)	shatar samay
viewfinder	व्यू फाइंडर (m)	vyū faindar
digital camera	डिजिटल कैमरा (m)	dijital kaimara
tripod	तिपाई (f)	tipaī
flash	फ़्लैश (m)	flaish
to photograph (vt)	फ़ोटो खींचना	foto khīnchana
to take pictures	फ़ोटो लेना	foto lena
to have one's picture taken	अपनी फ़ोटो खींचवाना	apanī foto khīnchavāna
focus	फ़ोकस (f)	fokas
to focus	फ़ोकस करना	fokas karana
sharp, in focus (adj)	फ़ोकस में	fokas men
sharpness	स्पष्टता (f)	spashtata
contrast	विपर्यास व्यतिरेक	viparyās vyatirek
contrast (as adj)	विपर्यासी	viparyāsī
picture (photo)	फ़ोटो (m)	foto
negative (n)	नेगेटिव (m)	negetiv
film (a roll of ~)	कैमरा फ़िल्म (f)	kaimara film

| frame (still) | फ्रेम (m) | frem |
| to print (photos) | छापना | chhāpana |

164. Beach. Swimming

beach	बालुतट (m)	bālutat
sand	रेत (f)	ret
deserted (beach)	वीरान	vīrān

suntan	धूप की कालिमा (f)	dhūp kī kālima
to get a tan	धूप में स्नान करना	dhūp men snān karana
tan (adj)	टैन	tain
sunscreen	धूप की क्रीम (f)	dhūp kī krīm

bikini	बिकीनी (f)	bikīnī
bathing suit	स्विम सूट (m)	svim sūt
swim trunks	स्विम ट्रंक (m)	svim trank

swimming pool	तरण-ताल (m)	taran-tāl
to swim (vi)	तैरना	tairana
shower	शावर (m)	shāvar
to change (one's clothes)	बदलना	badalana
towel	तौलिया (m)	tauliya

| boat | नाव (f) | nāv |
| motorboat | मोटरबोट (m) | motarabot |

| water ski | वॉटर स्की (f) | votar skī |
| paddle boat | चप्पू से चलने वाली नाव (f) | chappū se chalane vālī nāv |

| surfing | सर्फ़िंग (m) | sarfing |
| surfer | सर्फ़ करनेवाला (m) | sarf karanevāla |

scuba set	स्कूबा सेट (m)	skūba set
flippers (swim fins)	फ़्लिपर्स (m)	flipars
mask (diving ~)	डाइविंग के लिए मास्क (m)	daiving ke lie māsk
diver	गोताखोर (m)	gotākhor
to dive (vi)	डुबकी मारना	dubakī mārana
underwater (adv)	पानी के नीचे	pānī ke nīche

beach umbrella	बालुतट की छतरी (f)	bālutat kī chhatarī
sunbed (lounger)	बालूतट की कुर्सी (f)	bālūtat kī kursī
sunglasses	धूप का चश्मा (m)	dhūp ka chashma
air mattress	हवा वाला गद्दा (m)	hava vāla gadda

to play (amuse oneself)	खेलना	khelana
to go for a swim	तैरने के लिए जाना	tairane ke lie jāna
beach ball	बालूतट पर खेलने की गेंद (f)	bālutat par khelane kī gend

to inflate (vt)	हवा भराना	hava bharāna
inflatable, air (adj)	हवा से भरा	hava se bhara
wave	तरंग (m)	tarang
buoy (line of ~s)	बोया (m)	boya
to drown (ab. person)	डूब जाना	dūb jāna
to save, to rescue	बचाना	bachāna
life vest	बचाव पेटी (f)	bachāv petī
to observe, to watch	देखना	dekhana
lifeguard	जीवनरक्षक (m)	jīvanarakshak

TECHNICAL EQUIPMENT. TRANSPORTATION

Technical equipment

165. Computer

computer	कंप्यूटर (m)	kampyūtar
notebook, laptop	लैपटॉप (m)	laipatop
to turn on	चलाना	chalāna
to turn off	बंद करना	band karana
keyboard	कीबोर्ड (m)	kībord
key	कुंजी (f)	kunjī
mouse	माउस (m)	maus
mouse pad	माउस पैड (m)	maus paid
button	बटन (m)	batan
cursor	कर्सर (m)	karsar
monitor	मॉनिटर (m)	monitar
screen	स्क्रीन (m)	skrīn
hard disk	हार्ड डिस्क (m)	hārd disk
hard disk capacity	हार्ड डिस्क क्षमता (f)	hārd disk kshamata
memory	मेमोरी (f)	memorī
random access memory	रैंडम ऐक्सेस मेमोरी (f)	raindam aikses memorī
file	फ़ाइल (f)	fail
folder	फ़ोल्डर (m)	foldar
to open (vt)	खोलना	kholana
to close (vt)	बंद करना	band karana
to save (vt)	सहेजना	sahejana
to delete (vt)	हटाना	hatāna
to copy (vt)	कॉपी करना	kopī karana
to sort (vt)	व्यवस्थित करना	vyavasthit karana
to transfer (copy)	स्थानांतरित करना	sthānāntarit karana
program	प्रोग्राम (m)	progrām
software	सोफ़्टवेयर (m)	softaveyar
programmer	प्रोग्रामर (m)	progrāmar
to program (vt)	प्रोग्रम करना	program karana
hacker	हैकर (m)	haikar
password	पासवर्ड (m)	pāsavard

virus	वाइरस (m)	vairas
to find, to detect	तलाश करना	talāsh karana
byte	बाइट (m)	bait
megabyte	मेगाबाइट (m)	megābait
data	डाटा (m pl)	dāta
database	डाटाबेस (m)	dātābes
cable (USB, etc.)	तार (m)	tār
to disconnect (vt)	अलग करना	alag karana
to connect (sth to sth)	जोड़ना	jorana

166. Internet. E-mail

Internet	इन्टरनेट (m)	intaranet
browser	ब्राउज़र (m)	brauzar
search engine	सर्च इंजन (f)	sarch injan
provider	प्रोवाइडर (m)	provaidar
webmaster	वेब मास्टर (m)	veb māstar
website	वेब साइट (m)	veb sait
webpage	वेब पृष्ठ (m)	veb prshth
address (e-mail ~)	पता (m)	pata
address book	संपर्क पुस्तक (f)	sampark pustak
mailbox	मेलबॉक्स (m)	melaboks
mail	डाक (m)	dāk
message	संदेश (m)	sandesh
sender	प्रेषक (m)	preshak
to send (vt)	भेजना	bhejana
sending (of mail)	भेजना (m)	bhejana
receiver	प्रासकर्ता (m)	prāptakarta
to receive (vt)	प्रास करना	prāpt karana
correspondence	पत्राचार (m)	patrāchār
to correspond (vi)	पत्राचार करना	patrāchār karana
file	फ़ाइल (f)	fail
to download (vt)	डाउनलोड करना	daunalod karana
to create (vt)	बनाना	banāna
to delete (vt)	हटाना	hatāna
deleted (adj)	हटा दिया गया	hata diya gaya
connection (ADSL, etc.)	कनेक्शन (m)	kanekshan
speed	रफ़्तार (f)	rafatār
modem	मोडेम (m)	modem

access	पहुंच (m)	pahunch
port (e.g., input ~)	पोर्ट (m)	port
connection (make a ~)	कनेक्शन (m)	kanekshan
to connect to ... (vi)	जुड़ना	jurana
to select (vt)	चुनना	chunana
to search (for ...)	खोजना	khojana

167. Electricity

electricity	बिजली (f)	bijalī
electric, electrical (adj)	बिजली का	bijalī ka
electric power plant	बिजलीघर (m)	bijalīghar
energy	ऊर्जा (f)	ūrja
electric power	विद्युत शक्ति (f)	vidyut shakti
light bulb	बल्ब (m)	balb
flashlight	फ्लैशलाइट (f)	flaishalait
street light	सड़क की बत्ती (f)	sarak kī battī
light	बिजली (f)	bijalī
to turn on	चलाना	chalāna
to turn off	बंद करना	band karana
to turn off the light	बिजली बंद करना	bijalī band karana
to burn out (vi)	फ्यूज़ होना	fyūz hona
short circuit	शार्ट सर्किट (m)	shārt sarkit
broken wire	टूटा तार (m)	tūta tār
contact (electrical ~)	सॉकेट (m)	soket
light switch	स्विच (m)	svich
wall socket	सॉकेट (m)	soket
plug	प्लग (m)	plag
extension cord	एक्स्टेंशन कोर्ड (m)	ekstenshan kord
fuse	फ्यूज़ (m)	fyūz
cable, wire	तार (m)	tār
wiring	तार (m)	tār
ampere	ऐम्पेयर (m)	aimpeyar
amperage	विद्युत शक्ति (f)	vidyut shakti
volt	वोल्ट (m)	volt
voltage	वोल्टेज (f)	voltej
electrical device	विद्युत यंत्र (m)	vidyut yantr
indicator	सूचक (m)	sūchak
electrician	विद्युत कारीगर (m)	vidyut kārīgar
to solder (vt)	धातु जोड़ना	dhātu jorana

soldering iron	सोल्डरिंग आयरन (m)	soldaring āyaran
electric current	विद्युत प्रवाह (f)	vidyut pravāh

168. Tools

tool, instrument	औज़ार (m)	auzār
tools	औज़ार (m pl)	auzār
equipment (factory ~)	मशीन (f)	mashīn
hammer	हथौड़ी (f)	hathaurī
screwdriver	पेंचकस (m)	penchakas
ax	कुल्हाड़ी (f)	kulhārī
saw	आरी (f)	ārī
to saw (vt)	आरी से काटना	ārī se kātana
plane (tool)	रंदा (m)	randa
to plane (vt)	छीलना	chhīlana
soldering iron	सोल्डरिंग आयरन (m)	soldaring āyaran
to solder (vt)	धातु जोड़ना	dhātu jorana
file (tool)	रेती (f)	retī
carpenter pincers	संडसी (f pl)	sandasī
lineman's pliers	प्लायर (m)	plāyar
chisel	छेनी (f)	chhenī
drill bit	ड्रिल बिट (m)	dril bit
electric drill	विद्युतीय बरमा (m)	vidyutīy barama
to drill (vi, vt)	ड्रिल करना	dril karana
knife	छुरी (f)	chhurī
pocket knife	खुलने-बंद होने वाली छुरी (f)	khulane-band hone vālī chhurī
folding (~ knife)	खुलने-बंद होने वाली छुरी (f)	khulane-band hone vālī chhurī
blade	धार (f)	dhār
sharp (blade, etc.)	कटीला	katīla
dull, blunt (adj)	कुंद	kund
to get blunt (dull)	कुंद करना	kund karana
to sharpen (vt)	धारदार बनाना	dhāradār banāna
bolt	बोल्ट (m)	bolt
nut	नट (m)	nat
thread (of a screw)	चूड़ी (f)	chūrī
wood screw	पेंच (m)	pench
nail	कील (f)	kīl
nailhead	कील का सिरा (m)	kīl ka sira
ruler (for measuring)	स्केल (m)	skel
tape measure	इंची टेप (m)	inchī tep

spirit level	स्पिरिट लेवल (m)	spirit leval
magnifying glass	आवर्धक लेंस (m)	āvardhak lens
measuring instrument	मापक यंत्र (m)	māpak yantr
to measure (vt)	मापना	māpana
scale	स्केल (f)	skel
(of thermometer, etc.)		
readings	पाठ्यांक (m pl)	pāthyānk
compressor	कंप्रेसर (m)	kampresar
microscope	माइक्रोस्कोप (m)	maikroskop
pump (e.g., water ~)	पंप (m)	pamp
robot	रोबोट (m)	robot
laser	लेज़र (m)	lezar
wrench	रिंच (m)	rinch
adhesive tape	फ़ीता (m)	fīta
glue	लेई (f)	leī
sandpaper	रेगमाल (m)	regamāl
spring	कमानी (f)	kamānī
magnet	मैग्नेट (m)	maignet
gloves	दस्ताने (m pl)	dastāne
rope	रस्सी (f)	rassī
cord	डोरी (f)	dorī
wire (e.g., telephone ~)	तार (m)	tār
cable	केबल (m)	kebal
sledgehammer	हथौड़ा (m)	hathaura
prybar	रंभा (m)	rambha
ladder	सीढ़ी (f)	sīrhī
stepladder	सीढ़ी (f)	sīrhī
to screw (tighten)	कसना	kasana
to unscrew (lid, filter, etc.)	घुमाकर खोलना	ghumākar kholana
to tighten	कसना	kasana
(e.g., with a clamp)		
to glue, to stick	चिपकाना	chipakāna
to cut (vt)	काटना	kātana
malfunction (fault)	ख़राबी (f)	kharābī
repair (mending)	मरम्मत (f)	marammat
to repair, to fix (vt)	मरम्मत करना	marammat karana
to adjust (machine, etc.)	ठीक करना	thīk karana
to check (to examine)	जांचना	jānchana
checking	जांच (f)	jānch
readings	पाठ्यांक (m)	pāthyānk
reliable, solid (machine)	मज़बूत	mazabūt
complex (adj)	जटिल	jatil

to rust (get rusted)	ज़ंग लगना	zang lagana
rusty, rusted (adj)	ज़ंग लगा हुआ	zang laga hua
rust	ज़ंग (m)	zang

Transportation

169. Airplane

airplane	विमान (m)	vimān
air ticket	हवाई टिकट (m)	havaī tikat
airline	हवाई कम्पनी (f)	havaī kampanī
airport	हवाई अड्डा (m)	havaī adda
supersonic (adj)	पराध्वनिक	parādhvanik
captain	कप्तान (m)	kaptān
crew	वैमानिक दल (m)	vaimānik dal
pilot	विमान चालक (m)	vimān chālak
flight attendant (fem.)	एयर होस्टस (f)	eyar hostas
navigator	नैवीगेटर (m)	naivīgetar
wings	पंख (m pl)	pankh
tail	पूँछ (f)	pūnchh
cockpit	कॉकपिट (m)	kokapit
engine	इंजन (m)	injan
undercarriage (landing gear)	हवाई जहाज़ पहिये (m)	havaī jahāz pahiye
turbine	टरबाइन (f)	tarabain
propeller	प्रोपेलर (m)	propelar
black box	ब्लैक बॉक्स (m)	blaik boks
yoke (control column)	कंट्रोल कॉलम (m)	kantrol kolam
fuel	ईंधन (m)	īndhan
safety card	सुरक्षा-पत्र (m)	suraksha-patr
oxygen mask	ऑक्सीजन मास्क (m)	oksījan māsk
uniform	वर्दी (f)	vardī
life vest	बचाव पेटी (f)	bachāv petī
parachute	पैराशूट (m)	pairāshūt
takeoff	उड़ान (m)	urān
to take off (vi)	उड़ना	urana
runway	उड़ान पट्टी (f)	urān pattī
visibility	दृश्यता (f)	drshyata
flight (act of flying)	उड़ान (m)	urān
altitude	ऊंचाई (f)	ūnchaī
air pocket	वायु-पॉकेट (m)	vāyu-poket
seat	सीट (f)	sīt
headphones	हेडफ़ोन (m)	hedafon

folding tray (tray table)	ट्रे टेबल (f)	tre tebal
airplane window	हवाई जहाज़ की खिड़की (f)	havaī jahāz kī khirakī
aisle	गलियारा (m)	galiyāra

170. Train

train	रेलगाड़ी, ट्रेन (f)	relagārī, tren
commuter train	लोकल ट्रेन (f)	lokal tren
express train	तेज़ रेलगाड़ी (f)	tez relagārī
diesel locomotive	डीज़ल रेलगाड़ी (f)	dīzal relagārī
steam locomotive	स्टीम इंजन (f)	stīm injan

| passenger car | कोच (f) | koch |
| dining car | डाइनर (f) | dainar |

rails	पटरियाँ (f)	patariyān
railroad	रेलवे (f)	relave
railway tie	पटरियाँ (f)	patariyān

platform (railway ~)	प्लेटफॉर्म (m)	pletaform
track (~ 1, 2, etc.)	प्लेटफॉर्म (m)	pletaform
semaphore	सिग्नल (m)	signal
station	स्टेशन (m)	steshan

engineer (train driver)	इंजन ड्राइवर (m)	injan draivar
porter (of luggage)	कुली (m)	kulī
car attendant	कोच एटेंडेंट (m)	koch etendent
passenger	मुसाफ़िर (m)	musāfir
conductor (ticket inspector)	टीटी (m)	tītī

| corridor (in train) | गलियारा (m) | galiyāra |
| emergency brake | आपात ब्रेक (m) | āpāt brek |

compartment	डिब्बा (m)	dibba
berth	बर्थ (f)	barth
upper berth	ऊपरी बर्थ (f)	ūparī barth
lower berth	नीचली बर्थ (f)	nīchalī barth
bed linen, bedding	बिस्तर (m)	bistar

ticket	टिकट (m)	tikat
schedule	टाइम टैबुल (m)	taim taibul
information display	सूचना बोर्ड (m)	sūchana bord

to leave, to depart	चले जाना	chale jāna
departure (of train)	रवानगी (f)	ravānagī
to arrive (ab. train)	पहुंचना	pahunchana
arrival	आगमन (m)	āgaman
to arrive by train	गाड़ी से पहुंचना	gārī se pahunchana
to get on the train	गाड़ी पकड़ना	gādī pakarana

to get off the train	गाड़ी से उतरना	gārī se utarana
train wreck	दुर्घटनाग्रस्त (f)	durghatanāgrast
steam locomotive	स्टीम इंजन (m)	stīm injan
stoker, fireman	अग्निशामक (m)	agnishāmak
firebox	भट्ठी (f)	bhatthī
coal	कोयला (m)	koyala

171. Ship

ship	जहाज़ (m)	jahāz
vessel	जहाज़ (m)	jahāz
steamship	जहाज़ (m)	jahāz
riverboat	मोटर बोट (m)	motar bot
cruise ship	लाइनर (m)	lainar
cruiser	क्रूज़र (m)	krūzar
yacht	याख्ट (m)	yākht
tugboat	कर्षक पोत (m)	karshak pot
barge	बार्ज (f)	bārj
ferry	फेरी बोट (f)	ferī bot
sailing ship	पाल नाव (f)	pāl nāv
brigantine	बादबानी (f)	bādabānī
ice breaker	हिमभंजक पोत (m)	himabhanjak pot
submarine	पनडुब्बी (f)	panadubbī
boat (flat-bottomed ~)	नाव (m)	nāv
dinghy	किश्ती (f)	kishtī
lifeboat	जीवन रक्षा किश्ती (f)	jīvan raksha kishtī
motorboat	मोटर बोट (m)	motar bot
captain	कप्तान (m)	kaptān
seaman	मल्लाह (m)	mallāh
sailor	मल्लाह (m)	mallāh
crew	वैमानिक दल (m)	vaimānik dal
boatswain	बोसुन (m)	bosun
ship's boy	बोसुन (m)	bosun
cook	रसोइया (m)	rasoiya
ship's doctor	पोत डाक्टर (m)	pot dāktar
deck	डेक (m)	dek
mast	मस्तूल (m)	mastūl
sail	पाल (m)	pāl
hold	कार्गी (m)	kārgo
bow (prow)	जहाज़ का अगड़ा हिस्सा (m)	jahāz ka agara hissa

stern	ज़हाज़ का पिछला हिस्सा (m)	jahāz ka pichhala hissa
oar	चप्पू (m)	chappū
screw propeller	जहाज़ की पंखी चलाने का पेंच (m)	jahāz kī pankhī chalāne ka pench
cabin	कैबिन (m)	kaibin
wardroom	मेस (f)	mes
engine room	मशीन-कमरा (m)	mashīn-kamara
bridge	ब्रिज (m)	brij
radio room	रेडियो केबिन (m)	rediyo kebin
wave (radio)	रेडियो तरंग (f)	rediyo tarang
logbook	जहाज़ी रजिस्टर (m)	jahāzī rajistar
spyglass	टेलिस्कोप (m)	teliskop
bell	घंटा (m)	ghanta
flag	झंडा (m)	jhanda
hawser (mooring ~)	रस्सा (m)	rassa
knot (bowline, etc.)	जहाज़ी गांठ (f)	jahāzī gānth
deckrails	रेलिंग (f)	reling
gangway	सीढ़ी (f)	sīrhī
anchor	लंगर (m)	langar
to weigh anchor	लंगर उठाना	langar uthāna
to drop anchor	लंगर डालना	langar dālana
anchor chain	लंगर की ज़ंजीर (f)	langar kī zajīr
port (harbor)	बंदरगाह (m)	bandaragāh
quay, wharf	घाट (m)	ghāt
to berth (moor)	किनारे लगना	kināre lagana
to cast off	रवाना होना	ravāna hona
trip, voyage	यात्रा (f)	yātra
cruise (sea trip)	जलयात्रा (f)	jalayātra
course (route)	दिशा (f)	disha
route (itinerary)	मार्ग (m)	mārg
fairway (safe water channel)	नाव्य जलपथ (m)	nāvy jalapath
shallows	छिछला पानी (m)	chhichhala pānī
to run aground	छिछले पानी में धसना	chhichhale pānī men dhansana
storm	तूफ़ान (m)	tufān
signal	सिग्नल (m)	signal
to sink (vi)	डूबना	dūbana
SOS (distress signal)	एसओएस	esoes
ring buoy	लाइफ़ ब्वाय (m)	laif bvāy

172. Airport

airport	हवाई अड्डा (m)	havaī adda
airplane	विमान (m)	vimān
airline	हवाई कम्पनी (f)	havaī kampanī
air traffic controller	हवाई यातायात नियंत्रक (m)	havaī yātāyāt niyantrak
departure	प्रस्थान (m)	prasthān
arrival	आगमन (m)	āgaman
to arrive (by plane)	पहुंचना	pahunchana
departure time	उड़ान का समय (m)	urān ka samay
arrival time	आगमन का समय (m)	āgaman ka samay
to be delayed	देर से आना	der se āna
flight delay	उड़ान देरी (f)	urān derī
information board	सूचना बोर्ड (m)	sūchana bord
information	सूचना (f)	sūchana
to announce (vt)	घोषणा करना	ghoshana karana
flight (e.g., next ~)	फ्लाइट (f)	flait
customs	सीमाशुल्क कार्यालय (m)	sīmāshulk kāryālay
customs officer	सीमाशुल्क अधिकारी (m)	sīmāshulk adhikārī
customs declaration	सीमाशुल्क घोषणा (f)	sīmāshulk ghoshana
to fill out the declaration	सीमाशुल्क घोषणा भरना	sīmāshulk ghoshana bharana
passport control	पासपोर्ट जांच (f)	pāsport jānch
luggage	सामान (m)	sāmān
hand luggage	दस्ती सामान (m)	dastī sāmān
luggage cart	सामान के लिये गाड़ी (f)	sāmān ke liye gārī
landing	विमानारोहण (m)	vimānārohan
landing strip	विमानारोहण मार्ग (m)	vimānārohan mārg
to land (vi)	उतरना	utarana
airstairs	सीढ़ी (f)	sīrhī
check-in	चेक-इन (m)	chek-in
check-in counter	चेक-इन डेस्क (m)	chek-in desk
to check-in (vi)	चेक-इन करना	chek-in karana
boarding pass	बोर्डिंग पास (m)	bording pās
departure gate	प्रस्थान गेट (m)	prasthān get
transit	पारवहन (m)	pāravahan
to wait (vt)	इंतज़ार करना	intazār karana
departure lounge	प्रतीक्षालय (m)	pratīkshālay
to see off	विदा करना	vida karana
to say goodbye	विदा कहना	vida kahana

173. Bicycle. Motorcycle

bicycle	साइकिल (f)	saikil
scooter	स्कूटर (m)	skūtar
motorcycle, bike	मोटरसाइकिल (f)	motarasaikil
to go by bicycle	साइकिल से जाना	saikil se jāna
handlebars	हैंडल बार (m)	haindal bār
pedal	पेडल (m)	pedal
brakes	ब्रेक (m pl)	brek
bicycle seat (saddle)	सीट (f)	sīt
pump	पंप (m)	pamp
luggage rack	साइकिल का रैक (m)	sāiikal ka raik
front lamp	बत्ती (f)	battī
helmet	हेलमेट (f)	helamet
wheel	पहिया (m)	pahiya
fender	कीचड़ रोकने की पंखी (f)	kīchar rokane kī pankhī
rim	साइकिल रिम (f)	saikil rim
spoke	पहिये का आरा (m)	pahiye ka āra

Cars

174. Types of cars

automobile, car	कार (f)	kār
sports car	स्पोर्ट्स कार (f)	sports kār
limousine	लीमोज़ीन (m)	līmozīn
off-road vehicle	जीप (m)	jīp
convertible (n)	कन्वर्टिबल (m)	kanvartibal
minibus	मिनिबस (f)	minibas
ambulance	एम्बुलेंस (f)	embulens
snowplow	बर्फ़ हटाने की कार (f)	barf hatāne kī kār
truck	ट्रक (m)	trak
tanker truck	टैंकर-लॉरी (f)	tainkar-lorī
van (small truck)	वैन (m)	vain
road tractor (trailer truck)	ट्रक-ट्रेक्टर (m)	trak-trektar
trailer	ट्रेलर (m)	trelar
comfortable (adj)	सुविधाजनक	suvidhājanak
used (adj)	पुरानी	purānī

175. Cars. Bodywork

hood	बोनेट (f)	bonet
fender	कीचड़ रोकने की पंखी (f)	kīchar rokane kī pankhī
roof	छत (f)	chhat
windshield	विंडस्क्रीन (m)	vindaskrīn
rear-view mirror	रियरव्यू मिरर (m)	riyaravyū mirar
windshield washer	विंडशील्ड वॉशर (m)	vindashīld voshar
windshield wipers	वाइपर (m)	vaipar
side window	साइड की खिड़की (f)	said kī khirakī
window lift (power window)	विंडो-लिफ़्ट (f)	vindo-lift
antenna	एरियल (m)	eriyal
sunroof	सनरूफ़ (m)	sanarūf
bumper	बम्पर (m)	bampar
trunk	ट्रंक (m)	trank
door	दरवाज़ा (m)	daravāza
door handle	दरवाज़े का हैंडल (m)	daravāze ka haindal

door lock	ताला (m)	tāla
license plate	कार का नम्बर (m)	kār ka nambar
muffler	साइलेंसर (m)	sailensar
gas tank	पेट्रोल टैंक (m)	petrol taink
tailpipe	रेचक नलिका (f)	rechak nalika
gas, accelerator	गैस (m)	gais
pedal	पेडल (m)	pedal
gas pedal	गैस पेडल (m)	gais pedal
brake	ब्रैक (m)	braik
brake pedal	ब्रेक पेडल (m)	brek pedal
to brake (use the brake)	ब्रेक लगाना	brek lagāna
parking brake	पार्किंग पेडल (m)	pārking pedal
clutch	क्लच (m)	klach
clutch pedal	क्लच पेडल (m)	klach pedal
clutch disc	क्लच प्लेट (m)	klach plet
shock absorber	धक्का सह (m)	dhakka sah
wheel	पहिया (m)	pahiya
spare tire	स्पेयर टायर (m)	speyar tāyar
tire	टायर (m)	tāyar
hubcap	हबकैप (m)	habakaip
driving wheels	प्रधान पहिया (m)	pradhān pahiya
front-wheel drive (as adj)	आगे के पहियों से चलने वाली	āge ke pahiyon se chalane vālī
rear-wheel drive (as adj)	पीछे के पहियों से चलने वाली	pīchhe ke pahiyon se chalane vālī
all-wheel drive (as adj)	चार पहियों की कार	chār pahiyon kī kār
gearbox	गीयर बॉक्स (m)	gīyar boks
automatic (adj)	स्वचालित	svachālit
mechanical (adj)	मशीनी	mashīnī
gear shift	गीयर बॉक्स का साधन (m)	gīyar boks ka sādhan
headlight	हेडलाइट (f)	hedalait
headlights	हेडलाइटें (f pl)	hedalaiten
low beam	लो बीम (m)	lo bīm
high beam	हाई बीम (m)	haī bīm
brake light	ब्रेक लाइट (m)	brek lait
parking lights	पार्किंग लाइटें (f pl)	pārking laiten
hazard lights	खतरे की बत्तियां (f pl)	khatare kī battiyān
fog lights	कोहरे की बत्तियाँ (f pl)	kohare kī battiyān
turn signal	मुड़ने का सिग्नल (m)	murane ka signal
back-up light	पीछे जाने की लाइट (m)	pīchhe jāne kī lait

176. Cars. Passenger compartment

car inside (interior)	गाड़ी का भीतरी हिस्सा (m)	gārī ka bhītarī hissa
leather (as adj)	चमड़े का बना	chamare ka bana
velour (as adj)	मखमल का बना	makhamal ka bana
upholstery	अपहोल्स्टरी (f)	apaholstarī
instrument (gage)	यंत्र (m)	yantr
dashboard	यंत्र का पैनल (m)	yantr ka painal
speedometer	चालमापी (m)	chālamāpī
needle (pointer)	सूई (f)	sūī
odometer	ओडोमीटर (m)	odomītar
indicator (sensor)	इंडिकेटर (m)	indiketar
level	स्तर (m)	star
warning light	चेतावनी लाइट (m)	chetāvanī lait
steering wheel	स्टीयरिंग व्हील (m)	stīyaring vhīl
horn	हॉर्न (m)	horn
button	बटन (m)	batan
switch	स्विच (m)	svich
seat	सीट (m)	sīt
backrest	पीठ (f)	pīth
headrest	हेडरेस्ट (m)	hedarest
seat belt	सीट बेल्ट (m)	sīt belt
to fasten the belt	बेल्ट लगाना	belt lagāna
adjustment (of seats)	समायोजन (m)	samāyojan
airbag	एयरबैग (m)	eyarabaig
air-conditioner	एयर कंडीशनर (m)	eyar kandīshanar
radio	रेडियो (m)	rediyo
CD player	सीडी प्लेयर (m)	sīdī pleyar
to turn on	चलाना	chalāna
antenna	एरियल (m)	eriyal
glove box	दराज़ (m)	darāz
ashtray	राखदानी (f)	rākhadānī

177. Cars. Engine

engine	इंजन (m)	injan
motor	मोटर (m)	motar
diesel (as adj)	डीज़ल का	dīzal ka
gasoline (as adj)	तेल का	tel ka
engine volume	इंजन का परिमाण (m)	injan ka parimān
power	शक्ति (f)	shakti
horsepower	अश्व शक्ति (f)	ashv shakti

piston	पिस्टन (m)	pistan
cylinder	सिलिंडर (m)	silindar
valve	वाल्व (m)	vālv
injector	इंजेक्टर (m)	injektar
generator (alternator)	जनरेटर (m)	janaretar
carburetor	कार्बरेटर (m)	kārbaretar
motor oil	मोटर तेल (m)	motar tel
radiator	रेडिएटर (m)	redietar
coolant	शीतलक (m)	shītalak
cooling fan	पंखा (m)	pankha
battery (accumulator)	बैटरी (f)	baitarī
starter	स्टार्टर (m)	stārtar
ignition	इग्निशन (m)	ignishan
spark plug	स्पार्क प्लग (m)	spārk plag
terminal (of battery)	बैटरी टर्मिनल (m)	baitarī tarminal
positive terminal	प्लस टर्मिनल (m)	plas tarminal
negative terminal	माइनस टर्मिनल (m)	mainas tarminal
fuse	सेफ्टी फ्यूज़ (m)	seftī fyūz
air filter	वायु फ़िल्टर (m)	vāyu filtar
oil filter	तेल फ़िल्टर (m)	tel filtar
fuel filter	ईंधन फ़िल्टर (m)	īndhan filtar

178. Cars. Crash. Repair

car crash	दुर्घटना (f)	durghatana
traffic accident	दुर्घटना (f)	durghatana
to crash (into the wall, etc.)	टकराना	takarāna
to get smashed up	नष्ट हो जाना	nashth ho jāna
damage	नुकसान (m)	nukasān
intact (unscathed)	सुरक्षित	surakshit
to break down (vi)	ख़राब हो जाना	kharāb ho jāna
towrope	रस्सा (m)	rassa
puncture	पंक्चर (m)	pankchar
to be flat	पंक्चर होना	pankchar hona
to pump up	हवा भरना	hava bharana
pressure	दबाव (m)	dabāv
to check (to examine)	जांचना	jānchana
repair	मरम्मत (f)	marammat
auto repair shop	वाहन मरम्मत की दुकान (f)	vāhan marammat kī dukān
spare part	स्पेयर पार्ट (m)	speyar pārt

part	पुरज़ा (m)	puraza
bolt (with nut)	बोल्ट (m)	bolt
screw (fastener)	पेंच (m)	pench
nut	नट (m)	nat
washer	वॉशर (m)	voshar
bearing	बियरिंग (m)	biyaring

tube	ट्यूब (f)	tyūb
gasket (head ~)	गास्केट (m)	gāsket
cable, wire	तार (m)	tār

jack	जैक (m)	jaik
wrench	स्पैनर (m)	spainar
hammer	हथौड़ी (f)	hathaurī
pump	पंप (m)	pamp
screwdriver	पेंचकस (m)	penchakas

| fire extinguisher | अग्निशामक (m) | agnishāmak |
| warning triangle | चेतावनी त्रिकोण (m) | chetāvanī trikon |

to stall (vi)	बंद होना	band hona
stall (n)	बंद (m)	band
to be broken	टूटना	tūtana

to overheat (vi)	गरम होना	garam hona
to be clogged up	मैल जमना	mail jamana
to freeze up (pipes, etc.)	ठंडा हो जाना	thanda ho jāna
to burst (vi, ab. tube)	फटना	fatana

pressure	दबाव (m)	dabāv
level	स्तर (m)	star
slack (~ belt)	कमज़ोर	kamazor

dent	गड्ढा (m)	gadrha
knocking noise (engine)	खटखट की आवाज़ (f)	khatakhat kī āvāz
crack	दरार (f)	darār
scratch	खरोंच (f)	kharonch

179. Cars. Road

road	रास्ता (m)	rāsta
highway	राजमार्ग (m)	rājamārg
freeway	राजमार्ग (m)	rājamārg
direction (way)	दिशा (f)	disha
distance	दूरी (f)	dūrī

bridge	पुल (m)	pul
parking lot	पार्किन्ग (m)	pārking
square	मैदान (m)	maidān
interchange	फ्लाई ओवर (m)	flaī ovar

tunnel	सुरंग (m)	surang
gas station	पेट्रोल पम्प (f)	petrol pamp
parking lot	पार्किंग (m)	pārking
gas pump (fuel dispenser)	गैस पम्प (f)	gais pamp
auto repair shop	गराज (m)	garāj
to get gas (to fill up)	पेट्रोल भरवाना	petrol bharavāna
fuel	ईंधन (m)	īndhan
jerrycan	जेरिकेन (m)	jeriken
asphalt	तारकोल (m)	tārakol
road markings	मार्ग चिह्न (m)	mārg chihn
curb	फुटपाथ (m)	futapāth
guardrail	रेलिंग (f)	reling
ditch	नाली (f)	nālī
roadside (shoulder)	छोर (m)	chhor
lamppost	बिजली का खम्भा (m)	bijalī ka khambha
to drive (a car)	चलाना	chalāna
to turn (e.g., ~ left)	मोड़ना	morana
to make a U-turn	मुड़ना	murana
reverse (~ gear)	रिवर्स (m)	rivars
to honk (vi)	हॉर्न बजाना	horn bajāna
honk (sound)	हॉर्न (m)	horn
to get stuck (in the mud, etc.)	फंसना	fansana
to spin the wheels	पहिये को घुमाना	pahiye ko ghumāna
to cut, to turn off (vt)	इंजन बंद करना	injan band karana
speed	रफ़्तार (f)	rafatār
to exceed the speed limit	गति सीमा पार करना	gati sīma pār karana
to give a ticket	जुर्माना लगाना	jurmāna lagāna
traffic lights	ट्रैफ़िक-लाइट (m)	traifik-lait
driver's license	ड्राइवर-लाइसेंस (m)	draivar-laisens
grade crossing	रेल क्रॉसिंग (m)	rel krosing
intersection	चौराहा (m)	chaurāha
crosswalk	पार-पथ (m)	pār-path
bend, curve	मोड़ (m)	mor
pedestrian zone	पैदल सड़क (f)	paidal sarak

180. Traffic signs

rules of the road	यातायात के नियम (m pl)	yātāyāt ke niyam
road sign (traffic sign)	ट्रैफ़िक साइन (m)	traifik sain
passing (overtaking)	ओवरटेकिंग (f)	ovarateking
curve	मोड़ (m)	mor
U-turn	यू-टर्न (m)	yū-tarn
traffic circle	गोलचक्कर (m)	golachakkar
No entry	अंदर जाना मना है	andar jāna mana hai

No vehicles allowed	वाहन जाना मना है	vāhan jāna mana hai
No passing	ओवरटैकिंग मना है	ovarataiking mana hai
No parking	पार्किंग मना है	pārking mana hai
No stopping	रुकना मना है	rukana mana hai

dangerous bend	खतरनाक मोड़ (m)	khataranāk mor
steep descent	ढलवां उतार (m)	dhalavān utār
one-way traffic	इकतरफ़ा यातायात (f)	ikatarafa yātāyāt
crosswalk	पार-पथ (m)	pār-path
slippery road	फिसलाऊ रास्ता (m)	fisalaū rāsta
YIELD	निकलने देना	nikalane dena

PEOPLE. LIFE EVENTS

Life events

181. Holidays. Event

celebration, holiday	त्योहार (m)	tyohār
national day	राष्ट्रीय त्योहार (m)	rāshtrīy tyohār
public holiday	त्योहार का दिन (m)	tyohār ka din
to commemorate (vt)	पुण्यस्मरण करना	punyasmaran karana
event (happening)	घटना (f)	ghatana
event (organized activity)	आयोजन (m)	āyojan
banquet (party)	राजभोज (m)	rājabhoj
reception (formal party)	दावत (f)	dāvat
feast	दावत (f)	dāvat
anniversary	वर्षगांठ (m)	varshagānth
jubilee	वर्षगांठ (m)	varshagānth
to celebrate (vt)	मनाना	manāna
New Year	नव वर्ष (m)	nav varsh
Happy New Year!	नव वर्ष की शुभकामना!	nav varsh kī shubhakāmana!
Santa Claus	सांता क्लॉज़ (m)	sānta kloz
Christmas	बड़ा दिन (m)	bara din
Merry Christmas!	क्रिसमस की शुभकामनाएं!	krisamas kī shubhakāmanaen!
Christmas tree	क्रिस्मस ट्री (m)	krismas trī
fireworks (fireworks show)	अग्नि क्रीड़ा (f)	agni krīra
wedding	शादी (f)	shādī
groom	दूल्हा (m)	dulha
bride	दुल्हन (f)	dulhan
to invite (vt)	आमंत्रित करना	āmantrit karana
invitation card	निमंत्रण पत्र (m)	nimantran patr
guest	मेहमान (m)	mehamān
to visit (~ your parents, etc.)	मिलने जाना	milane jāna
to meet the guests	मेहमानों से मिलना	mehamānon se milana
gift, present	उपहार (m)	upahār
to give (sth as present)	उपहार देना	upahār dena

to receive gifts	उपहार मिलना	upahār milana
bouquet (of flowers)	गुलदस्ता (m)	guladasta
congratulations	बधाई (f)	badhaī
to congratulate (vt)	बधाई देना	badhaī dena
greeting card	बधाई पोस्टकार्ड (m)	badhaī postakārd
to send a postcard	पोस्टकार्ड भेजना	postakārd bhejana
to get a postcard	पोस्टकार्ड पाना	postakārd pāna
toast	टोस्ट (m)	tost
to offer (a drink, etc.)	ऑफ़र करना	ofar karana
champagne	शैम्पेन (f)	shaimpen
to enjoy oneself	मज़े करना	maze karana
merriment (gaiety)	आमोद (m)	āmod
joy (emotion)	खुशी (f)	khushī
dance	नाच (m)	nāch
to dance (vi, vt)	नाचना	nāchana
waltz	वॉल्ट्ज़ (m)	voltz
tango	टैंगो (m)	taingo

182. Funerals. Burial

cemetery	कब्रिस्तान (m)	kabristān
grave, tomb	कब्र (m)	kabr
cross	क्रॉस (m)	kros
gravestone	सामाधि शिला (f)	sāmādhi shila
fence	बाड़ (f)	bār
chapel	चैपल (m)	chaipal
death	मृत्यु (f)	mrtyu
to die (vi)	मरना	marana
the deceased	मृतक (m)	mrtak
mourning	शोक (m)	shok
to bury (vt)	दफनाना	dafanāna
funeral home	दफ़नालय (m)	dafanālay
funeral	अंतिम संस्कार (m)	antim sanskār
wreath	फूलमाला (f)	fūlamāla
casket, coffin	ताबूत (m)	tābūt
hearse	शव मंच (m)	shav manch
shroud	कफन (m)	kafan
funerary urn	भस्मी कलश (m)	bhasmī kalash
crematory	दाहगृह (m)	dāhagrh
obituary	निधन सूचना (f)	nidhan sūchana

| to cry (weep) | रोना | rona |
| to sob (vi) | रोना | rona |

183. War. Soldiers

platoon	दस्ता (m)	dasta
company	कंपनी (f)	kampanī
regiment	रेजीमेंट (f)	rejīment
army	सेना (f)	sena
division	डिवीज़न (m)	divīzan

| section, squad | दल (m) | dal |
| host (army) | फौज (m) | fauj |

| soldier | सिपाही (m) | sipāhī |
| officer | अफ़्सर (m) | afsar |

private	सैनिक (m)	sainik
sergeant	सार्जेंट (m)	sārjent
lieutenant	लेफ्टिनेंट (m)	leftinent
captain	कप्तान (m)	kaptān
major	मेज़र (m)	mejar
colonel	कर्नेल (m)	karnal
general	जनरल (m)	janaral

sailor	मल्लाह (m)	mallāh
captain	कप्तान (m)	kaptān
boatswain	बोसुन (m)	bosun

artilleryman	तोपची (m)	topachī
paratrooper	पैराट्रूपर (m)	pairātrūpar
pilot	पाइलट (m)	pailat
navigator	नैवीगेटर (m)	naivīgetar
mechanic	मैकेनिक (m)	maikenik

pioneer (sapper)	सैपर (m)	saipar
parachutist	छतरीबाज़ (m)	chhatarībāz
reconnaissance scout	जासूस (m)	jāsūs
sniper	निशानची (m)	nishānachī

patrol (group)	गश्त (m)	gasht
to patrol (vt)	गश्त लगाना	gasht lagāna
sentry, guard	प्रहरी (m)	praharī

warrior	सैनिक (m)	sainik
hero	हिरो (m)	hiro
heroine	हिरोइन (f)	hiroin
patriot	देशभक्त (m)	deshabhakt
traitor	गद्दार (m)	gaddār
deserter	भगोड़ा (m)	bhagora

to desert (vi)	भाग जाना	bhāg jāna
mercenary	भाड़े का सैनिक (m)	bhāre ka sainik
recruit	रंगरूट (m)	rangarūt
volunteer	स्वयंसेवी (m)	svayansevī

dead (n)	मृतक (m)	mrtak
wounded (n)	घायल (m)	ghāyal
prisoner of war	युद्ध क़ैदी (m)	yuddh qaidī

184. War. Military actions. Part 1

war	युद्ध (m)	yuddh
to be at war	युद्ध करना	yuddh karana
civil war	गृहयुद्ध (m)	grhayuddh

treacherously (adv)	विश्वासघाती ढंग से	vishvāsaghātī dhang se
declaration of war	युद्ध का एलान (m)	yuddh ka elān
to declare (~ war)	एलान करना	elān karana
aggression	हमला (m)	hamala
to attack (invade)	हमला करना	hamala karana

to invade (vt)	हमला करना	hamala karana
invader	आक्रमणकारी (m)	ākramanakārī
conqueror	विजेता (m)	vijeta

defense	हिफ़ाज़त (f)	hifāzat
to defend (a country, etc.)	हिफ़ाज़त करना	hifāzat karana
to defend (against …)	के विरुद्ध हिफ़ाज़त करना	ke viruddh hifāzat karana

enemy	दुश्मन (m)	dushman
foe, adversary	विपक्ष (m)	vipaksh
enemy (as adj)	दुश्मनों का	dushmanon ka

| strategy | रणनीति (f) | rananīti |
| tactics | युक्ति (f) | yukti |

order	हुक्म (m)	hukm
command (order)	आज्ञा (f)	āgya
to order (vt)	हुक्म देना	hukm dena
mission	मिशन (m)	mishan
secret (adj)	गुप्त	gupt

| battle | लड़ाई (f) | laraī |
| combat | युद्ध (m) | yuddh |

attack	आक्रमण (m)	ākraman
charge (assault)	धावा (m)	dhāva
to storm (vt)	धावा करना	dhāva karana
siege (to be under ~)	घेरा (m)	ghera
offensive (n)	आक्रमण (m)	ākraman

to go on the offensive	आक्रमण करना	ākraman karana
retreat	अपयान (m)	apayān
to retreat (vi)	अपयान करना	apayān karana
encirclement	घेराई (f)	gheraī
to encircle (vt)	घेरना	gherana
bombing (by aircraft)	बमबारी (f)	bamabārī
to drop a bomb	बम गिराना	bam girāna
to bomb (vt)	बमबारी करना	bamabārī karana
explosion	विस्फोट (m)	visfot
shot	गोली (m)	golī
to fire (~ a shot)	गोली चलाना	golī chalāna
firing (burst of ~)	गोलीबारी (f)	golībārī
to aim (to point a weapon)	निशाना लगाना	nishāna lagāna
to point (a gun)	निशाना बांधना	nishāna bāndhana
to hit (the target)	गोली मारना	golī mārana
to sink (~ a ship)	डुबाना	dubāna
hole (in a ship)	छेद (m)	chhed
to founder, to sink (vi)	डूबना	dūbana
front (war ~)	मोरचा (m)	moracha
evacuation	निकास (m)	nikās
to evacuate (vt)	निकास करना	nikās karana
barbwire	कांटेदार तार (m)	kāntedār tār
barrier (anti tank ~)	बाड़ (m)	bār
watchtower	बुर्ज (m)	burj
military hospital	सैनिक अस्पताल (m)	sainik aspatāl
to wound (vt)	घायल करना	ghāyal karana
wound	घाव (m)	ghāv
wounded (n)	घायल (m)	ghāyal
to be wounded	घायल होना	ghāyal hona
serious (wound)	गम्भीर	gambhīr

185. War. Military actions. Part 2

captivity	क़ैद (f)	qaid
to take captive	क़ैद करना	qaid karana
to be held captive	क़ैद में रखना	qaid men rakhana
to be taken captive	क़ैद में लेना	qaid men lena
concentration camp	कन्सेंट्रेशन कैंप (m)	kansentreshan kaimp
prisoner of war	युद्ध-क़ैदी (m)	yuddh-qaidī
to escape (vi)	क़ैद से भाग जाना	qaid se bhāg jāna
to betray (vt)	गद्दारी करना	gaddārī karana

| betrayer | गद्दार (m) | gaddār |
| betrayal | गद्दारी (f) | gaddārī |

| to execute (by firing squad) | फाँसी देना | fānsī dena |
| execution (by firing squad) | प्राणदण्ड (f) | prānadand |

equipment (military gear)	फौजी पोशक (m)	faujī poshak
shoulder board	कंधे का फीता (m)	kandhe ka fīta
gas mask	गैस मास्क (m)	gais māsk

field radio	ट्रांस-रिसिवर (m)	trāns-risivar
cipher, code	गुप्तलेख (m)	guptalekh
secrecy	गुप्तता (f)	guptata
password	पासवर्ड (m)	pāsavard

land mine	बारूदी सुरंग (f)	bārūdī surang
to mine (road, etc.)	सुरंग खोदना	surang khodana
minefield	सुरंग-क्षेत्र (m)	surang-kshetr

air-raid warning	हवाई हमले की चेतावनी (f)	havaī hamale kī chetāvanī
alarm (alert signal)	चेतावनी (f)	chetāvanī
signal	सिग्नल (m)	signal
signal flare	सिग्नल रॉकेट (m)	signal roket

headquarters	सैनिक मुख्यालय (m)	sainik mukhyālay
reconnaissance	जासूसी देख-भाल (m)	jāsūsī dekh-bhāl
situation	हालत (f)	hālat
report	रिपोर्ट (m)	riport
ambush	घात (f)	ghāt
reinforcement (of army)	बलवृद्धि (m)	balavrddhi

target	निशाना (m)	nishāna
proving ground	प्रशिक्षण क्षेत्र (m)	prashikshan kshetr
military exercise	युद्धाभ्यास (m pl)	yuddhābhyās

panic	भगदड़ (f)	bhagadar
devastation	तबाही (f)	tabāhī
destruction, ruins	विनाश (m pl)	vināsh
to destroy (vt)	नष्ट करना	nasht karana

to survive (vi, vt)	जीवित रहना	jīvit rahana
to disarm (vt)	निरस्त्र करना	nirastr karana
to handle (~ a gun)	हथियार चलाना	hathiyār chalāna

| Attention! | सावधान! | sāvadhān! |
| At ease! | आराम! | ārām! |

act of courage	साहस का कार्य (m)	sāhas ka kāry
oath (vow)	शपथ (f)	shapath
to swear (an oath)	शपथ लेना	shapath lena
decoration (medal, etc.)	पदक (m)	padak

to award (give medal to)	इनाम देना	inām dena
medal	मेडल (m)	medal
order (e.g., ~ of Merit)	आर्डर (m)	ārdar
victory	विजय (m)	vijay
defeat	हार (f)	hār
armistice	युद्धविराम (m)	yuddhavirām
standard (battle flag)	झंडा (m)	jhanda
glory (honor, fame)	प्रताप (m)	pratāp
parade	परेड (m)	pared
to march (on parade)	मार्च करना	mārch karana

186. Weapons

weapons	हथियार (m)	hathiyār
firearms	हथियार (m)	hathiyār
cold weapons (knives, etc.)	पैने हथियार (m)	paine hathiyār
chemical weapons	रसायनिक शस्त्र (m)	rasāyanik shastr
nuclear (adj)	आण्विक	ānvik
nuclear weapons	आण्विक-शस्त्र (m)	ānvik-shastr
bomb	बम (m)	bam
atomic bomb	परमाणु बम (m)	paramānu bam
pistol (gun)	पिस्तौल (m)	pistaul
rifle	बंदूक (m)	bandūk
submachine gun	टामी गन (f)	tāmī gan
machine gun	मशीन गन (f)	mashīn gan
muzzle	नालमुख (m)	nālamukh
barrel	नाल (m)	nāl
caliber	नली का व्यास (m)	nalī ka vyās
trigger	घोड़ा (m)	ghora
sight (aiming device)	लक्षक (m)	lakshak
magazine	मैगज़ीन (m)	maigazīn
butt (shoulder stock)	कुंदा (m)	kunda
hand grenade	ग्रेनेड (m)	grened
explosive	विस्फोटक (m)	visfotak
bullet	गोली (f)	golī
cartridge	कारतूस (m)	kāratūs
charge	गति (f)	gati
ammunition	गोला बारूद (m pl)	gola bārūd
bomber (aircraft)	बमबार (m)	bamabār
fighter	लड़ाकू विमान (m)	larākū vimān

helicopter	हेलिकॉप्टर (m)	helikoptar
anti-aircraft gun	विमान-विध्वंस तोप (f)	vimān-vidhvans top
tank	टैंक (m)	taink
tank gun	तोप (m)	top

artillery	तोपें (m)	topen
to lay (a gun)	निशाना बांधना	nishāna bāndhana

shell (projectile)	गोला (m)	gola
mortar bomb	मोटार बम (m)	mortār bam
mortar	मोटार (m)	mortār
splinter (shell fragment)	किरच (m)	kirach

submarine	पनडुब्बी (f)	panadubbī
torpedo	टोरपीडो (m)	torapīdo
missile	रॉकेट (m)	roket

to load (gun)	बंदूक भरना	bandūk bharana
to shoot (vi)	गोली चलाना	golī chalāna
to point at (the cannon)	निशाना लगाना	nishāna lagāna
bayonet	किरिच (m)	kirich

rapier	खंजर (m)	khanjar
saber (e.g., cavalry ~)	कृपाण (m)	krpān
spear (weapon)	भाला (m)	bhāla
bow	धनुष (m)	dhanush
arrow	बाण (m)	bān
musket	मसकट (m)	masakat
crossbow	क्रॉसबो (m)	krosabo

187. Ancient people

primitive (prehistoric)	आदिकालीन	ādikālīn
prehistoric (adj)	प्रागैतिहासिक	prāgaitihāsik
ancient (~ civilization)	प्राचीन	prāchīn

Stone Age	पाषाण युग (m)	pāshān yug
Bronze Age	कांस्य युग (m)	kānsy yug
Ice Age	हिम युग (m)	him yug

tribe	जनजाति (f)	janajāti
cannibal	नरभक्षी (m)	narabhakshī
hunter	शिकारी (m)	shikārī
to hunt (vi, vt)	शिकार करना	shikār karana
mammoth	प्राचीन युग हाथी (m)	prāchīn yug hāthī

cave	गुफ़ा (f)	gufa
fire	अग्नि (m)	agni
campfire	अलाव (m)	alāv
cave painting	शिला चित्र (m)	shila chitr

tool (e.g., stone ax)	औज़ार (m)	auzār
spear	भाला (m)	bhāla
stone ax	पत्थर की कुल्हाड़ी (f)	patthar kī kulhārī
to be at war	युद्ध पर होना	yuddh par hona
to domesticate (vt)	जानवरों को पालतू बनाना	jānavaron ko pālatū banāna
idol	मूर्ति (f)	mūrti
to worship (vt)	पूजना	pūjana
superstition	अंधविश्वास (m)	andhavishvās
rite	अनुष्ठान (m)	anushthān
evolution	उद्भव (m)	udbhav
development	विकास (m)	vikās
disappearance (extinction)	गायब (m)	gāyab
to adapt oneself	अनुकूल बनाना	anukūl banāna
archeology	पुरातत्व (m)	purātatv
archeologist	पुरातत्वविद (m)	purātatvavid
archeological (adj)	पुरातात्विक	purātātvik
excavation site	खुदाई क्षेत्र (m pl)	khudaī kshetr
excavations	उत्खनन (f)	utkhanan
find (object)	खोज (f)	khoj
fragment	टुकड़ा (m)	tukara

188. Middle Ages

people (ethnic group)	लोग (m)	log
peoples	लोग (m pl)	log
tribe	जनजाति (f)	janajāti
tribes	जनजातियाँ (f pl)	janajātiyān
barbarians	बर्बर (m pl)	barbar
Gauls	गॉल्स (m pl)	gols
Goths	गोथ्स (m pl)	goths
Slavs	स्लैव्स (m pl)	slaivs
Vikings	वाइकिंग्स (m pl)	vaikings
Romans	रोमन (m pl)	roman
Roman (adj)	रोमन	roman
Byzantines	बाइज़ेंटीनी (m pl)	baizentīnī
Byzantium	बाइज़ेंटीयम (m)	baizentīyam
Byzantine (adj)	बाइज़ेंटीन	baizentīn
emperor	सम्राट् (m)	samrāt
leader, chief (tribal ~)	सरदार (m)	saradār
powerful (~ king)	प्रबल	prabal
king	बादशाह (m)	bādashāh

ruler (sovereign)	शासक (m)	shāsak
knight	योद्धा (m)	yoddha
feudal lord	सामंत (m)	sāmant
feudal (adj)	सामंतिक	sāmantik
vassal	जागीरदार (m)	jāgīradār
duke	ड्यूक (m)	dyūk
earl	अर्ल (m)	arl
baron	बैरन (m)	bairan
bishop	बिशप (m)	bishap
armor	कवच (m)	kavach
shield	ढाल (m)	dhāl
sword	तलवार (f)	talavār
visor	मुखावरण (m)	mukhāvaran
chainmail	कवच (m)	kavach
Crusade	धर्मयुद्ध (m)	dharmayuddh
crusader	धर्मयोद्धा (m)	dharmayoddha
territory	प्रदेश (m)	pradesh
to attack (invade)	हमला करना	hamala karana
to conquer (vt)	जीतना	jītana
to occupy (invade)	कब्ज़ा करना	kabza karana
siege (to be under ~)	घेरा (m)	ghera
besieged (adj)	घेरा हुआ	ghera hua
to besiege (vt)	घेरना	gherana
inquisition	न्यायिक जांच (m)	nyāyik jānch
inquisitor	न्यायिक जांचकर्ता (m)	nyāyik jānchakarta
torture	घोर शारीरिक यंत्रणा (f)	ghor sharīrik yantrana
cruel (adj)	निर्दयी	nirdayī
heretic	विधर्मी (m)	vidharmī
heresy	विधर्म (m)	vidharm
seafaring	जहाज़रानी (f)	jahāzarānī
pirate	समुद्री लूटेरा (m)	samudrī lūtera
piracy	समुद्री डकैती (f)	samudrī dakaitī
boarding (attack)	बोर्डिंग (m)	bording
loot, booty	लूट का माल (m)	lūt ka māl
treasures	खज़ाना (m)	khazāna
discovery	खोज (f)	khoj
to discover (new land, etc.)	नई ज़मीन खोजना	naī zamīn khojana
expedition	अभियान (m)	abhiyān
musketeer	बंदूक धारी सिपाही (m)	bandūk dhārī sipāhī
cardinal	कार्डिनल (m)	kārdinal
heraldry	शौर्यशास्त्र (f)	shauryashāstr
heraldic (adj)	हेरल्डिक	heraldik

189. Leader. Chief. Authorities

king	बादशाह (m)	bādashāh
queen	महारानी (f)	mahārānī
royal (adj)	राजसी	rājasī
kingdom	राज्य (m)	rājy
prince	राजकुमार (m)	rājakumār
princess	राजकुमारी (f)	rājakumārī
president	राष्ट्रपति (m)	rāshtrapati
vice-president	उपराष्ट्रपति (m)	uparāshtrapati
senator	सांसद (m)	sānsad
monarch	सम्राट (m)	samrāt
ruler (sovereign)	शासक (m)	shāsak
dictator	तानाशाह (m)	tānāshāh
tyrant	तानाशाह (m)	tānāshāh
magnate	रईस (m)	raïs
director	निदेशक (m)	nideshak
chief	मुखिया (m)	mukhiya
manager (director)	मैनेजर (m)	mainejar
boss	साहब (m)	sāhab
owner	मालिक (m)	mālik
head (~ of delegation)	मुखिया (m)	mukhiya
authorities	अधिकारी वर्ग (m pl)	adhikārī varg
superiors	अधिकारी (m)	adhikārī
governor	राज्यपाल (m)	rājyapāl
consul	वाणिज्य-दूत (m)	vānijy-dūt
diplomat	राजनयिक (m)	rājanayik
mayor	महापालिकाध्यक्ष (m)	mahāpālikādhyaksh
sheriff	प्रधान हाकिम (m)	pradhān hākim
emperor	सम्राट (m)	samrāt
tsar, czar	राजा (m)	rāja
pharaoh	फिरौन (m)	firaun
khan	ख़ान (m)	khān

190. Road. Way. Directions

road	रास्ता (m)	rāsta
way (direction)	मार्ग (m)	mārg
freeway	राजमार्ग (m)	rājamārg
highway	राजमार्ग (m)	rājamārg
interstate	अंतरराज्यीय (m)	antararājyīy

| main road | मुख्य मार्ग (m) | mukhy mārg |
| dirt road | कच्ची सड़क (f) | kachchī sarak |

| pathway | पगडंडी (f) | pagadandī |
| footpath (troddenpath) | कच्चा रास्ता (m) | kachcha rāsta |

Where?	कहाँ?	kahān?
Where (to)?	किधर?	kidhar?
From where?	कहाँ से?	kahān se?

| direction (way) | तरफ़ (f) | taraf |
| to point (~ the way) | दिखाना | dikhāna |

to the left	बाईं ओर	baīn or
to the right	दाईं ओर	daīn or
straight ahead (adv)	सीधा	sīdha
back (e.g., to turn ~)	पीछे	pīchhe

bend, curve	मोड़ (m)	mor
to turn (e.g., ~ left)	मोड़ना	morana
to make a U-turn	यू-टर्न लेना	yū-tarn lena
to be visible (mountains, castle, etc.)	दिखाई देना	dikhaī dena
to appear (come into view)	नज़र आना	nazar āna

stop, halt (e.g., during a trip)	ठहराव (m)	thaharāv
to rest, to pause (vi)	आराम करना	ārām karana
rest (pause)	विराम (m)	virām

to lose one's way	रास्ता भूलना	rāsta bhūlana
to lead to … (ab. road)	ले जाना	le jāna
to come out (e.g., on the highway)	निकलना	nikalana
stretch (of road)	रास्ते का हिस्सा (m)	rāste ka hissa

asphalt	तारकोल (m)	tārakol
curb	फुटपाथ (m)	futapāth
ditch	खाई (f)	khaī
manhole	मैनहोल (m)	mainahol
roadside (shoulder)	सड़क का किनारा (m)	sarak ka kināra
pit, pothole	खड्ढा (m)	khaddha

| to go (on foot) | जाना | jāna |
| to pass (overtake) | आगे निकलना | āge nikalana |

| step (footstep) | कदम (m) | kadam |
| on foot (adv) | पैदल | paidal |

to block (road)	रास्ता रोक देना	rāsta rok dena
boom gate	बैरियर (m)	bairiyar
dead end	बंद गली (f)	band galī

191. Breaking the law. Criminals. Part 1

bandit	डाकू (m)	dākū
crime	जुर्म (m)	jurm
criminal (person)	अपराधी (m)	aparādhī
thief	चोर (m)	chor
stealing, theft	चोरी (f)	chorī
to kidnap (vt)	अपहरण करना	apaharan karana
kidnapping	अपहरण (m)	apaharan
kidnapper	अपहरणकर्ता (m)	apaharanakartta
ransom	फ़िरौती (f)	firautī
to demand ransom	फ़िरौती मांगना	firautī māngana
to rob (vt)	लूटना	lūtana
robber	लुटेरा (m)	lutera
to extort (vt)	ऐंठना	ainthana
extortionist	वसूलिकर्ता (m)	vasūlikarta
extortion	जबरन वसूली (m)	jabaran vasūlī
to murder, to kill	मारना	mārana
murder	हत्या (f)	hatya
murderer	हत्यारा (m)	hatyāra
gunshot	गोली (m)	golī
to fire (~ a shot)	गोली चलाना	golī chalāna
to shoot to death	गोली मारकर हत्या करना	golī mārakar hatya karana
to shoot (vi)	गोली चलाना	golī chalāna
shooting	गोलीबारी (f)	golībārī
incident (fight, etc.)	घटना (f)	ghatana
fight, brawl	झगड़ा (m)	jhagara
Help!	बचाओ!	bachao!
victim	शिकार (m)	shikār
to damage (vt)	हानि पहुँचाना	hāni pahunchāna
damage	नुक्सान (m)	nuksān
dead body, corpse	शव (m)	shav
grave (~ crime)	गंभीर	gambhīr
to attack (vt)	आक्रमण करना	ākraman karana
to beat (to hit)	पीटना	pītana
to beat up	पीट जाना	pīt jāna
to take (rob of sth)	लूटना	lūtana
to stab to death	चाकू से मार डालना	chākū se mār dālana
to maim (vt)	अपाहिज करना	apāhij karana
to wound (vt)	घाव करना	ghāv karana
blackmail	ब्लैकमेल (m)	blaikamel

| to blackmail (vt) | धमकी से रुपया ऐंठना | dhamakī se rupaya ainthana |
| blackmailer | ब्लैकमेलर (m) | blaikamelar |

protection racket	ठग व्यापार (m)	thag vyāpār
racketeer	ठग व्यापारी (m)	thag vyāpārī
gangster	गैंगस्टर (m)	gaingastar
mafia, Mob	माफ़िया (f)	māfiya

pickpocket	जेबकतरा (m)	jebakatara
burglar	सेंधमार (m)	sendhamār
smuggling	तस्करी (m)	taskarī
smuggler	तस्कर (m)	taskar

forgery	जालसाज़ी (f)	jālasāzī
to forge (counterfeit)	जलसाज़ी करना	jalasāzī karana
fake (forged)	नक़ली	naqalī

192. Breaking the law. Criminals. Part 2

rape	बलात्कार (m)	balātkār
to rape (vt)	बलात्कार करना	balātkār karana
rapist	बलात्कारी (m)	balātkārī
maniac	कामोन्मादी (m)	kāmonmādī

prostitute (fem.)	वैश्या (f)	vaishya
prostitution	वेश्यावृत्ति (m)	veshyāvrtti
pimp	भड़ुआ (m)	bharua

| drug addict | नशेबाज़ (m) | nashebāz |
| drug dealer | नशीली दवा के विक्रेता (m) | nashīlī dava ke vikreta |

to blow up (bomb)	विस्फोट करना	visfot karana
explosion	विस्फोट (m)	visfot
to set fire	आग जलाना	āg jalāna
arsonist	आग जलानेवाला (m)	āg jalānevāla

terrorism	आतंकवाद (m)	ātankavād
terrorist	आतंकवादी (m)	ātankavādī
hostage	बंधक (m)	bandhak

to swindle (deceive)	धोखा देना	dhokha dena
swindle, deception	धोखा (m)	dhokha
swindler	धोखेबाज़ (m)	dhokhebāz

to bribe (vt)	रिश्वत देना	rishvat dena
bribery	रिश्वतखोरी (m)	rishvatakhorī
bribe	रिश्वत (m)	rishvat
poison	ज़हर (m)	zahar
to poison (vt)	ज़हर खिलाना	zahar khilāna

to poison oneself	ज़हर खाना	zahar khāna
suicide (act)	आत्महत्या (f)	ātmahatya
suicide (person)	आत्महत्यारा (m)	ātmahatyāra
to threaten (vt)	धमकाना	dhamakāna
threat	धमकी (f)	dhamakī
to make an attempt	प्रयत्न करना	prayatn karana
attempt (attack)	हत्या का प्रयत्न (m)	hatya ka prayatn
to steal (a car)	चुराना	churāna
to hijack (a plane)	विमान का अपहरण करना	vimān ka apaharan karana
revenge	बदला (m)	badala
to avenge (get revenge)	बदला लेना	badala lena
to torture (vt)	घोर शरीरिक यंत्रणा पहुँचाना	ghor sharīrik yantrana pahunchāna
torture	घोर शरीरिक यंत्रणा (f)	ghor sharīrik yantrana
to torment (vt)	सताना	satāna
pirate	समुद्री लूटेरा (m)	samudrī lūtera
hooligan	बदमाश (m)	badamāsh
armed (adj)	सशस्त्र	sashastr
violence	अत्यचार (m)	atyachār
spying (espionage)	जासूसी (f)	jāsūsī
to spy (vi)	जासूसी करना	jāsūsī karana

193. Police. Law. Part 1

justice	मुक़दमा (m)	muqadama
court (see you in ~)	न्यायालय (m)	nyāyālay
judge	न्यायाधीश (m)	nyāyādhīsh
jurors	जूरी सदस्य (m pl)	jūrī sadasy
jury trial	जूरी (f)	jūrī
to judge (vt)	मुक़दमा सुनना	muqadama sunana
lawyer, attorney	वकील (m)	vakīl
defendant	मुलज़िम (m)	mulazim
dock	अदालत का कठघरा (m)	adālat ka kathaghara
charge	आरोप (m)	ārop
accused	मुलज़िम (m)	mulazim
sentence	निर्णय (m)	nirnay
to sentence (vt)	निर्णय करना	nirnay karana
guilty (culprit)	दोषी (m)	doshī
to punish (vt)	सज़ा देना	saza dena

punishment	सज़ा (f)	saza
fine (penalty)	जुर्माना (m)	jurmāna
life imprisonment	आजीवन करावास (m)	ājīvan karāvās
death penalty	मृत्युदंड (m)	mrtyudand
electric chair	बिजली की कुर्सी (f)	bijalī kī kursī
gallows	फांसी का तख्ता (m)	fānsī ka takhta
to execute (vt)	फांसी देना	fānsī dena
execution	मौत की सज़ा (f)	maut kī saza
prison, jail	जेल (f)	jel
cell	जेल का कमरा (m)	jel ka kamara
escort	अनुरक्षक दल (m)	anurakshak dal
prison guard	जेल का पहरेदार (m)	jel ka paharedār
prisoner	क़ैदी (m)	qaidī
handcuffs	हथकड़ी (f)	hathakarī
to handcuff (vt)	हथकड़ी लगाना	hathakarī lagāna
prison break	काराभंग (m)	kārābhang
to break out (vi)	जेल से फरार हो जाना	jel se farār ho jāna
to disappear (vi)	ग़ायब हो जाना	gāyab ho jāna
to release (from prison)	जेल से आज़ाद होना	jel se āzād hona
amnesty	राजक्षमा (f)	rājakshama
police	पुलिस (m)	pulis
police officer	पुलिसवाला (m)	pulisavāla
police station	थाना (m)	thāna
billy club	रबड़ की लाठी (f)	rabar kī lāthī
bullhorn	मेगाफ़ोन (m)	megāfon
patrol car	गश्त कार (f)	gasht kār
siren	साइरन (f)	sairan
to turn on the siren	साइरन बजाना	sairan bajāna
siren call	साइरन की चिल्लाहट (m)	sairan kī chillāhat
crime scene	घटना स्थल (m)	ghatana sthal
witness	गवाह (m)	gavāh
freedom	आज़ादी (f)	āzādī
accomplice	सह अपराधी (m)	sah aparādhī
to flee (vi)	भाग जाना	bhāg jāna
trace (to leave a ~)	निशान (m)	nishān

194. Police. Law. Part 2

search (investigation)	तफ़्तीश (f)	tafatīsh
to look for ...	तफ़्तीश करना	tafatīsh karana
suspicion	शक (m)	shak
suspicious (e.g., ~ vehicle)	शक करना	shak karana

to stop (cause to halt)	रोकना	rokana
to detain (keep in custody)	रोक के रखना	rok ke rakhana
case (lawsuit)	मुक़दमा (m)	mukadama
investigation	जाँच (f)	jānch
detective	जासूस (m)	jāsūs
investigator	जाँचकर्ता (m)	jānchakartta
hypothesis	अंदाज़ा (m)	andāza
motive	वजह (f)	vajah
interrogation	पूछताछ (f)	pūchhatāchh
to interrogate (vt)	पूछताछ करना	pūchhatāchh karana
to question (~ neighbors, etc.)	पूछताछ करना	puchhatāchh karana
check (identity ~)	जांच (f)	jānch
round-up	घेराव (m)	gherāv
search (~ warrant)	तलाशी (f)	talāshī
chase (pursuit)	पीछा (m)	pīchha
to pursue, to chase	पीछा करना	pīchha karana
to track (a criminal)	खोज निकालना	khoj nikālana
arrest	गिरफ़्तारी (f)	giraftārī
to arrest (sb)	गिरफ़्तार करना	giraftār karana
to catch (thief, etc.)	पकड़ना	pakarana
capture	पकड़ (m)	pakar
document	दस्तावेज़ (m)	dastāvez
proof (evidence)	सबूत (m)	sabūt
to prove (vt)	साबित करना	sābit karana
footprint	पैरों के निशान (m)	pairon ke nishān
fingerprints	उंगलियों के निशान (m)	ungaliyon ke nishān
piece of evidence	सबूत (m)	sabūt
alibi	अन्यत्रता (m)	anyatrata
innocent (not guilty)	बेगुनाह	begunāh
injustice	अन्याय (m)	anyāy
unjust, unfair (adj)	अन्यायपूर्ण	anyāyapūrn
criminal (adj)	आपराधिक	āparādhik
to confiscate (vt)	कुर्क करना	kurk karana
drug (illegal substance)	अवैध पदार्थ (m)	avaidh padārth
weapon, gun	हथियार (m)	hathiyār
to disarm (vt)	निरस्त्र करना	nirastr karana
to order (command)	हुक्म देना	hukm dena
to disappear (vi)	ग़ायब होना	gāyab hona
law	कानून (m)	kānūn
legal, lawful (adj)	कानूनी	kānūnī
illegal, illicit (adj)	अवैध	avaidh
responsibility (blame)	ज़िम्मेदारी (f)	zimmedārī
responsible (adj)	ज़िम्मेदार	zimmedār

NATURE

The Earth. Part 1

195. Outer space

space	अंतरिक्ष (m)	antariksh
space (as adj)	अंतरिक्षीय	antarikshīy
outer space	अंतरिक्ष (m)	antariksh
universe	ब्रह्माण्ड (m)	brahmānd
galaxy	आकाशगंगा (f)	ākāshaganga
star	सितारा (m)	sitāra
constellation	नक्षत्र (m)	nakshatr
planet	ग्रह (m)	grah
satellite	उपग्रह (m)	upagrah
meteorite	उल्का पिंड (m)	ulka pind
comet	पुच्छल तारा (m)	puchchhal tāra
asteroid	ग्रहिका (f)	grahika
orbit	ग्रहपथ (m)	grahapath
to revolve	चक्कर लगना	chakkar lagana
(~ around the Earth)		
atmosphere	वातावरण (m)	vātāvaran
the Sun	सूरज (m)	sūraj
solar system	सौर प्रणाली (f)	saur pranālī
solar eclipse	सूर्य ग्रहण (m)	sūry grahan
the Earth	पृथ्वी (f)	prthvī
the Moon	चांद (m)	chānd
Mars	मंगल (m)	mangal
Venus	शुक्र (m)	shukr
Jupiter	बृहस्पति (m)	brhaspati
Saturn	शनि (m)	shani
Mercury	बुध (m)	budh
Uranus	अरुण (m)	arun
Neptune	वरूण (m)	varūn
Pluto	प्लूटो (m)	plūto
Milky Way	आकाश गंगा (f)	ākāsh ganga
Great Bear (Ursa Major)	सप्तर्षिमंडल (m)	saptarshimandal

North Star	धुव तारा (m)	dhruv tāra
Martian	मंगल ग्रह का निवासी (m)	mangal grah ka nivāsī
extraterrestrial (n)	अन्य नक्षत्र का निवासी (m)	any nakshatr ka nivāsī
alien	अन्य नक्षत्र का निवासी (m)	any nakshatr ka nivāsī
flying saucer	उड़न तश्तरी (f)	uran tashtarī
spaceship	अंतरिक्ष विमान (m)	antariksh vimān
space station	अंतरिक्ष अड्डा (m)	antariksh adda
blast-off	चालू करना (m)	chālū karana
engine	इंजन (m)	injan
nozzle	नोज़ल (m)	nozal
fuel	ईंधन (m)	īndhan
cockpit, flight deck	केबिन (m)	kebin
antenna	एरियल (m)	eriyal
porthole	विमान गवाक्ष (m)	vimān gavāksh
solar panel	सौर पेनल (m)	saur penal
spacesuit	अंतरिक्ष पोशाक (m)	antariksh poshāk
weightlessness	भारहीनता (m)	bhārahīnata
oxygen	आक्सीजन (m)	āksījan
docking (in space)	डॉकिंग (f)	doking
to dock (vi, vt)	डॉकिंग करना	doking karana
observatory	वेधशाला (m)	vedhashāla
telescope	दूरबीन (f)	dūrabīn
to observe (vt)	देखना	dekhana
to explore (vt)	जाँचना	jānchana

196. The Earth

the Earth	पृथ्वी (f)	prthvī
the globe (the Earth)	गोला (m)	gola
planet	ग्रह (m)	grah
atmosphere	वातावरण (m)	vātāvaran
geography	भूगोल (m)	bhūgol
nature	प्रकृति (f)	prakrti
globe (table ~)	गोलक (m)	golak
map	नक्शा (m)	naksha
atlas	मानचित्रावली (f)	mānachitrāvalī
Europe	यूरोप (m)	yūrop
Asia	एशिया (f)	eshiya
Africa	अफ्रीका (m)	afrīka

Australia	ऑस्ट्रेलिया (m)	ostreliya
America	अमेरिका (f)	amerika
North America	उत्तरी अमेरिका (f)	uttarī amerika
South America	दक्षिणी अमेरिका (f)	dakshinī amerika
Antarctica	अंटार्कटिक (m)	antārkatik
the Arctic	आर्कटिक (m)	ārkatik

197. Cardinal directions

north	उत्तर (m)	uttar
to the north	उत्तर की ओर	uttar kī or
in the north	उत्तर में	uttar men
northern (adj)	उत्तरी	uttarī
south	दक्षिण (m)	dakshin
to the south	दक्षिण की ओर	dakshin kī or
in the south	दक्षिण में	dakshin men
southern (adj)	दक्षिणी	dakshinī
west	पश्चिम (m)	pashchim
to the west	पश्चिम की ओर	pashchim kī or
in the west	पश्चिम में	pashchim men
western (adj)	पश्चिमी	pashchimī
east	पूर्व (m)	pūrv
to the east	पूर्व की ओर	pūrv kī or
in the east	पूर्व में	pūrv men
eastern (adj)	पूर्वी	pūrvī

198. Sea. Ocean

sea	सागर (m)	sāgar
ocean	महासागर (m)	mahāsāgar
gulf (bay)	खाड़ी (f)	khārī
straits	जलग्रीवा (m)	jalagrīva
continent (mainland)	महाद्वीप (m)	mahādvīp
island	द्वीप (m)	dvīp
peninsula	प्रायद्वीप (m)	prāyadvīp
archipelago	द्वीप समूह (m)	dvīp samūh
bay, cove	तट-खाड़ी (f)	tat-khārī
harbor	बंदरगाह (m)	bandaragāh
lagoon	लैगून (m)	laigūn
cape	अंतरीप (m)	antarīp
atoll	एटोल (m)	etol
reef	रीफ़ (m)	rīf

| coral | प्रवाल (m) | pravāl |
| coral reef | प्रवाल रीफ़ (m) | pravāl rīf |

deep (adj)	गहरा	gahara
depth (deep water)	गहराई (f)	gaharaī
abyss	रसातल (m)	rasātal
trench (e.g., Mariana ~)	गढ्ढा (m)	garha

| current (Ocean ~) | धारा (f) | dhāra |
| to surround (bathe) | घिरा होना | ghira hona |

| shore | किनारा (m) | kināra |
| coast | तटबंध (m) | tatabandh |

flow (flood tide)	ज्वार (m)	jvār
ebb (ebb tide)	भाटा (m)	bhāta
shoal	रेती (m)	retī
bottom (~ of the sea)	तला (m)	tala

wave	तरंग (f)	tarang
crest (~ of a wave)	तरंग शिखर (f)	tarang shikhar
spume (sea foam)	झाग (m)	jhāg

hurricane	तूफ़ान (m)	tufān
tsunami	सुनामी (f)	sunāmī
calm (dead ~)	शांत (m)	shānt
quiet, calm (adj)	शांत	shānt

| pole | ध्रुव (m) | dhruv |
| polar (adj) | ध्रुवीय | dhruvīy |

latitude	अक्षांश (m)	akshānsh
longitude	देशान्तर (m)	deshāntar
parallel	समांतर-रेखा (f)	samāntar-rekha
equator	भूमध्य रेखा (f)	bhūmadhy rekha

sky	आकाश (f)	ākāsh
horizon	क्षितिज (m)	kshitij
air	हवा (f)	hava

lighthouse	प्रकाशस्तंभ (m)	prakāshastambh
to dive (vi)	गोता मारना	gota mārana
to sink (ab. boat)	डूब जाना	dūb jāna
treasures	खज़ाना (m)	khazāna

199. Seas' and Oceans' names

Atlantic Ocean	अटलांटिक महासागर (m)	atalāntik mahāsāgar
Indian Ocean	हिन्द महासागर (m)	hind mahāsāgar
Pacific Ocean	प्रशांत महासागर (m)	prashānt mahāsāgar

Arctic Ocean	उत्तरी ध्रुव महासागर (m)	uttarī dhruv mahāsāgar
Black Sea	काला सागर (m)	kāla sāgar
Red Sea	लाल सागर (m)	lāl sāgar
Yellow Sea	पीला सागर (m)	pīla sāgar
White Sea	सफ़ेद सागर (m)	safed sāgar
Caspian Sea	कैस्पियन सागर (m)	kaispiyan sāgar
Dead Sea	मृत सागर (m)	mrt sāgar
Mediterranean Sea	भूमध्य सागर (m)	bhūmadhy sāgar
Aegean Sea	ईजियन सागर (m)	ījiyan sāgar
Adriatic Sea	एड्रिएटिक सागर (m)	edrietik sāgar
Arabian Sea	अरब सागर (m)	arab sāgar
Sea of Japan	जापान सागर (m)	jāpān sāgar
Bering Sea	बेरिंग सागर (m)	bering sāgar
South China Sea	दक्षिण चीन सागर (m)	dakshin chīn sāgar
Coral Sea	कोरल सागर (m)	koral sāgar
Tasman Sea	तस्मान सागर (m)	tasmān sāgar
Caribbean Sea	करिबियन सागर (m)	karibiyan sāgar
Barents Sea	बैरेंट्स सागर (m)	bairents sāgar
Kara Sea	काड़ा सागर (m)	kāra sāgar
North Sea	उत्तर सागर (m)	uttar sāgar
Baltic Sea	बाल्टिक सागर (m)	bāltik sāgar
Norwegian Sea	नार्वे सागर (m)	nārve sāgar

200. Mountains

mountain	पहाड़ (m)	pahār
mountain range	पर्वत माला (f)	parvat māla
mountain ridge	पहाड़ों का सिलसिला (m)	pahāron ka silasila
summit, top	चोटी (f)	chotī
peak	शिखर (m)	shikhar
foot (~ of the mountain)	तलहटी (f)	talahatī
slope (mountainside)	ढलान (f)	dhalān
volcano	ज्वालामुखी (m)	jvālāmukhī
active volcano	सक्रिय ज्वालामुखी (m)	sakriy jvālāmukhī
dormant volcano	निष्क्रिय ज्वालामुखी (m)	nishkriy jvālāmukhī
eruption	विस्फोटन (m)	visfotan
crater	ज्वालामुखी का मुख (m)	jvālāmukhī ka mukh
magma	मैग्मा (m)	maigma
lava	लावा (m)	lāva
molten (~ lava)	पिघला हुआ	pighala hua
canyon	घाटी (m)	ghātī

gorge	तंग घाटी (f)	tang ghātī
crevice	दरार (m)	darār
pass, col	मार्ग (m)	mārg
plateau	पठार (m)	pathār
cliff	शिला (f)	shila
hill	टीला (m)	tīla
glacier	हिमनद (m)	himanad
waterfall	झरना (m)	jharana
geyser	उष्ण जल स्रोत (m)	ushn jal srot
lake	तालाब (m)	tālāb
plain	समतल प्रदेश (m)	samatal pradesh
landscape	परिदृश्य (m)	paridrshy
echo	गूँज (f)	gūnj
alpinist	पर्वतारोही (m)	parvatārohī
rock climber	पर्वतारोही (m)	parvatārohī
to conquer (in climbing)	चोटी पर पहुँचना	chotī par pahunchana
climb (an easy ~)	चढ़ाव (m)	charhāv

201. Mountains names

The Alps	आल्पस (m)	ālpas
Mont Blanc	मोन्ट ब्लैंक (m)	mont blaink
The Pyrenees	पाइरीनीज़ (f pl)	pairīnīz
The Carpathians	कार्पाथियेन्स (m)	kārpāthiyens
The Ural Mountains	यूराल (m)	yūral
The Caucasus Mountains	कोकेशिया के पहाड़ (m)	kokeshiya ke pahār
Mount Elbrus	एल्ब्रस पर्वत (m)	elbras parvat
The Altai Mountains	अल्टाई पर्वत (m)	altaī parvat
The Tian Shan	तियान शान (m)	tiyān shān
The Pamir Mountains	पामीर पर्वत (m)	pāmīr parvat
The Himalayas	हिमालय (m)	himālay
Mount Everest	माउंट एवरेस्ट (m)	maunt evarest
The Andes	एंडीज़ (f pl)	endīz
Mount Kilimanjaro	किलीमन्जारो (m)	kilīmanjāro

202. Rivers

river	नदी (f)	nadī
spring (natural source)	झरना (m)	jharana
riverbed (river channel)	नदी तल (m)	nadī tal
basin (river valley)	बेसिन (m)	besin

to flow into …	गिरना	girana
tributary	उपनदी (f)	upanadī
bank (of river)	तट (m)	tat
current (stream)	धारा (f)	dhāra
downstream (adv)	बहाव के साथ	bahāv ke sāth
upstream (adv)	बहाव के विरुद्ध	bahāv ke virūddh
inundation	बाढ़ (f)	bārh
flooding	बाढ़ (f)	bārh
to overflow (vi)	उमड़ना	umarana
to flood (vt)	पानी से भरना	pānī se bharana
shallow (shoal)	छिछला पानी (m)	chhichhala pānī
rapids	तेज़ उतार (m)	tez utār
dam	बांध (m)	bāndh
canal	नहर (f)	nahar
reservoir (artificial lake)	जलाशय (m)	jalāshay
sluice, lock	स्लूस (m)	slūs
water body (pond, etc.)	जल स्रोत (m)	jal srot
swamp (marshland)	दलदल (f)	daladal
bog, marsh	दलदल (f)	daladal
whirlpool	भंवर (m)	bhanvar
stream (brook)	झरना (m)	jharana
drinking (ab. water)	पीने का	pīne ka
fresh (~ water)	ताज़ा	tāza
ice	बर्फ़ (m)	barf
to freeze over (ab. river, etc.)	जम जाना	jam jāna

203. Rivers' names

Seine	सीन (f)	sīn
Loire	लॉयर (f)	loyar
Thames	थेम्स (f)	thems
Rhine	राइन (f)	rain
Danube	डेन्यूब (f)	denyūb
Volga	वोल्गा (f)	volga
Don	डॉन (f)	don
Lena	लेना (f)	lena
Yellow River	ह्वांग हे (f)	hvāng he
Yangtze	यांग्त्ज़ी (f)	yāngtzī
Mekong	मेकांग (f)	mekāng

Ganges	गंगा (f)	ganga
Nile River	नील (f)	nīl
Congo River	कांगो (f)	kāngo
Okavango River	ओकावान्गो (f)	okāvāngo
Zambezi River	ज़म्बेज़ी (f)	zambezī
Limpopo River	लिम्पोपो (f)	limpopo
Mississippi River	मिसिसिपी (f)	misisipī

204. Forest

forest, wood	जंगल (m)	jangal
forest (as adj)	जंगली	jangalī
thick forest	घना जंगल (m)	ghana jangal
grove	उपवान (m)	upavān
forest clearing	खुला छोटा मैदान (m)	khula chhota maidān
thicket	झाड़ियाँ (f pl)	jhāriyān
scrubland	झाड़ियों भरा मैदान (m)	jhāriyon bhara maidān
footpath (troddenpath)	फुटपाथ (m)	futapāth
gully	नाली (f)	nālī
tree	पेड़ (m)	per
leaf	पत्ता (m)	patta
leaves (foliage)	पत्तियां (f)	pattiyān
fall of leaves	पतझड़ (m)	patajhar
to fall (ab. leaves)	गिरना	girana
top (of the tree)	शिखर (m)	shikhar
branch	टहनी (f)	tahanī
bough	शाखा (f)	shākha
bud (on shrub, tree)	कलिका (f)	kalika
needle (of pine tree)	सुई (f)	suī
pine cone	शंकुफल (m)	shankufal
hollow (in a tree)	खोखला (m)	khokhala
nest	घोंसला (m)	ghonsala
burrow (animal hole)	बिल (m)	bil
trunk	तना (m)	tana
root	जड़ (f)	jar
bark	छाल (f)	chhāl
moss	काई (f)	kaī
to uproot (remove trees or tree stumps)	उखाड़ना	ukhārana
to chop down	काटना	kātana
to deforest (vt)	जंगल काटना	jangal kātana

tree stump	ठूंठ (m)	thūnth
campfire	अलाव (m)	alāv
forest fire	जंगल की आग (f)	jangal kī āg
to extinguish (vt)	आग बुझाना	āg bujhāna
forest ranger	वनरक्षक (m)	vanarakshak
protection	रक्षा (f)	raksha
to protect (~ nature)	रक्षा करना	raksha karana
poacher	चोर शिकारी (m)	chor shikārī
steel trap	फंदा (m)	fanda
to gather, to pick (vt)	बटोरना	batorana
to lose one's way	रास्ता भूलना	rāsta bhūlana

205. Natural resources

natural resources	प्राकृतिक संसाधन (m pl)	prākrtik sansādhan
minerals	खनिज पदार्थ (m pl)	khanij padārth
deposits	तह (f pl)	tah
field (e.g., oilfield)	क्षेत्र (m)	kshetr
to mine (extract)	खोदना	khodana
mining (extraction)	खनिकर्म (m)	khanikarm
ore	अयस्क (m)	ayask
mine (e.g., for coal)	खान (f)	khān
shaft (mine ~)	शैफ़ट (m)	shaifat
miner	खनिक (m)	khanik
gas (natural ~)	गैस (m)	gais
gas pipeline	गैस पाइप लाइन (m)	gais paip lain
oil (petroleum)	पेट्रोल (m)	petrol
oil pipeline	तेल पाइप लाइन (m)	tel paip lain
oil well	तेल का कुँआ (m)	tel ka kuna
derrick (tower)	डेरिक (m)	derik
tanker	टैंकर (m)	tainkar
sand	रेत (m)	ret
limestone	चूना पत्थर (m)	chūna patthar
gravel	बजरी (f)	bajarī
peat	पीट (m)	pīt
clay	मिट्टी (f)	mittī
coal	कोयला (m)	koyala
iron (ore)	लोहा (m)	loha
gold	सोना (m)	sona
silver	चाँदी (f)	chāndī
nickel	गिलट (m)	gilat
copper	ताँबा (m)	tānba
zinc	जस्ता (m)	jasta

manganese	अयस (m)	ayas
mercury	पारा (f)	pāra
lead	सीसा (f)	sīsa
mineral	खनिज (m)	khanij
crystal	क्रिस्टल (m)	kristal
marble	संगमरमर (m)	sangamaramar
uranium	यूरेनियम (m)	yūreniyam

The Earth. Part 2

206. Weather

weather	मौसम (m)	mausam
weather forecast	मौसम का पूर्वानुमान (m)	mausam ka pūrvānumān
temperature	तापमान (m)	tāpamān
thermometer	थर्मामीटर (m)	tharmāmītar
barometer	बैरोमीटर (m)	bairomītar
humidity	नमी (f)	namī
heat (extreme ~)	गरमी (f)	garamī
hot (torrid)	गरम	garam
it's hot	गरमी है	garamī hai
it's warm	गरम है	garam hai
warm (moderately hot)	गरम	garam
it's cold	ठंडक है	thandak hai
cold (adj)	ठंडा	thanda
sun	सूरज (m)	sūraj
to shine (vi)	चमकना	chamakana
sunny (day)	धूपदार	dhūpadār
to come up (vi)	उगना	ugana
to set (vi)	डूबना	dūbana
cloud	बादल (m)	bādal
cloudy (adj)	मेघाच्छादित	meghāchchhādit
rain cloud	घना बादल (m)	ghana bādal
somber (gloomy)	बदली	badalī
rain	बारिश (f)	bārish
it's raining	बारिश हो रही है	bārish ho rahī hai
rainy (~ day, weather)	बरसाती	barasātī
to drizzle (vi)	बूंदाबांदी होना	būndābāndī hona
pouring rain	मूसलधार बारिश (f)	mūsaladhār bārish
downpour	मूसलधार बारिश (f)	mūsaladhār bārish
heavy (e.g., ~ rain)	भारी	bhārī
puddle	पोखर (m)	pokhar
to get wet (in rain)	भीगना	bhīgana
fog (mist)	कुहरा (m)	kuhara
foggy	कुहरेदार	kuharedār
snow	बर्फ़ (f)	barf
it's snowing	बर्फ़ पड़ रही है	barf par rahī hai

207. Severe weather. Natural disasters

thunderstorm	गरजवाला तुफ़ान (m)	garajavāla tufān
lightning (~ strike)	बिजली (m)	bijalī
to flash (vi)	चमकना	chamakana
thunder	गरज (m)	garaj
to thunder (vi)	बादल गरजना	bādal garajana
it's thundering	बादल गरज रहा है	bādal garaj raha hai
hail	ओला (m)	ola
it's hailing	ओले पड़ रहे हैं	ole par rahe hain
to flood (vt)	बाढ़ आ जाना	bārh ā jāna
flood, inundation	बाढ़ (f)	bārh
earthquake	भूकंप (m)	bhūkamp
tremor, quake	झटका (m)	jhataka
epicenter	अधिकेंद्र (m)	adhikendr
eruption	उद्गार (m)	udgār
lava	लावा (m)	lāva
twister	बवंडर (m)	bavandar
tornado	टोर्नेडो (m)	tornedo
typhoon	रतूफ़ान (m)	ratūfān
hurricane	समुद्री तूफ़ान (m)	samudrī tūfān
storm	तूफ़ान (m)	tufān
tsunami	सुनामी (f)	sunāmī
cyclone	चक्रवात (m)	chakravāt
bad weather	ख़राब मौसम (m)	kharāb mausam
fire (accident)	आग (f)	āg
disaster	प्रलय (m)	pralay
meteorite	उल्का पिंड (m)	ulka pind
avalanche	हिमस्खलन (m)	himaskhalan
snowslide	हिमस्खलन (m)	himaskhalan
blizzard	बर्फ़ का तुफ़ान (m)	barf ka tufān
snowstorm	बफ़ीला तुफ़ान (m)	barfila tufān

208. Noises. Sounds

silence (quiet)	सन्नाटा (m)	sannāta
sound	ध्वनि (m)	dhvani
noise	शोर (m)	shor
to make noise	शोर मचाना	shor machāna
noisy (adj)	कोलाहलमय	kolāhalamay

loudly (to speak, etc.)	ऊँचा	ūncha
loud (voice, etc.)	ऊंचा	ūncha
constant (e.g., ~ noise)	लगातार	lagātār
cry, shout (n)	चिल्लाहट (f)	chillāhat
to cry, to shout (vi)	चिल्लाना	chillāna
whisper	फुसफुस (m)	fusafus
to whisper (vi, vt)	फुसफुसाना	fusafusāna
barking (dog's ~)	भौं-भौं (f)	bhaun-bhaun
to bark (vi)	भौंकना	bhaunkana
groan (of pain, etc.)	कराह (m)	karāh
to groan (vi)	कराहना	karāhana
cough	खाँस (f)	khāns
to cough (vi)	खाँसना	khānsana
whistle	सीटी (f)	sītī
to whistle (vi)	सीटी बजाना	sītī bajāna
knock (at the door)	खटखट (f)	khatakhat
to knock (at the door)	खटखटाना	khatakhatāna
to crack (vi)	चीर पड़ना	chīr parana
crack (cracking sound)	कड़क (m)	karak
siren	साइरन (f)	sairan
whistle (factory ~, etc.)	साइरन (m)	sairan
to whistle (ab. train)	सीटी बजना	sītī bajana
honk (car horn sound)	होर्न (m)	horn
to honk (vi)	होर्न बजाना	horn bajāna

209. Winter

winter (n)	सर्दी (f)	sardī
winter (as adj)	सर्दी का	sardī ka
in winter	सर्दियों में	sardiyon men
snow	बर्फ़ (f)	barf
it's snowing	बर्फ़ पड़ रही है	barf par rahī hai
snowfall	बर्फ़बारी (f)	barfabārī
snowdrift	बर्फ़ का ढेर (m)	barf ka rher
snowflake	हिमकण (m)	himakan
snowball	बर्फ़ का गोला (m)	barf ka gola
snowman	हिम मानव (m)	him mānav
icicle	हिमलंब (m)	himalamb
December	दिसम्बर (m)	disambar
January	जनवरी (f)	janavarī
February	फ़रवरी (m)	faravarī

frost (severe ~, freezing cold)	पाला (m)	pāla
frosty (weather, air)	शीत	shīt
below zero (adv)	शून्य से नीचे	shūny se nīche
first frost	पहली ठंड (f)	pahalī thand
hoarfrost	पाला (m)	pāla
cold (cold weather)	ठंडक (m)	thandak
it's cold	ठंडक है	thandak hai
fur coat	फरकोट (m)	farakot
mittens	दस्ताने (m pl)	dastāne
to get sick	बीमार पड़ जाना	bīmār par jāna
cold (illness)	जुकाम (m)	zukām
to catch a cold	जुकाम होना	zukām hona
ice	बर्फ़ (m)	barf
black ice	बर्फ़ की परत (f)	barf kī parat
to freeze over (ab. river, etc.)	जम जाना	jam jāna
ice floe	हिमखंड (m)	himakhand
skis	स्की (m pl)	skī
skier	स्कीयर (m)	skīyar
to ski (vi)	स्कीइंग करना	skīing karana
to skate (vi)	स्केटिंग करना	sketing karana

Fauna

210. Mammals. Predators

predator	परभक्षी (m)	parabhakshī
tiger	बाघ (m)	bāgh
lion	शेर (m)	sher
wolf	भेड़िया (m)	bheriya
fox	लोमड़ी (f)	lomri
jaguar	जागुआर (m)	jāguār
leopard	तेंदुआ (m)	tendua
cheetah	चीता (m)	chīta
black panther	काला तेंदुआ (m)	kāla tendua
puma	पहाड़ी बिलाव (m)	pahādī bilāv
snow leopard	हिम तेंदुआ (m)	him tendua
lynx	वन बिलाव (m)	van bilāv
coyote	कोयोट (m)	koyot
jackal	गीदड़ (m)	gīdar
hyena	लकड़बग्घा (m)	lakarabaggha

211. Wild animals

animal	जानवर (m)	jānavar
beast (animal)	जानवर (m)	jānavar
squirrel	गिलहरी (f)	gilaharī
hedgehog	कांटा-चूहा (m)	kānta-chūha
hare	खरगोश (m)	kharagosh
rabbit	खरगोश (m)	kharagosh
badger	बिज्जू (m)	bijjū
raccoon	रैकून (m)	raikūn
hamster	हैम्स्टर (m)	haimstar
marmot	मारमोट (m)	māramot
mole	छछूंदर (m)	chhachhūndar
mouse	चूहा (m)	chūha
rat	घूस (m)	ghūs
bat	चमगादड़ (m)	chamagādar
ermine	नेवला (m)	nevala
sable	सेबल (m)	sebal

marten	मारटेन (m)	māraten
weasel	नेवला (m)	nevala
mink	मिंक (m)	mink

| beaver | ऊदबिलाव (m) | ūdabilāv |
| otter | ऊदबिलाव (m) | ūdabilāv |

horse	घोड़ा (m)	ghora
moose	मूस (m)	mūs
deer	हिरण (m)	hiran
camel	ऊंट (m)	ūnt

bison	बाइसन (m)	baisan
aurochs	जंगली बैल (m)	jangalī bail
buffalo	भैंस (m)	bhains

zebra	ज़ेबरा (m)	zebara
antelope	मृग (f)	mrg
roe deer	मृग्नी (f)	mrgnī
fallow deer	चीतल (m)	chītal
chamois	शैमी (f)	shaimī
wild boar	जंगली सुअर (m)	jangalī suār

whale	ह्वेल (f)	hvel
seal	सील (m)	sīl
walrus	वॉलरस (m)	volaras
fur seal	फर सील (f)	far sīl
dolphin	डॉल्फ़िन (f)	dolafin

bear	रीछ (m)	rīchh
polar bear	सफ़ेद रीछ (m)	safed rīchh
panda	पांडा (m)	pānda

monkey	बंदर (m)	bandar
chimpanzee	वनमानुष (m)	vanamānush
orangutan	वनमानुष (m)	vanamānush
gorilla	गोरिला (m)	gorila
macaque	अफ़्रीकिन लंगूर (m)	afrikan langūr
gibbon	गिब्बन (m)	gibban

elephant	हाथी (m)	hāthī
rhinoceros	गैंडा (m)	gainda
giraffe	ज़िराफ़ (m)	jirāf
hippopotamus	दरियाई घोड़ा (m)	dariyaī ghora

| kangaroo | कंगारू (m) | kangārū |
| koala (bear) | कोआला (m) | koāla |

mongoose	नेवला (m)	nevala
chinchilla	चिनचीला (f)	chinachīla
skunk	स्कंक (m)	skank
porcupine	शल्यक (f)	shalyak

212. Domestic animals

cat	बिल्ली (f)	billī
tomcat	बिल्ला (m)	billa
dog	कुत्ता (m)	kutta
horse	घोड़ा (m)	ghora
stallion (male horse)	घोड़ा (m)	ghora
mare	घोड़ी (f)	ghorī
cow	गाय (f)	gāy
bull	बैल (m)	bail
ox	बैल (m)	bail
sheep (ewe)	भेड़ (f)	bher
ram	भेड़ा (m)	bhera
goat	बकरी (f)	bakarī
billy goat, he-goat	बकरा (m)	bakara
donkey	गधा (m)	gadha
mule	खच्चर (m)	khachchar
pig, hog	सुअर (m)	suar
piglet	घेंटा (m)	ghenta
rabbit	खरगोश (m)	kharagosh
hen (chicken)	मुर्गी (f)	murgī
rooster	मुर्गा (m)	murga
duck	बत्तख़ (f)	battakh
drake	नर बत्तख़ (m)	nar battakh
goose	हंस (m)	hans
tom turkey, gobbler	नर टर्की (m)	nar tarkī
turkey (hen)	टर्की (f)	tarkī
domestic animals	घरेलू पशु (m pl)	gharelū pashu
tame (e.g., ~ hamster)	पालतू	pālatū
to tame (vt)	पालतू बनाना	pālatū banāna
to breed (vt)	पालना	pālana
farm	खेत (m)	khet
poultry	मुर्गी पालन (f)	murgī pālan
cattle	मवेशी (m)	maveshī
herd (cattle)	पशु समूह (m)	pashu samūh
stable	अस्तबल (m)	astabal
pigpen	सुअरखाना (m)	sūarakhāna
cowshed	गोशाला (f)	goshāla
rabbit hutch	खरगोश का दरबा (m)	kharagosh ka daraba
hen house	मुर्गीखाना (m)	murgīkhāna

213. Dogs. Dog breeds

dog	कुत्ता (m)	kutta
sheepdog	गड़रिये का कुत्ता (m)	garariye ka kutta
poodle	पूडल (m)	pūdal
dachshund	डॉक्सहूण्ड (m)	dāksahūnd
bulldog	बुलडॉग (m)	buladog
boxer	बॉक्सर (m)	boksar
mastiff	मास्टिफ़ (m)	māstif
Rottweiler	रॉटवायलर (m)	rotavāyalar
Doberman	डोबरमैन (m)	dobaramain
basset	बास्सेट (m)	bāsset
bobtail	बोब्टेल (m)	bobtel
Dalmatian	डालमेशियन (m)	dālameshiyan
cocker spaniel	कॉकर स्पैनियल (m)	kokar spainiyal
Newfoundland	न्यूफाउंडलंड (m)	nyūfaundaland
Saint Bernard	सेंट बर्नार्ड (m)	sent barnārd
husky	हस्की (m)	haskī
Chow Chow	चाउ-चाउ (m)	chau-chau
spitz	स्पीट्ज़ (m)	spītz
pug	पग (m)	pag

214. Sounds made by animals

barking (n)	भौं-भौं (f)	bhaun-bhaun
to bark (vi)	भौंकना	bhaunkana
to meow (vi)	म्याऊं-म्याऊं करना	myaūn-myaun karana
to purr (vi)	घुरघुराना	ghuraghurāna
to moo (vi)	रँभाना	ranbhāna
to bellow (bull)	गर्जना	garjana
to growl (vi)	गुर्राना	gurrāna
howl (n)	गुर्राहट (f)	gurrāhat
to howl (vi)	चिल्लाना (m)	chillāna
to whine (vi)	रिरियाना	ririyāna
to bleat (sheep)	मिमियाना	mimiyāna
to oink, to grunt (pig)	घुरघुराना	ghuraghurāna
to squeal (vi)	किंकियाना	kikiyāna
to croak (vi)	टर्-टर् करना	tarr-tarr karana
to buzz (insect)	भनभनाना	bhanabhanāna
to chirp (crickets, grasshopper)	चरचराना	characharāna

215. Young animals

cub	पशुशावक (m)	pashushāvak
kitten	बिल्लौटा (m)	billauta
baby mouse	चुहिया (f)	chuhiya
puppy	पिल्ला (m)	pilla
leveret	खरगोश का बच्चा (m)	kharagosh ka bachcha
baby rabbit	खरगोश का बच्चा (m)	kharagosh ka bachcha
wolf cub	भेड़िये का शावक (m)	bheriye ka shāvak
fox cub	लोमड़ी का शावक (m)	lomri ka shāvak
bear cub	भालू का बच्चा (m)	bhālū ka bachcha
lion cub	शेर का बच्चा (m)	sher ka bachcha
tiger cub	बाघ का बच्चा (m)	bāgh ka bachcha
elephant calf	हाथी का बच्चा (m)	hāthī ka bachcha
piglet	घेंटा (m)	ghenta
calf (young cow, bull)	बछड़ा (m)	bachhara
kid (young goat)	बकरी का बच्चा (m)	bakarī ka bachcha
lamb	भेड़ का बच्चा (m)	bher ka bachcha
fawn (young deer)	मृग का बच्चा (m)	mrg ka bachcha
young camel	ऊट का बच्चा (m)	ūnt ka bachcha
snakelet (baby snake)	सर्प का बच्चा (m)	sarp ka bachcha
froglet (baby frog)	मेंढक का बच्चा (m)	mendhak ka bachcha
baby bird	चिड़िया का बच्चा (m)	chiriya ka bachcha
chick (of chicken)	मुर्गी का बच्चा (m)	murgī ka bachcha
duckling	बतख़ का बच्चा (m)	battakh ka bachcha

216. Birds

bird	चिड़िया (f)	chiriya
pigeon	कबूतर (m)	kabūtar
sparrow	गौरैया (f)	gauraiya
tit (great tit)	टिटरी (f)	titarī
magpie	नीलकण्ठ पक्षी (f)	nīlakanth pakshī
raven	काला कौआ (m)	kāla kaua
crow	कौआ (m)	kaua
jackdaw	कौआ (m)	kaua
rook	कौआ (m)	kaua
duck	बतख़ (f)	battakh
goose	हंस (m)	hans
pheasant	तीतर (m)	tītar
eagle	चील (f)	chīl
hawk	बाज़ (m)	bāz

falcon	बाज़ (m)	bāz
vulture	गिद्ध (m)	giddh
condor (Andean ~)	कॉन्डोर (m)	kondor
swan	राजहंस (m)	rājahans
crane	सारस (m)	sāras
stork	लकलक (m)	lakalak
parrot	तोता (m)	tota
hummingbird	हमिंग बर्ड (f)	haming bard
peacock	मोर (m)	mor
ostrich	शुतुरमुर्ग (m)	shuturamurg
heron	बगुला (m)	bagula
flamingo	फ्लेमिन्गो (m)	flemingo
pelican	हवासिल (m)	havāsil
nightingale	बुलबुल (m)	bulabul
swallow	अबाबील (f)	abābīl
thrush	मुखब्रण (f)	mukhavran
song thrush	मुखब्रण (f)	mukhavran
blackbird	ब्लैकबर्ड (m)	blaikabard
swift	बतासी (f)	batāsī
lark	भरत (m)	bharat
quail	वर्तक (m)	varttak
woodpecker	कठफोड़ा (m)	kathafora
cuckoo	कोयल (f)	koyal
owl	उल्लू (m)	ullū
eagle owl	गरुड़ उल्लू (m)	garūr ullū
wood grouse	तीतर (m)	tītar
black grouse	काला तीतर (m)	kāla tītar
partridge	चकोर (m)	chakor
starling	तिलिया (f)	tiliya
canary	कनारी (f)	kanārī
hazel grouse	पिंगल तीतर (m)	pingal tītar
chaffinch	फ़िंच (m)	finch
bullfinch	बुलफ़िंच (m)	bulafinch
seagull	गंगा-चिल्ली (f)	ganga-chillī
albatross	अल्बात्रोस (m)	albātros
penguin	पेंगुइन (m)	penguin

217. Birds. Singing and sounds

to sing (vi)	गाना	gāna
to call (animal, bird)	बुलाना	bulāna

to crow (rooster)	बाँग देना	bāng dena
cock-a-doodle-doo	कुकड़ूकू	kukarūnkū
to cluck (hen)	कुड़कुड़ाना	kurakurāna
to caw (vi)	कांय कांय करना	kāny kāny karana
to quack (duck)	कुवैक कुवैक करना	kuvaik kuvaik karana
to cheep (vi)	चीं चीं करना	chīn chīn karana
to chirp, to twitter	चहकना	chahakana

218. Fish. Marine animals

bream	ब्रीम (f)	brīm
carp	कार्प (f)	kārp
perch	पर्च (f)	parch
catfish	कैटफ़िश (f)	kaitafish
pike	पाइक (f)	paik
salmon	सैल्मन (f)	sailman
sturgeon	स्टर्जन (f)	starjan
herring	हेरिंग (f)	hering
Atlantic salmon	अटलांटिक सैल्मन (f)	atalāntik sailman
mackerel	माक्रैल (f)	mākrail
flatfish	फ्लैटफ़िश (f)	flaitafish
zander, pike perch	पाइक पर्च (f)	paik parch
cod	कॉड (f)	kod
tuna	टूना (f)	tūna
trout	ट्राउट (f)	traut
eel	सर्पमीन (f)	sarpamīn
electric ray	विद्युत शंकुश (f)	vidyut shankush
moray eel	मोरे सर्पमीन (f)	more sarpamīn
piranha	पिरान्हा (f)	pirānha
shark	शार्क (f)	shārk
dolphin	डॉलफ़िन (f)	dolafin
whale	ह्वेल (f)	hvel
crab	केकड़ा (m)	kekara
jellyfish	जेली फ़िश (f)	jelī fish
octopus	आक्टोपस (m)	āktopas
starfish	स्टार फ़िश (f)	stār fish
sea urchin	जलसाही (f)	jalasāhī
seahorse	समुद्री घोड़ा (m)	samudrī ghora
oyster	कस्तूरा (m)	kastūra
shrimp	झींगा (f)	jhīnga
lobster	लॉब्स्टर (m)	lobsatar
spiny lobster	स्पाइनी लॉब्स्टर (m)	spainī lobsatar

219. Amphibians. Reptiles

snake	सर्प (m)	sarp
venomous (snake)	विषैला	vishaila
viper	वाइपर (m)	vaipar
cobra	नाग (m)	nāg
python	अजगर (m)	ajagar
boa	अजगर (m)	ajagar
grass snake	साँप (f)	sānp
rattle snake	रैटल सर्प (m)	raital sarp
anaconda	एनाकोन्डा (f)	enākonda
lizard	छिपकली (f)	chhipakalī
iguana	इग्युएना (m)	igyūena
monitor lizard	मॉनिटर छिपकली (f)	monitar chhipakalī
salamander	सैलामैंडर (m)	sailāmaindar
chameleon	गिरगिट (m)	giragit
scorpion	वृश्चिक (m)	vrshchik
turtle	कछुआ (m)	kachhua
frog	मेंढक (m)	mendhak
toad	भेक (m)	bhek
crocodile	मगर (m)	magar

220. Insects

insect, bug	कीट (m)	kīt
butterfly	तितली (f)	titalī
ant	चींटी (f)	chīntī
fly	मक्खी (f)	makkhī
mosquito	मच्छर (m)	machchhar
beetle	भृंग (m)	bhrng
wasp	हड्डा (m)	hadda
bee	मधुमक्खी (f)	madhumakkhī
bumblebee	भंवरा (m)	bhanvara
gadfly (botfly)	गोमक्खी (f)	gomakkhī
spider	मकड़ी (f)	makarī
spiderweb	मकड़ी का जाल (m)	makarī ka jāl
dragonfly	व्याध-पतंग (m)	vyādh-patang
grasshopper	टिड्डा (m)	tidda
moth (night butterfly)	पतंगा (m)	patanga
cockroach	तिलचट्टा (m)	tilachatta
tick	जुँआ (m)	juna

flea	पिस्सू (m)	pissū
midge	भुनगा (m)	bhunaga
locust	टिड्डी (f)	tiddī
snail	घोंघा (m)	ghongha
cricket	झींगुर (m)	jhīngur
lightning bug	जुगनू (m)	juganū
ladybug	सोनपंखी (f)	sonapankhī
cockchafer	कोकचाफ़ (m)	kokachāf
leech	जोंक (m)	jok
caterpillar	इल्ली (f)	illī
earthworm	केंचुआ (m)	kenchua
larva	कीटडिंभ (m)	kītadimbh

221. Animals. Body parts

beak	चोंच (f)	chonch
wings	पंख (m pl)	pankh
foot (of bird)	पंजा (m)	panja
feathers (plumage)	पक्षी के पर (m)	pakshī ke par
feather	पर (m)	par
crest	कलगी (f)	kalagī
gills	गलफड़ा (m)	galafara
spawn	अंडा (m)	anda
larva	लार्वा (f)	lārva
fin	मछली का पंख (m)	machhalī ka pankh
scales (of fish, reptile)	स्केल (f)	skel
fang (canine)	खांग (m)	khāng
paw (e.g., cat's ~)	पंजा (m)	panja
muzzle (snout)	थूथन (m)	thūthan
mouth (of cat, dog)	मुंह (m)	munh
tail	पूँछ (f)	pūnchh
whiskers	मूंछें (f pl)	mūnchhen
hoof	खुर (m)	khur
horn	शृंग (m)	shrng
carapace	कवच (m)	kavach
shell (of mollusk)	कौड़ी (f)	kaurī
eggshell	अंडे का छिलका (m)	ande ka chhilaka
animal's hair (pelage)	जानवर के बाल (m)	jānavar ke bāl
pelt (hide)	पशुचर्म (m)	pashucharm

222. Actions of animals

to fly (vi)	उड़ना	urana
to fly in circles	चक्कर लगाना	chakkar lagāna
to fly away	उड़ जाना	ur jāna
to flap (~ the wings)	पंख फड़फड़ाना	pankh farafarāna
to peck (vi)	चुगना	chugana
to sit on eggs	अंडे सेना	ande sena
to hatch out (vi)	अंडे से बाहर निकलना	ande se bāhar nikalana
to build a nest	घोंसला बनाना	ghonsala banāna
to slither, to crawl	रेंगना	rengana
to sting, to bite (insect)	डसना	dasana
to bite (ab. animal)	काटना	kātana
to sniff (vt)	सूंघना	sūnghana
to bark (vi)	भौंकना	bhaunkana
to hiss (snake)	फुफकारना	fufakārana
to scare (vt)	डराना	darāna
to attack (vt)	हमला करना	hamala karana
to gnaw (bone, etc.)	कुतरना	kutarana
to scratch (with claws)	कुरेदना	kuredana
to hide (vi)	छिपाना	chhipāna
to play (kittens, etc.)	खेलना	khelana
to hunt (vi, vt)	शिकार करना	shikār karana
to hibernate (vi)	सीतनिद्रा में होना	sītanidra men hona
to go extinct	समाप्त हो जाना	samāpt ho jāna

223. Animals. Habitats

habitat	निवास-स्थान (m)	nivās-sthān
migration	देशांतरण (m)	deshāntaran
mountain	पहाड़ (m)	pahār
reef	रीफ़ (m)	rīf
cliff	शिला (f)	shila
forest	वन (m)	van
jungle	जंगल (m)	jangal
savanna	सवान्ना (m)	savānna
tundra	तुंड्रा (m)	tundra
steppe	घास का मैदान (m)	ghās ka maidān
desert	रेगिस्तान (m)	registān
oasis	नख़लिस्तान (m)	nakhalistān
sea	सागर (m)	sāgar

lake	तालाब (m)	tālāb
ocean	महासागर (m)	mahāsāgar
swamp (marshland)	दलदल (m)	daladal
freshwater (adj)	मीठे पानी का	mīthe pānī ka
pond	ताल (m)	tāl
river	नदी (f)	nadī
den (bear's ~)	गुफ़ा (f)	gufa
nest	घोंसला (m)	ghonsala
hollow (in a tree)	खोखला (m)	khokhala
burrow (animal hole)	बिल (m)	bil
anthill	बांबी (f)	bāmbī

224. Animal care

zoo	चिड़ियाघर (m)	chiriyāghar
nature preserve	पशुविहार (m)	pashuvihār
breeder (cattery, kennel, etc.)	पशुफ़ार्म (m)	pashufārm
open-air cage	अहाता (m)	ahāta
cage	पिंजरा (m)	pinjara
doghouse (kennel)	कुत्ताघर (m)	kuttāghar
dovecot	कबूतरखाना (m)	kabūtarkhāna
aquarium (fish tank)	मछलीघर (m)	machhalīghar
dolphinarium	डॉलफ़िनघर (m)	dolafinaghar
to breed (animals)	पालन करना	pālan karana
brood, litter	बच्चे (m)	bachche
to tame (vt)	पालतू बनाना	pālatū banāna
feed (fodder, etc.)	चारा (m)	chāra
to feed (vt)	खिलाना	khilāna
to train (animals)	सधाना	sadhāna
pet store	पालतू जानवरों की दुकान (f)	pālatū jānavaron kī dukān
muzzle (for dog)	थूथन (f)	thūthan
collar (e.g., dog ~)	पट्टा (m)	patta
name (of animal)	नाम (m)	nām
pedigree (of dog)	वंशावली (f)	vanshāvalī

225. Animals. Miscellaneous

pack (wolves)	झुंड (m)	jhund
flock (birds)	झुंड (m)	jhund
shoal, school (fish)	झुंड (m)	jhund

herd (horses)	झुंड (m)	jhund
male (n)	नर (m)	nar
female (n)	मादा (f)	māda
hungry (adj)	भूखा	bhūkha
wild (adj)	जंगली	jangalī
dangerous (adj)	खतरनाक	khataranāk

226. Horses

horse	घोड़ा (m)	ghora
breed (race)	नस्ल (f)	nasl
foal	बछड़ा (m)	bachhara
mare	घोड़ी (f)	ghorī
mustang	मुस्तांग (m)	mustāng
pony	टट्टू (m)	tattū
draft horse	भारवाही घोड़ा (m)	bhāravāhī ghora
mane	अयाल (m)	ayāl
tail	पूँछ (f)	pūnchh
hoof	खुर (m)	khur
horseshoe	अश्वनाल (f)	ashvanāl
to shoe (vt)	नाल जड़ना	nāl jarana
blacksmith	लोहार (m)	lohār
saddle	काठी (f)	kāthī
stirrup	रक़ाब (m)	raqāb
bridle	लगाम (f)	lagām
reins	लगाम (f)	lagām
whip (for riding)	चाबूक (m)	chābūk
rider	सवार (m)	savār
to saddle up (vt)	काठी कसना	kāthī kasana
to mount a horse	काठी पर बैठना	kāthī par baithana
gallop	सरपट (f)	sarapat
to gallop (vi)	सरपट दौड़ना	sarapat daurana
trot (n)	दुलकी चाल (m)	dulakī chāl
at a trot (adv)	दुलकी चाल चलना	dulakī chāl chalana
racehorse	दौड़ का घोड़ा (m)	daur ka ghora
horse racing	घुड़दौड़ (m pl)	ghuradaur
stable	अस्तबल (m)	astabal
to feed (vt)	खिलाना	khilāna
hay	सूखी घास (f)	sūkhī ghās
to water (animals)	पिलाना	pilāna

to wash (horse)	नहलाना	nahalāna
to graze (vi)	चरना	charana
to neigh (vi)	हिनहिनाना	hinahināna
to kick (about horse)	लात मारना	lāt mārana

Flora

227. Trees

tree	पेड़ (m)	per
deciduous (adj)	पर्णपाती	parnapātī
coniferous (adj)	शंकुधर	shankudhar
evergreen (adj)	सदाबहार	sadābahār
apple tree	सेब वृक्ष (m)	seb vrksh
pear tree	नाश्पाती का पेड़ (m)	nāshpātī ka per
cherry tree	चेरी का पेड़ (f)	cherī ka per
plum tree	आलूबुखारे का पेड़ (m)	ālūbukhāre ka per
birch	सनोबर का पेड़ (m)	sanobar ka per
oak	बलूत (m)	balūt
linden tree	लिनडेन वृक्ष (m)	linaden vrksh
aspen	आस्पेन वृक्ष (m)	āspen vrksh
maple	मेपल (m)	mepal
spruce	फर का पेड़ (m)	far ka per
pine	देवदार (m)	devadār
larch	लार्च (m)	lārch
fir tree	फर (m)	far
cedar	देवदर (m)	devadar
poplar	पोप्लर वृक्ष (m)	poplar vrksh
rowan	रोवाण (m)	rovān
willow	विलो (f)	vilo
alder	आल्डर वृक्ष (m)	āldar vrksh
beech	बीच (m)	bīch
elm	एल्म वृक्ष (m)	elm vrksh
ash (tree)	एश-वृक्ष (m)	esh-vrksh
chestnut	चेस्टनट (m)	chestanat
magnolia	मैगनोलिया (f)	maiganoliya
palm tree	ताड़ का पेड़ (m)	tār ka per
cypress	सरो (m)	saro
mangrove	मैनग्रोव (m)	mainagrov
baobab	गोरक्षी (m)	gorakshī
eucalyptus	यूकेलिप्टस (m)	yūkeliptas
sequoia	सेकोइया (f)	sekoiya

228. Shrubs

bush	झाड़ी (f)	jhārī
shrub	झाड़ी (f)	jhārī
grapevine	अंगूर की बेल (f)	angūr kī bel
vineyard	अंगूर का बाग़ (m)	angūr ka bāg
raspberry bush	रास्पबेरी की झाड़ी (f)	rāspaberī kī jhārī
redcurrant bush	लाल करेंट की झाड़ी (f)	lāl karent kī jhārī
gooseberry bush	गूज़बेरी की झाड़ी (f)	gūzaberī kī jhārī
acacia	ऐकेशिय (m)	aikeshiy
barberry	बारबेरी झाड़ी (f)	bāraberī jhārī
jasmine	चमेली (f)	chamelī
juniper	जूनिपर (m)	jūnipar
rosebush	गुलाब की झाड़ी (f)	gulāb kī jhārī
dog rose	जंगली गुलाब (m)	jangalī gulāb

229. Mushrooms

mushroom	गगन-धूलि (f)	gagan-dhūli
edible mushroom	खाने योग्य गगन-धूलि (f)	khāne yogy gagan-dhūli
poisonous mushroom	ज़हरीली गगन-धूलि (f)	zaharīlī gagan-dhūli
cap (of mushroom)	छतरी (f)	chhatarī
stipe (of mushroom)	डंठल (f)	danthal
cep (Boletus edulis)	सफ़ेद गगन-धूलि (f)	safed gagan-dhūli
orange-cap boletus	नारंगी छतरी वाली गगन-धूलि (f)	nārangī chhatarī vālī gagan-dhūli
birch bolete	बर्च बोलेट (f)	barch bolet
chanterelle	शैंटरेल (f)	shentarel
russula	रसुला (f)	rasula
morel	मोरेल (f)	morel
fly agaric	फ्लाई ऐगेरिक (f)	flaī aigerik
death cap	डेथ कैप (f)	deth kaip

230. Fruits. Berries

fruit	फल (m)	fal
fruits	फल (m pl)	fal
apple	सेब (m)	seb
pear	नाश्पाती (f)	nāshpātī
plum	आलूबुख़ारा (m)	ālūbukhāra
strawberry (garden ~)	स्ट्रॉबेरी (f)	stroberī

| cherry | चेरी (f) | cherī |
| grape | अंगूर (m) | angūr |

raspberry	रास्पबेरी (f)	rāspaberī
blackcurrant	काली करेंट (f)	kālī karent
redcurrant	लाल करेंट (f)	lāl karent
gooseberry	गूज़बेरी (f)	gūzaberī
cranberry	क्रैनबेरी (f)	krenaberī

orange	संतरा (m)	santara
mandarin	नारंगी (f)	nārangī
pineapple	अनानास (m)	anānās
banana	केला (m)	kela
date	खजूर (m)	khajūr

lemon	नींबू (m)	nīmbū
apricot	खुबानी (f)	khūbānī
peach	आड़ू (m)	ārū
kiwi	चीकू (m)	chīkū
grapefruit	ग्रेपफ्रूट (m)	grepafrūt

berry	बेरी (f)	berī
berries	बेरियां (f pl)	beriyān
cowberry	काओबेरी (f)	kaoberī
wild strawberry	जंगली स्ट्रॉबेरी (f)	jangalī stroberī
bilberry	बिलबेरी (f)	bilaberī

231. Flowers. Plants

| flower | फूल (m) | fūl |
| bouquet (of flowers) | गुलदस्ता (m) | guladasta |

rose (flower)	गुलाब (f)	gulāb
tulip	ट्यूलिप (m)	tyūlip
carnation	गुलनार (m)	gulanār
gladiolus	ग्लेडियोलस (m)	glediyolas

cornflower	नीलकूपी (m)	nīlakūpī
harebell	ब्लूबेल (m)	blūbel
dandelion	कुकरौंधा (m)	kukaraundha
camomile	कैमोमाइल (m)	kaimomail

aloe	मुसब्बर (m)	musabbar
cactus	कैक्टस (m)	kaiktas
rubber plant, ficus	रबड़ का पौधा (m)	rabar ka paudha

lily	कुमुदिनी (f)	kumudinī
geranium	जेरनियम (m)	jeraniyam
hyacinth	हायसिंथ (m)	hāyasinth
mimosa	मिमोसा (m)	mimosa

narcissus	नरगिस (f)	naragis
nasturtium	नस्टाशयम (m)	nastāshayam
orchid	आर्किड (m)	ārkid
peony	पियोनी (m)	piyonī
violet	वॉयलेट (m)	voyalet
pansy	पैंज़ी (m pl)	painzī
forget-me-not	फर्गेंट मी नाट (m)	fargent mī nāt
daisy	गुलबहार (f)	gulabahār
poppy	खशखाश (m)	khashakhāsh
hemp	भांग (f)	bhāng
mint	पुदीना (m)	pudīna
lily of the valley	कामुदिनी (f)	kāmudinī
snowdrop	सफ़ेद फूल (m)	safed fūl
nettle	बिच्छू बूटी (f)	bichchhū būtī
sorrel	सोरेल (m)	sorel
water lily	कुमुदिनी (f)	kumudinī
fern	फर्न (m)	farn
lichen	शैवाक (m)	shaivāk
greenhouse (tropical ~)	शीशाघर (m)	shīshāghar
lawn	घास का मैदान (m)	ghās ka maidān
flowerbed	फुलवारी (f)	fulavārī
plant	पौधा (m)	paudha
grass	घास (f)	ghās
blade of grass	तिनका (m)	tinaka
leaf	पत्ती (f)	pattī
petal	पंखड़ी (f)	pankharī
stem	डंडी (f)	dandī
tuber	कंद (m)	kand
young plant (shoot)	अंकुर (m)	ankur
thorn	कांटा (m)	kānta
to blossom (vi)	खिलना	khilana
to fade, to wither	मुरझाना	murajhāna
smell (odor)	बू (m)	bū
to cut (flowers)	काटना	kātana
to pick (a flower)	तोड़ना	torana

232. Cereals, grains

| grain | दाना (m) | dāna |
| cereal crops | अनाज की फ़सलें (m pl) | anāj kī fasalen |

ear (of barley, etc.)	बाल (f)	bāl
wheat	गेहूं (m)	gehūn
rye	रई (f)	raī
oats	जई (f)	jaī
millet	बाजरा (m)	bājara
barley	जौ (m)	jau
corn	मक्का (m)	makka
rice	चावल (m)	chāval
buckwheat	मोथी (m)	mothī
pea plant	मटर (m)	matar
kidney bean	राजमा (f)	rājama
soy	सोया (m)	soya
lentil	दाल (m)	dāl
beans (pulse crops)	फली (f pl)	falī

233. Vegetables. Greens

vegetables	सब्जियाँ (f pl)	sabziyān
greens	हरी सब्जियाँ (f)	harī sabjiyān
tomato	टमाटर (m)	tamātar
cucumber	खीरा (m)	khīra
carrot	गाजर (f)	gājar
potato	आलू (m)	ālū
onion	प्याज़ (f)	pyāz
garlic	लहसुन (m)	lahasun
cabbage	बंदगोभी (f)	bandagobhī
cauliflower	फूल गोभी (f)	fūl gobhī
Brussels sprouts	ब्रसेल्स स्प्राउट्स (m)	brasels sprauts
beetroot	चुकन्दर (m)	chukandar
eggplant	बैंगन (m)	baingan
zucchini	लौकी (f)	laukī
pumpkin	कद्दू (m)	kaddū
turnip	शलजम (f)	shalajam
parsley	अजमोद (f)	ajamod
dill	सोआ (m)	soa
lettuce	सलाद पत्ता (m)	salād patta
celery	सेलरी (m)	selarī
asparagus	एस्परैगस (m)	esparaigas
spinach	पालक (m)	pālak
pea	मटर (m)	matar
beans	फली (f pl)	falī
corn (maize)	मकई (f)	makī
kidney bean	राजमा (f)	rājama

pepper	मिर्च (f)	mirch
radish	मूली (f)	mūlī
artichoke	अतिशोक (m)	artishok

REGIONAL GEOGRAPHY

Countries. Nationalities

234. Western Europe

Europe	यूरोप (m)	yūrop
European Union	यूरोपीय संघ (m)	yūropīy sangh
European (n)	यरोपीय (m)	yaropīy
European (adj)	यरोपीय	yaropīy
Austria	ऑसट्रिया (m)	ostriya
Austrian (masc.)	ऑसट्रियाई (m)	ostriyaī
Austrian (fem.)	ऑस्ट्रीयाई (f)	ostrīyaī
Austrian (adj)	ऑस्ट्रीयाई	ostrīyaī
Great Britain	ग्रेट ब्रिटेन (m)	gret briten
England	इंग्लैंड (m)	inglaind
British (masc.)	ब्रिटिश (m)	british
British (fem.)	ब्रिटिश (f)	british
English, British (adj)	अंग्रेज़	angrez
Belgium	बेल्जियम (m)	beljiyam
Belgian (masc.)	बेल्जियाई (m)	beljiyaī
Belgian (fem.)	बेल्जियाई (f)	beljiyaī
Belgian (adj)	बेल्जियाई	beljiyaī
Germany	जर्मन (m)	jarman
German (masc.)	जर्मन (m)	jarman
German (fem.)	जर्मन (f)	jarman
German (adj)	जर्मन	jarman
Netherlands	नीदरलैंड्स (m)	nīdaralainds
Holland	हॉलैंड (m)	holaind
Dutch (masc.)	डच (m)	dach
Dutch (fem.)	डच (f)	dach
Dutch (adj)	डच	dach
Greece	ग्रीस (m)	grīs
Greek (masc.)	ग्रीक (m)	grīk
Greek (fem.)	ग्रीक (f)	grīk
Greek (adj)	ग्रीक	grīk
Denmark	डेन्मार्क (m)	denmārk
Dane (masc.)	डेनिश (m)	denish

| Dane (fem.) | डेनिश (f) | denish |
| Danish (adj) | डेनिश | denish |

Ireland	आयरलैंड (m)	āyaralaind
Irish (masc.)	आयरिश (m)	āyarish
Irish (fem.)	आयरिश (f)	āyarish
Irish (adj)	आयरिश	āyarish

Iceland	आयसलैंड (m)	āyasalaind
Icelander (masc.)	आयसलैंडर (m)	āyasalaindar
Icelander (fem.)	आयसलैंडर (f)	āyasalaindar
Icelandic (adj)	आयसलैंडर	āyasalaindar

Spain	स्पेन (m)	spen
Spaniard (masc.)	स्पेनी (m)	spenī
Spaniard (fem.)	स्पेनी (f)	spenī
Spanish (adj)	स्पेनी	spenī

Italy	इटली (m)	italī
Italian (masc.)	इतालवी (m)	itālavī
Italian (fem.)	इतालवी (f)	itālavī
Italian (adj)	इतालवी	itālavī

Cyprus	साइप्रस (m)	saipras
Cypriot (masc.)	साइप्रस वासी (m)	saipras vāsī
Cypriot (fem.)	साइप्रस वासी (f)	saipras vāsī
Cypriot (adj)	साइप्रसी	saiprasī

Malta	माल्टा (m)	mālta
Maltese (masc.)	मोलतिज़ (m)	molatiz
Maltese (fem.)	मोलतिज़ (f)	molatiz
Maltese (adj)	मोलतिज़	molatiz

Norway	नार्वे (m)	nārve
Norwegian (masc.)	नार्वेजियन (m)	nārvejiyan
Norwegian (fem.)	नार्वेजियन (f)	nārvejiyan
Norwegian (adj)	नार्वेजियन	nārvejiyan

Portugal	पुर्तगाल (m)	purtagāl
Portuguese (masc.)	पुर्तगाली (m)	purtagālī
Portuguese (fem.)	पुर्तगाली (f)	purtagālī
Portuguese (adj)	पुर्तगाली	purtagālī

Finland	फ़िनलैंड (m)	finalaind
Finn (masc.)	फ़िनिश (m)	finish
Finn (fem.)	फ़िनिश (f)	finish
Finnish (adj)	फ़िनिश	finish

France	फ़्रांस (m)	frāns
French (masc.)	फ़्रांसीसी (m)	frānsīsī
French (fem.)	फ़्रांसीसी (f)	frānsīsī
French (adj)	फ़्रांसीसी	frānsīsī

Sweden	स्वीडन (m)	svīdan
Swede (masc.)	स्वीड (m)	svīd
Swede (fem.)	स्वीड (f)	svīd
Swedish (adj)	स्वीडिश	svīdish
Switzerland	स्विट्ज़रलैंड (m)	svitzaralaind
Swiss (masc.)	स्विस (m)	svis
Swiss (fem.)	स्विस (f)	svis
Swiss (adj)	स्विस	svis
Scotland	स्कॉटलैंड (m)	skotalaind
Scottish (masc.)	स्कॉटिश (m)	skotish
Scottish (fem.)	स्कॉटिश (f)	skotish
Scottish (adj)	स्कॉटिश	skotish
Vatican	वेटिकन (m)	vetikan
Liechtenstein	लिकटेंस्टीन (m)	likatenstīn
Luxembourg	लक्ज़मबर्ग (m)	lakzamabarg
Monaco	मोनाको (m)	monāko

235. Central and Eastern Europe

Albania	अल्बानिया (m)	albāniya
Albanian (masc.)	अल्बानियाई (m)	albāniyaī
Albanian (fem.)	अल्बानियाई (f)	albāniyaī
Albanian (adj)	अल्बानियाई	albāniyaī
Bulgaria	बुल्गारिया (m)	bulgāriya
Bulgarian (masc.)	बल्ग़ोरियाई (m)	balgeriyaī
Bulgarian (fem.)	बल्ग़ोरियाई (f)	balgeriyaī
Bulgarian (adj)	बल्ग़ोरियाई	balgeriyaī
Hungary	हंगरी (m)	hangarī
Hungarian (masc.)	हंगेरियाई (m)	hangeriyaī
Hungarian (fem.)	हंगेरियाई (f)	hangeriyaī
Hungarian (adj)	हंगेरियाई	hangeriyaī
Latvia	लाटविया (m)	lātaviya
Latvian (masc.)	लाटवियाई (m)	lātaviyaī
Latvian (fem.)	हंगेरियाई (f)	hangeriyaī
Latvian (adj)	लाटवियाई	lātaviyaī
Lithuania	लिथुआनिया (m)	lithuāniya
Lithuanian (masc.)	लिथुआनियन (m)	lithuāniyan
Lithuanian (fem.)	लिथुआनियन (f)	lithuāniyan
Lithuanian (adj)	लिथुआनियन	lithuāniyan
Poland	पोलैंड (m)	polaind
Pole (masc.)	पोलिश (m)	polish
Pole (fem.)	पोलिश (f)	polish

Polish (adj)	पोलिश	polish
Romania	रोमानिया (m)	romāniya
Romanian (masc.)	रोमानियाई (m)	romāniyaī
Romanian (fem.)	रोमानियाई (f)	romāniyaī
Romanian (adj)	रोमानियाई	romāniyaī
Serbia	सर्बिया (m)	sarbiya
Serbian (masc.)	सर्बियाई (m)	sarbiyaī
Serbian (fem.)	सर्बियाई (f)	sarbiyaī
Serbian (adj)	सर्बियाई	sarbiyaī
Slovakia	स्लोवाकिया (m)	slovākiya
Slovak (masc.)	स्लोवाकियन (m)	slovākiyan
Slovak (fem.)	स्लोवाकियन (f)	slovākiyan
Slovak (adj)	स्लोवाकियन	slovākiyan
Croatia	क्रोएशिया (m)	kroeshiya
Croatian (masc.)	क्रोएशियन (m)	kroeshiyan
Croatian (fem.)	क्रोएशियन (f)	kroeshiyan
Croatian (adj)	क्रोएशियन	kroeshiyan
Czech Republic	चेक गणतंत्र (m)	chek ganatantr
Czech (masc.)	चेक (m)	chek
Czech (fem.)	चेक (f)	chek
Czech (adj)	चेक	chek
Estonia	एस्तोनिया (m)	estoniya
Estonian (masc.)	एस्तोनियन (m)	estoniyan
Estonian (fem.)	एस्तोनियन (f)	estoniyan
Estonian (adj)	एस्तोनियन	estoniyan
Bosnia and Herzegovina	बोस्निया और हर्ज़ेगोविना	bosniya aur harzegovina
Macedonia (Republic of ~)	मेसेडोनिया (m)	mesedoniya
Slovenia	स्लोवेनिया (m)	sloveniya
Montenegro	मोंटेनेग्रो (m)	montenegro

236. Former USSR countries

Azerbaijan	आज़रबाइजान (m)	āzarabaijān
Azerbaijani (masc.)	आज़रबाइजानी (m)	āzarabaijānī
Azerbaijani (fem.)	आज़रबाइजानी (f)	āzarabaijānī
Azerbaijani, Azeri (adj)	आज़रबाइजानी	āzarabaijānī
Armenia	आर्मीनिया (m)	ārmīniya
Armenian (masc.)	आर्मीनियन (m)	ārmīniyan
Armenian (fem.)	आर्मीनियन (f)	ārmīniyan
Armenian (adj)	आर्मीनियाई	ārmīniyaī
Belarus	बेलारूस (m)	belārūs
Belarusian (masc.)	बेलारूसी (m)	belārūsī

| Belarusian (fem.) | बेलारूसी (f) | belārūsī |
| Belarusian (adj) | बेलारूसी | belārūsī |

Georgia	जॉर्जिया (m)	jorjiya
Georgian (masc.)	जॉर्जियन (m)	jorjiyan
Georgian (fem.)	जॉर्जियन (f)	jorjiyan
Georgian (adj)	जॉर्जिया	jorjiya
Kazakhstan	कज़ाकस्तान (m)	kazākastān
Kazakh (masc.)	कज़ाकी (m)	kazākī
Kazakh (fem.)	कज़ाकी (f)	kazākī
Kazakh (adj)	कज़ाकी	kazākī

Kirghizia	किर्गीज़िया (m)	kirgīziya
Kirghiz (masc.)	किर्गीज़ (m)	kirgīz
Kirghiz (fem.)	किर्गीज़ (f)	kirgīz
Kirghiz (adj)	किर्गीज़	kirgīz

Moldova, Moldavia	मोलदोवा (m)	moladova
Moldavian (masc.)	मोलदोवियन (m)	moladoviyan
Moldavian (fem.)	मोलदोवियन (f)	moladoviyan
Moldavian (adj)	मोलदोवियन	moladoviyan
Russia	रूस (m)	rūs
Russian (masc.)	रूसी (m)	rūsī
Russian (fem.)	रूसी (f)	rūsī
Russian (adj)	रूसी	rūsī

Tajikistan	ताजिकिस्तान (m)	tājikistān
Tajik (masc.)	ताजिक (m)	tājik
Tajik (fem.)	ताजिक (f)	tājik
Tajik (adj)	ताजिक	tājik

Turkmenistan	तुर्कमानिस्तान (m)	turkamānistān
Turkmen (masc.)	तुर्कमानी (m)	turkamānī
Turkmen (fem.)	तुर्कमानी (f)	turkamānī
Turkmenian (adj)	तुर्कमानी	turkamānī

Uzbekistan	ऊज़्बेकिस्तान (m)	uzbekistān
Uzbek (masc.)	ऊज़्बेकी (m)	uzbekī
Uzbek (fem.)	ऊज़्बेकी (f)	uzbekī
Uzbek (adj)	ऊज़्बेकि	uzbeki

Ukraine	यूक्रेन (m)	yūkren
Ukrainian (masc.)	यूक्रेनी (m)	yūkrenī
Ukrainian (fem.)	यूक्रेनी (f)	yūkrenī
Ukrainian (adj)	यूक्रेनी	yūkrenī

237. Asia

| Asia | एशिया (f) | eshiya |
| Asian (adj) | एशियई | eshiyī |

Vietnam	वियतनाम (m)	viyatanām
Vietnamese (masc.)	वियतनामी (m)	viyatanāmī
Vietnamese (fem.)	वियतनामी (f)	viyatanāmī
Vietnamese (adj)	वियतनामी	viyatanāmī
India	भारत (m)	bhārat
Indian (masc.)	भारतीय (m)	bhāratīy
Indian (fem.)	भारतीय (f)	bhāratīy
Indian (adj)	भारतीय	bhāratīy
Israel	इस्रायल (m)	isrāyal
Israeli (masc.)	इस्राइली (m)	israilī
Israeli (fem.)	इस्राइली (f)	israilī
Israeli (adj)	इस्राइली	israilī
Jew (n)	यहूदी (m)	yahūdī
Jewess (n)	यहूदी (f)	yahūdī
Jewish (adj)	यहूदी	yahūdī
China	चीन (m)	chīn
Chinese (masc.)	चीनी (m)	chīnī
Chinese (fem.)	चीनी (f)	chīnī
Chinese (adj)	चीनी	chīnī
Korean (masc.)	कोरियन (m)	koriyan
Korean (fem.)	कोरियन (f)	koriyan
Korean (adj)	कोरियन	koriyan
Lebanon	लेबनान (m)	lebanān
Lebanese (masc.)	लेबनानी (m)	lebanānī
Lebanese (fem.)	लेबनानी (f)	lebanānī
Lebanese (adj)	लेबनानी	lebanānī
Mongolia	मंगोलिया (m)	mangoliya
Mongolian (masc.)	मंगोलियन (m)	mangoliyan
Mongolian (fem.)	मंगोलियन (f)	mangoliyan
Mongolian (adj)	मंगोलियन	mangoliyan
Malaysia	मलेशिया (m)	maleshiya
Malaysian (masc.)	मलेशियाई (m)	maleshiyaī
Malaysian (fem.)	मलेशियाई (f)	maleshiyaī
Malaysian (adj)	मलेशियाई	maleshiyaī
Pakistan	पाकिस्तान (m)	pākistān
Pakistani (masc.)	पाकिस्तानी (m)	pākistānī
Pakistani (fem.)	पाकिस्तानी (f)	pākistānī
Pakistani (adj)	पाकिस्तानी	pākistānī
Saudi Arabia	सऊदी अरब (m)	saūdī arab
Arab (masc.)	अरब (m)	arab
Arab (fem.)	अरबी (f)	arabī
Arab, Arabic (adj)	अरबी	arabī

Thailand	थाईलैंड (m)	thaïlaind
Thai (masc.)	थाई (m)	thaï
Thai (fem.)	थाई (f)	thaï
Thai (adj)	थाई	thaï

Taiwan	ताइवान (m)	taivān
Taiwanese (masc.)	ताइवानी (m)	taivānī
Taiwanese (fem.)	ताइवानी (f)	taivānī
Taiwanese (adj)	ताइवानी	taivānī

Turkey	तुर्की (m)	turkī
Turk (masc.)	तुर्क (m)	turk
Turk (fem.)	तुर्क (m)	turk
Turkish (adj)	तुर्किश	turkish

Japan	जापान (m)	jāpān
Japanese (masc.)	जापानी (m)	jāpānī
Japanese (fem.)	जापानी (f)	jāpānī
Japanese (adj)	जापानी	jāpānī

Afghanistan	अफ़ग़ानिस्तान (m)	afagānistān
Bangladesh	बांग्लादेश (m)	bānglādesh
Indonesia	इण्डोनेशिया (m)	indoneshiya
Jordan	जॉर्डन (m)	jordan

Iraq	इराक़ (m)	irāq
Iran	इरान (m)	irān
Cambodia	कम्बोडिया (m)	kambodiya
Kuwait	कुवैत (m)	kuvait

Laos	लाओस (m)	laos
Myanmar	म्यांमर (m)	myāmmar
Nepal	नेपाल (m)	nepāl
United Arab Emirates	संयुक्त अरब अमीरात (m)	sanyukt arab amīrāt

| Syria | सीरिया (m) | sīriya |
| Palestine | फिलिस्तीन (m) | filistīn |

| South Korea | दक्षिण कोरिया (m) | dakshin koriya |
| North Korea | उत्तर कोरिया (m) | uttar koriya |

238. North America

United States of America	संयुक्त राज्य अमरीका (m)	sanyukt rājy amarīka
American (masc.)	अमरीकी (m)	amarīkī
American (fem.)	अमरीकी (f)	amarīkī
American (adj)	अमरीकी	amarīkī

| Canada | कनाडा (m) | kanāda |
| Canadian (masc.) | कैनेडियन (m) | kainediyan |

| Canadian (fem.) | कैनेडियन (f) | kainediyan |
| Canadian (adj) | कैनेडियन | kainediyan |

Mexico	मेक्सिको (m)	meksiko
Mexican (masc.)	मेक्सिकन (m)	meksikan
Mexican (fem.)	मेक्सिकन (f)	meksikan
Mexican (adj)	मेक्सिकन	meksikan

239. Central and South America

Argentina	अर्जेंटीना (m)	arjentīna
Argentinian (masc.)	अर्जेंटीनी (m)	arjentīnī
Argentinian (fem.)	अर्जेंटीनी (f)	arjentīnī
Argentinian (adj)	अर्जेंटीनी	arjentīnī

Brazil	ब्राज़ील (m)	brāzīl
Brazilian (masc.)	ब्राज़ीली (m)	brāzīlī
Brazilian (fem.)	ब्राज़ीली (f)	brāzīlī
Brazilian (adj)	ब्राज़ीली	brāzīlī

Colombia	कोलम्बिया (m)	kolambiya
Colombian (masc.)	कोलम्बियन (m)	kolambiyan
Colombian (fem.)	कोलम्बियन (f)	kolambiyan
Colombian (adj)	कोलम्बियन	kolambiyan

Cuba	क्यूबा (m)	kyūba
Cuban (masc.)	क्यूबन (m)	kyūban
Cuban (fem.)	क्यूबन (f)	kyūban
Cuban (adj)	क्यूबाई	kyūbaī

Chile	चिली (m)	chilī
Chilean (masc.)	चीलीयन (m)	chīlīyan
Chilean (fem.)	चीलीयन (f)	chīlīyan
Chilean (adj)	चीलीयन	chīlīyan

Bolivia	बोलीविया (m)	bolīviya
Venezuela	वेनेज़ुएला (m)	venezuela
Paraguay	परागुआ (m)	parāgua
Peru	पेरू (m)	perū

Suriname	सूरीनाम (m)	sūrīnām
Uruguay	उरुग्वे (m)	urugve
Ecuador	इक्वेडोर (m)	ikvedor

| The Bahamas | बहामा (m) | bahāma |
| Haiti | हाइटी (m) | haitī |

Dominican Republic	डोमिनिकन रिपब्लिक (m)	dominikan ripablik
Panama	पनामा (m)	panāma
Jamaica	जमैका (m)	jamaika

240. Africa

Egypt	मिस्र (m)	misr
Egyptian (masc.)	मिसरी (m)	misrī
Egyptian (fem.)	मिसरी (f)	misrī
Egyptian (adj)	मिसरी	misrī

Morocco	मोरक्को (m)	morakko
Moroccan (masc.)	मोरकन (m)	morakan
Moroccan (fem.)	मोरकन (f)	morakan
Moroccan (adj)	मोरकन	morakan

Tunisia	ट्युनीसिया (m)	tyunīsiya
Tunisian (masc.)	ट्युनीसियन (m)	tyunīsiyan
Tunisian (fem.)	ट्युनीसियन (f)	tyunīsiyan
Tunisian (adj)	ट्युनीसियन	tyunīsiyan

Ghana	घाना (m)	ghāna
Zanzibar	ज़ैंज़िबार (m)	zainzibār
Kenya	केन्या (m)	kenya

Libya	लीबिया (m)	lībiya
Madagascar	मडागास्कार (m)	madāgāskār
Namibia	नामीबिया (m)	nāmībiya

Senegal	सेनेगाल (m)	senegāl

Tanzania	तंज़ानिया (m)	tanzāniya
South Africa	दक्षिण अफ़्रीका (m)	dakshin afrīka

African (masc.)	अफ़्रीकी (m)	afrīkī
African (fem.)	अफ़्रीकी (f)	afrīkī
African (adj)	अफ़्रीकी	afrīkī

241. Australia. Oceania

Australia	आस्ट्रेलिया (m)	āstreliya
Australian (masc.)	आस्ट्रेलियन (m)	āstreliyan
Australian (fem.)	आस्ट्रेलियन (f)	āstreliyan
Australian (adj)	आस्ट्रेलियन	āstreliyan

New Zealand	न्यू ज़ीलैंड (m)	nyū zīlaind
New Zealander (masc.)	न्यू ज़ीलैंडियन (m)	nyū zīlaindiyan
New Zealander (fem.)	न्यू ज़ीलैंडियन (f)	nyū zīlaindiyan
New Zealand (as adj)	न्यू ज़ीलैंडियन	nyū zīlaindiyan

Tasmania	तास्मानिया (m)	tāsmāniya
French Polynesia	फ्रेंच पॉलीनेशिया (m)	french polīneshiya

242. Cities

Amsterdam	एम्स्टर्डैम (m)	emstardam
Ankara	अंकारा (m)	ankāra
Athens	एथेन्स (m)	ethens
Baghdad	बगदाद (m)	bagadād
Bangkok	बैंकॉक (m)	bainkok
Barcelona	बार्सिलोना (m)	bārsilona
Beijing	बीजिंग (m)	bījing
Beirut	बेरूत (m)	berūt
Berlin	बर्लिन (m)	barlin
Mumbai (Bombay)	मुम्बई (m)	mumbī
Bonn	बॉन (m)	bon
Bordeaux	बोर्दो (m)	bordo
Bratislava	ब्राटीस्लावा (m)	brātīslāva
Brussels	ब्रसेल्स (m)	brasels
Bucharest	बुखारेस्ट (m)	bukhārest
Budapest	बुडापेस्ट (m)	budāpest
Cairo	काहिरा (m)	kāhira
Kolkata (Calcutta)	कोलकाता (m)	kolakāta
Chicago	शिकागो (m)	shikāgo
Copenhagen	कोपनहेगन (m)	kopanahegan
Dar-es-Salaam	दार-एस-सलाम (m)	dār-es-salām
Delhi	दिल्ली (f)	dillī
Dubai	दुबई (m)	dubī
Dublin	डब्लिन (m)	dablin
Düsseldorf	डसेलडोर्फ़ (m)	daseladorf
Florence	फ़्लोरेंस (m)	florens
Frankfurt	फ़्रैंकफ़र्ट (m)	frainkfart
Geneva	जेनेवा (m)	jeneva
The Hague	हेग (m)	heg
Hamburg	हैम्बर्ग (m)	haimbarg
Hanoi	हनोई (m)	hanoī
Havana	हवाना (m)	havāna
Helsinki	हेलसिंकी (m)	helasinkī
Hiroshima	हिरोशीमा (m)	hiroshīma
Hong Kong	हांगकांग (m)	hāngakāng
Istanbul	इस्तांबुल (m)	istāmbul
Jerusalem	यरूशलम (m)	yarūshalam
Kyiv	कीव (m)	kīv
Kuala Lumpur	कुआला लुम्पुर (m)	kuāla lumpur
Lisbon	लिस्बन (m)	lisban
London	लंदन (m)	landan
Los Angeles	लॉस एंजेलेस (m)	los enjeles

Lyons	लिओन (m)	lion
Madrid	मेड्रिड (m)	medrid
Marseille	मार्सेल (m)	mārsel
Mexico City	मेक्सिको सिटी (f)	meksiko sitī
Miami	मियामी (m)	miyāmī
Montreal	मांट्रियल (m)	māntriyal
Moscow	मॉस्को (m)	mosko
Munich	म्यूनिख़ (m)	myūnikh

Nairobi	नैरोबी (m)	nairobī
Naples	नेपल्स (m)	nepals
New York	न्यू यॉर्क (m)	nyū york
Nice	नीस (m)	nīs
Oslo	ओस्लो (m)	oslo
Ottawa	ओटावा (m)	otāva

Paris	पेरिस (m)	peris
Prague	प्राग (m)	prāg
Rio de Janeiro	रिओ डे जैनेरो (m)	rio de jainero
Rome	रोम (m)	rom

Saint Petersburg	सेंट पीटरस्बर्ग (m)	sent pītarasbarg
Seoul	सियोल (m)	siyol
Shanghai	शंघाई (m)	shanghaī
Singapore	सिंगापुर (m)	singāpur
Stockholm	स्टॉकहोम (m)	stokahom
Sydney	सिडनी (m)	sidanī

Taipei	ताइपे (m)	taipe
Tokyo	टोकियो (m)	tokiyo
Toronto	टोरोन्टो (m)	toronto

Venice	वीनिस (m)	vīnis
Vienna	विएना (m)	viena
Warsaw	वॉरसों (m)	voraso
Washington	वॉशिंग्टन (m)	voshingtan

243. Politics. Government. Part 1

politics	राजनीति (f)	rājanīti
political (adj)	राजनीतिक	rājanītik
politician	राजनीतिज्ञ (m)	rājanītigy

state (country)	राज्य (m)	rājy
citizen	नागरिक (m)	nāgarik
citizenship	नागरिकता (f)	nāgarikata

national emblem	राष्ट्रीय प्रतीक (m)	rāshtrīy pratīk
national anthem	राष्ट्रीय धुन (f)	rāshtrīy dhun
government	सरकार (m)	sarakār

head of state	देश का नेता (m)	desh ka neta
parliament	संसद (m)	sansad
party	दल (m)	dal
capitalism	पुंजीवाद (m)	punjīvād
capitalist (adj)	पुंजीवादी	punjīvādī
socialism	समाजवाद (m)	samājavād
socialist (adj)	समाजवादी	samājavādī
communism	साम्यवाद (m)	sāmyavād
communist (adj)	साम्यवादी	sāmyavādī
communist (n)	साम्यवादी (m)	sāmyavādī
democracy	प्रजातंत्र (m)	prajātantr
democrat	प्रजातंत्रवादी (m)	prajātantravādī
democratic (adj)	प्रजातंत्रवादी	prajātantravādī
Democratic party	प्रजातंत्रवादी पार्टी (m)	prajātantravādī pārtī
liberal (n)	उदारवादी (m)	udāravādī
liberal (adj)	उदारवादी	udāravādī
conservative (n)	रूढ़िवादी (m)	rūrhivādī
conservative (adj)	रूढ़िवादी	rūrhivādī
republic (n)	गणतंत्र (m)	ganatantr
republican (n)	गणतंत्रवादी (m)	ganatantravādī
Republican party	गणतंत्रवादी पार्टी (m)	ganatantravādī pārtī
elections	चुनाव (m pl)	chunāv
to elect (vt)	चुनना	chunana
elector, voter	मतदाता (m)	matadāta
election campaign	चुनाव प्रचार (m)	chunāv prachār
voting (n)	मतदान (m)	matadān
to vote (vi)	मत डालना	mat dālana
suffrage, right to vote	मताधिकार (m)	matādhikār
candidate	उम्मीदवार (m)	ummīdavār
to be a candidate	चुनाव लड़ना	chunāv larana
campaign	अभियान (m)	abhiyān
opposition (as adj)	विरोधी	virodhī
opposition (n)	विरोध (m)	virodh
visit	यात्रा (f)	yātra
official visit	सरकारी यात्रा (f)	sarakārī yātra
international (adj)	अंतरराष्ट्रीय	antarrāshtrīy
negotiations	वार्ता (f pl)	vārtta
to negotiate (vi)	वार्ता करना	vārtta karana

244. Politics. Government. Part 2

society	समाज (m)	samāj
constitution	संविधान (m)	sanvidhān
power (political control)	शासन (m)	shāsan
corruption	भ्रष्टाचार (m)	bhrashtāchār
law (justice)	कानून (m)	kānūn
legal (legitimate)	कानूनी	kānūnī
justice (fairness)	न्याय (m)	nyāy
just (fair)	न्यायी	nyāyī
committee	समिति (f)	samiti
bill (draft law)	विधेयक (m)	vidheyak
budget	बजट (m)	bajat
policy	नीति (f)	nīti
reform	सुधार (m)	sudhār
radical (adj)	आमूल	āmūl
power (strength, force)	ताकत (f)	tākat
powerful (adj)	प्रबल	prabal
supporter	समर्थक (m)	samarthak
influence	असर (m)	asar
regime (e.g., military ~)	शासन (m)	shāsan
conflict	टकराव (m)	takarāv
conspiracy (plot)	साज़िश (f)	sāzish
provocation	उकसाव (m)	ukasāv
to overthrow (regime, etc.)	तख़्ता पलटना	takhta palatana
overthrow (of government)	तख़्ता पलट (m)	takhta palat
revolution	क्रांति (f)	krānti
coup d'état	तख़्ता पलट (m)	takhta palat
military coup	फ़ौजी बगावत (f)	faujī bagāvat
crisis	संकट (m)	sankat
economic recession	आर्थिक मंदी (f)	ārthik mandī
demonstrator (protester)	प्रदर्शक (m)	pradarshak
demonstration	प्रदर्शन (m)	pradarshan
martial law	फ़ौजी कानून (m)	faujī kānūn
military base	सैन्य अड्डा (m)	sainy adda
stability	स्थिरता (f)	sthirata
stable (adj)	स्थिर	sthir
exploitation	शोषण (m)	shoshan
to exploit (workers)	शोषण करना	shoshan karana
racism	जातिवाद (m)	jātivād
racist	जातिवादी (m)	jātivādī

| fascism | फ़ासिवादी (m) | fāsivādī |
| fascist | फ़ासिस्ट (m) | fāsist |

245. Countries. Miscellaneous

foreigner	विदेशी (m)	videshī
foreign (adj)	विदेश	videsh
abroad (in a foreign country)	परदेश में	paradesh men

emigrant	प्रवासी (m)	pravāsī
emigration	प्रवासन (m)	pravāsan
to emigrate (vi)	प्रवास करना	pravās karana

the West	पश्चिम (m)	pashchim
the East	पूर्व (m)	pūrv
the Far East	सुदूर पूर्व (m)	sudūr pūrv

civilization	सभ्यता (f)	sabhyata
humanity (mankind)	मानवजाति (f)	mānavajāti
the world (earth)	संसार (m)	sansār
peace	शांति (f)	shānti
worldwide (adj)	विश्वव्यापी	vishvavyāpī

homeland	मातृभूमि (f)	mātrbhūmi
people (population)	जनता (m)	janata
population	जनता (m)	janata

people (a lot of ~)	लोग (m)	log
nation (people)	जाति (f)	jāti
generation	पीढ़ी (f)	pīrhī

territory (area)	प्रदेश (m)	pradesh
region	क्षेत्र (m)	kshetr
state (part of a country)	राज्य (m)	rājy

tradition	रिवाज़ (m)	rivāz
custom (tradition)	परम्परा (m)	parampara
ecology	परिस्थितिकी (f)	paristhitikī

Indian (Native American)	रेड इंडियन (m)	red indiyan
Gypsy (masc.)	जिप्सी (f)	jipsī
Gypsy (fem.)	जिप्सी (f)	jipsī
Gypsy (adj)	जिप्सी	jipsī

empire	साम्राज्य (m)	sāmrājy
colony	उपनिवेश (m)	upanivesh
slavery	दासता (f)	dāsata
invasion	हमला (m)	hamala
famine	भूखमरी (f)	bhūkhamarī

246. Major religious groups. Confessions

religion	धर्म (m)	dharm
religious (adj)	धार्मिक	dhārmik
faith, belief	धर्म (m)	dharm
to believe (in God)	आस्था रखना	āstha rakhana
believer	आस्तिक (m)	āstik
atheism	नास्तिकवाद (m)	nāstikavād
atheist	नास्तिक (m)	nāstik
Christianity	ईसाई धर्म (m)	īsaī dharm
Christian (n)	ईसाई (m)	īsaī
Christian (adj)	ईसाई	īsaī
Catholicism	कैथोलिक धर्म (m)	kaitholik dharm
Catholic (n)	कैथोलिक (m)	kaitholik
Catholic (adj)	कैथोलिक	kaitholik
Protestantism	प्रोटेस्टेंट धर्म (m)	protestent dharm
Protestant Church	प्रोटेस्टेंट चर्च (m)	protestent charch
Protestant (n)	प्रोटेस्टेंट (m)	protestent
Orthodoxy	ऑर्थीडॉक्सी (m)	orthodoksī
Orthodox Church	ऑर्थीडॉक्स चर्च (m)	orthodoks charch
Orthodox (n)	ऑर्थीडॉक्सी (m)	orthodoksī
Presbyterianism	प्रेस्बिटेरियनवाद (m)	presbiteriyanavād
Presbyterian Church	प्रेस्बिटेरियन चर्च (m)	presbiteriyan charch
Presbyterian (n)	प्रेस्बिटेरियन (m)	presbiteriyan
Lutheranism	लुथर धर्म (m)	luthar dharm
Lutheran (n)	लुथर (m)	luthar
Baptist Church	बैप्टिस्ट चर्च (m)	baiptist charch
Baptist (n)	बैप्टिस्ट (m)	baiptist
Anglican Church	अंग्रेज़ी चर्च (m)	angrezī charch
Anglican (n)	अंग्रेज़ी (m)	angrezī
Mormonism	मोर्मनवाद (m)	mormanavād
Mormon (n)	मोर्मन (m)	morman
Judaism	यहूदी धर्म (m)	yahūdī dharm
Jew (n)	यहूदी (m)	yahūdī
Buddhism	बौद्ध धर्म (m)	bauddh dharm
Buddhist (n)	बौद्ध (m)	bauddh
Hinduism	हिन्दू धर्म (m)	hindū dharm
Hindu (n)	हिन्दू (m)	hindū

Islam	इस्लाम (m)	islām
Muslim (n)	मुस्लिम (m)	muslim
Muslim (adj)	मुस्लिम	muslim

Shiah Islam	शिया इस्लाम (m)	shiya islām
Shiite (n)	शिया (m)	shiya
Sunni Islam	सुन्नी इस्लाम (m)	sunnī islām
Sunnite (n)	सुन्नी (m)	sunnī

247. Religions. Priests

| priest | पादरी (m) | pādarī |
| the Pope | पोप (m) | pop |

monk, friar	मठवासी (m)	mathavāsī
nun	नन (f)	nan
pastor	पादरी (m)	pādarī

abbot	एब्बट (m)	ebbat
vicar (parish priest)	विकार (m)	vikār
bishop	बिशप (m)	bishap
cardinal	कार्डिनल (m)	kārdinal

preacher	प्रीचर (m)	prīchar
preaching	धर्मोपदेश (m)	dharmopadesh
parishioners	ग्रामवासी (m)	grāmavāsī

| believer | आस्तिक (m) | āstik |
| atheist | नास्तिक (m) | nāstik |

248. Faith. Christianity. Islam

| Adam | आदम (m) | ādam |
| Eve | हव्वा (f) | havva |

God	भगवान (m)	bhagavān
the Lord	ईश्वर (m)	īshvar
the Almighty	सर्वशक्तिशाली (m)	sarvashaktishālī

sin	पाप (m)	pāp
to sin (vi)	पाप करना	pāp karana
sinner (masc.)	पापी (m)	pāpī
sinner (fem.)	पापी (f)	pāpī

hell	नरक (m)	narak
paradise	जन्नत (m)	jannat
Jesus	ईसा (m)	īsa
Jesus Christ	ईसा मसीह (m)	īsa masīh

the Holy Spirit	पवित्र आत्मा (m)	pavitr ātma
the Savior	मुक्तिदाता (m)	muktidāta
the Virgin Mary	वर्जिन मैरी (f)	varjin mairī

the Devil	शैतान (m)	shaitān
devil's (adj)	शैतानी	shaitānī
Satan	शैतान (m)	shaitān
satanic (adj)	शैतानी	shaitānī

angel	फरिश्ता (m)	farishta
guardian angel	देवदूत (m)	devadūt
angelic (adj)	देवदूतीय	devadūtīy

apostle	धर्मदूत (m)	dharmadūt
archangel	महादेवदूत (m)	mahādevadūt
the Antichrist	ईसा मसीह का शत्रु (m)	īsa masīh ka shatru

Church	गिरजाघर (m)	girajāghar
Bible	बाइबिल (m)	baibil
biblical (adj)	बाइबिल का	baibil ka

Old Testament	ओल्ड टेस्टामेंट (m)	old testāment
New Testament	न्यू टेस्टामेंट (m)	nyū testāment
Gospel	धर्मसिद्धान्त (m)	dharmasiddhānt
Holy Scripture	धर्म ग्रंथ (m)	dharm granth
Heaven	स्वर्ग (m)	svarg

Commandment	धर्मादेश (m)	dharmādesh
prophet	पैगंबर (m)	paigambar
prophecy	आगामवाणी (f)	āgāmavānī

Allah	अल्लाह (m)	allāh
Mohammed	मुहम्मद (m)	muhammad
the Koran	क़ुरान (m)	qurān

mosque	मस्जिद (m)	masjid
mullah	मुल्ला (m)	mulla
prayer	दुआ (f)	dua
to pray (vi, vt)	दुआ करना	dua karana

pilgrimage	तीर्थ यात्रा (m)	tīrth yātra
pilgrim	तीर्थ यात्री (m)	tīrth yātrī
Mecca	मक्का (m)	makka

church	गिरजाघर (m)	girajāghar
temple	मंदिर (m)	mandir
cathedral	गिरजाघर (m)	girajāghar
Gothic (adj)	गोथिक	gothik
synagogue	सीनागोग (m)	sīnāgog
mosque	मस्जिद (m)	masjid
chapel	चैपल (m)	chaipal
abbey	ईसाई मठ (m)	īsaī math

convent	मठ (m)	math
monastery	मठ (m)	math
bell (church ~s)	घंटा (m)	ghanta
bell tower	घंटाघर (m)	ghantāghar
to ring (ab. bells)	बजाना	bajāna
cross	क्रॉस (m)	kros
cupola (roof)	गुंबद (m)	gumbad
icon	देव प्रतिमा (f)	dev pratima
soul	आत्मा (f)	ātma
fate (destiny)	भाग्य (f)	bhāgy
evil (n)	बुराई (f)	buraī
good (n)	भलाई (f)	bhalaī
vampire	पिशाच (m)	pishāch
witch (evil ~)	डायन (f)	dāyan
demon	असुर (m)	asur
spirit	आत्मा (f)	ātma
redemption (giving us ~)	प्रायश्चित (m)	prayāshchit
to redeem (vt)	प्रायश्चित करना	prayāshchit karana
church service, mass	धार्मिक सेवा (m)	dhārmik seva
to say mass	उपासना करना	upāsana karana
confession	पापस्वीकरण (m)	pāpasvīkaran
to confess (vi)	पापस्वीकरण करना	pāpasvīkaran karana
saint (n)	संत (m)	sant
sacred (holy)	पवित्र	pavitr
holy water	पवित्र पानी (m)	pavitr pānī
ritual (n)	अनुष्ठान (m)	anushthān
ritual (adj)	सांस्कारिक	sānskārik
sacrifice	कुरबानी (f)	kurabānī
superstition	अंधविश्वास (m)	andhavishvās
superstitious (adj)	अंधविश्वासी	andhavishvāsī
afterlife	परलोक (m)	paralok
eternal life	अमर जीवन (m)	amar jīvan

MISCELLANEOUS

249. Various useful words

background (green ~)	पृष्टिका (f)	prshtika
balance (of situation)	संतुलन (m)	santulan
barrier (obstacle)	बाधा (f)	bādha
base (basis)	आधार (m)	ādhār
beginning	शुरु (m)	shurū
category	श्रेणी (f)	shrenī
cause (reason)	कारण (m)	kāran
choice	चुनाव (m)	chunāv
coincidence	समकालीनता (f)	samakālīnata
comfortable (~ chair)	आरामदेह	ārāmadeh
comparison	तुलना (f)	tulana
compensation	क्षतिपुर्ति (f)	kshatipurti
degree (extent, amount)	मात्रा (f)	mātra
development	विकास (m)	vikās
difference	फ़र्क़ (m)	fark
effect (e.g., of drugs)	प्रभाव (m)	prabhāv
effort (exertion)	प्रयत्न (m)	prayatn
element	तत्व (m)	tatv
end (finish)	ख़त्म (m)	khatm
example (illustration)	उदाहरण (m)	udāharan
fact	तथ्य (m)	tathy
frequent (adj)	बारंबार	bārambār
growth (development)	वृद्धि (f)	vrddhi
help	सहायता (f)	sahāyata
ideal	आदर्श (m)	ādarsh
kind (sort, type)	प्रकार (m)	prakār
labyrinth	भूलभुलैया (f)	bhūlabhulaiya
mistake, error	ग़लती (f)	galatī
moment	पल (m)	pal
object (thing)	चीज़ें (f)	chīzen
obstacle	अवरोध (m)	avarodh
original (original copy)	मूल (m)	mūl
part (~ of sth)	भाग (m)	bhāg
particle, small part	टुकड़ा (m)	tukara
pause (break)	विराम (m)	virām

position	स्थिति (f)	sthiti
principle	उसूल (m)	usūl
problem	समस्या (f)	samasya
process	प्रक्रिया (f)	prakriya
progress	उन्नति (f)	unnati
property (quality)	गुण (m)	gun
reaction	प्रतिक्रिया (f)	pratikriya
risk	जोखिम (m)	jokhim
secret	रहस्य (m)	rahasy
series	श्रृंखला (f)	shrrnkhala
shape (outer form)	रूप (m)	rūp
situation	स्थिति (f)	sthiti
solution	हल (m)	hal
standard (adj)	मानक	mānak
standard (level of quality)	मानक (m)	mānak
stop (pause)	विराम (m)	virām
style	शैली (f)	shailī
system	प्रणाली (f)	pranālī
table (chart)	सारणी (f)	sāranī
tempo, rate	गति (f)	gati
term (word, expression)	पारिभाषिक शब्द (m)	pāribhāshik shabd
thing (object, item)	वस्तु (f)	vastu
truth (e.g., moment of ~)	सच (m)	sach
turn (please wait your ~)	बारी (f)	bārī
type (sort, kind)	ढंग (m)	dhang
urgent (adj)	अत्यावश्यक	atyāvashyak
urgently (adv)	तत्काल	tatkāl
utility (usefulness)	उपयोग (m)	upayog
variant (alternative)	विकल्प (m)	vikalp
way (means, method)	तरीका (m)	tarīka
zone	क्षेत्र (m)	kshetr

250. Modifiers. Adjectives. Part 1

additional (adj)	अतिरिक्त	atirikt
ancient (~ civilization)	प्राचीन	prāchīn
artificial (adj)	कृत्रिम	krtrim
back, rear (adj)	पिछा	pichha
bad (adj)	बुरा	bura
beautiful (~ palace)	सुंदर	sundar
beautiful (person)	सुंदर	sundar
big (in size)	बड़ा	bara

bitter (taste)	कड़वा	karava
blind (sightless)	अंधा	andha
calm, quiet (adj)	शांत	shānt
careless (negligent)	लापरवाह	lāparavāh
caring (~ father)	विचारशील	vichārashīl
central (adj)	केंद्रीय	kendrīy
cheap (low-priced)	सस्ता	sasta
cheerful (adj)	हँसमुख	hansamukh
children's (adj)	बच्चों का	bachchon ka
civil (~ law)	नागरिक	nāgarik
clandestine (secret)	गुप्त	gupt
clean (free from dirt)	साफ़	sāf
clear (explanation, etc.)	साफ़	sāf
clever (smart)	बुद्धिमान	buddhimān
close (near in space)	समीप	samīp
closed (adj)	बंद	band
cloudless (sky)	निर्मेघ	nirmegh
cold (drink, weather)	ठंडा	thanda
compatible (adj)	अनुकूल	anukūl
contented (satisfied)	संतुष्ट	santusht
continuous (uninterrupted)	निरंतर	nirantar
cool (weather)	ठंडा	thanda
dangerous (adj)	खतरनाक	khataranāk
dark (room)	अंधेरा	andhera
dead (not alive)	मृत	mrt
dense (fog, smoke)	घना	ghana
destitute (extremely poor)	गरीब	garīb
different (not the same)	भिन्न	bhinn
difficult (decision)	मुश्किल	mushkil
difficult (problem, task)	कठिन	kathin
dim, faint (light)	धुंधला	dhundhala
dirty (not clean)	मैला	maila
distant (in space)	दूर	dūr
dry (clothes, etc.)	सूखा	sūkha
easy (not difficult)	आसान	āsān
empty (glass, room)	खाली	khālī
even (e.g., ~ surface)	समतल	samatal
exact (amount)	ठीक	thīk
excellent (adj)	उत्कृष्ट	utkrsht
excessive (adj)	अत्यधिक	atyadhik
expensive (adj)	महंगा	mahanga
exterior (adj)	बाहरी	bāharī
far (the ~ East)	सुदूर	sudūr

fast (quick)	तेज़	tez
fatty (food)	चरबीला	charabīla
fertile (land, soil)	उपजाऊ	upajaū
flat (~ panel display)	सपाट	sapāt
foreign (adj)	विदेश	videsh
fragile (china, glass)	नाज़ुक	nāzuk
free (at no cost)	मुफ़्त	muft
free (unrestricted)	मुक्त	mukt
fresh (~ water)	ताज़ा	tāza
fresh (e.g., ~ bread)	ताज़ा	tāza
frozen (food)	जमा	jama
full (completely filled)	भरा	bhara
gloomy (house, forecast)	विषादपूर्ण	vishādapūrn
good (book, etc.)	अच्छा	achchha
good, kind (kindhearted)	नेक	nek
grateful (adj)	आभारी	ābhārī
happy (adj)	प्रसन्न	prasann
hard (not soft)	कड़ा	kara
heavy (in weight)	भारी	bhārī
hostile (adj)	शत्रुतापूर्ण	shatrutāpūrn
hot (adj)	गरम	garam
huge (adj)	विशाल	vishāl
humid (adj)	नमी	namī
hungry (adj)	भूखा	bhūkha
ill (sick, unwell)	बीमार	bīmār
immobile (adj)	अचल	achal
important (adj)	महत्वपूर्ण	mahatvapūrn
impossible (adj)	असंभव	asambhav
incomprehensible	समझ से बाहर	samajh se bāhar
indispensable (adj)	ज़रूरी	zarūrī
inexperienced (adj)	अनुभवहीन	anubhavahīn
insignificant (adj)	महत्वहीन	mahatvahīn
interior (adj)	आंतरिक	āntarik
joint (~ decision)	संयुक्त	sanyukt
last (e.g., ~ week)	पिछला	pichhala
last (final)	आखिरी	ākhirī
left (e.g., ~ side)	बायाँ	bāyān
legal (legitimate)	कानूनी	kānūnī
light (in weight)	हल्का	halka
light (pale color)	हल्का	halka
limited (adj)	सीमित	sīmit
liquid (fluid)	तरल	taral
long (e.g., ~ hair)	लंबा	lamba

| loud (voice, etc.) | ऊंचा | ūncha |
| low (voice) | धीमा | dhīma |

251. Modifiers. Adjectives. Part 2

main (principal)	मुख्य	mukhy
matt, matte	मैट	mait
meticulous (job)	सुव्यवस्थित	suvvavasthit
mysterious (adj)	रहस्यपूर्ण	rahasyapūrn
narrow (street, etc.)	तंग	tang

native (~ country)	देसी	desī
nearby (adj)	निकट	nikat
nearsighted (adj)	निकटदर्शी	nikatadarshī
needed (necessary)	ज़रूरी	zarūrī
negative (~ response)	नकारात्मक	nakārātmak

neighboring (adj)	पड़ोस	paros
nervous (adj)	बेचैन	bechain
new (adj)	नया	naya
next (e.g., ~ week)	अगला	agala

nice (kind)	दयालु	dayālu
nice (voice)	अच्छा	achchha
normal (adj)	साधारण	sādhāran
not big (adj)	बड़ा नहीं	bara nahin
not difficult (adj)	आसान	āsān

obligatory (adj)	अनिवार्य	anivāry
old (house)	पुराना	purāna
open (adj)	खुला	khula
opposite (adj)	उल्टा	ulta

ordinary (usual)	आम	ām
original (unusual)	मूल	mūl
past (recent)	बीता हुआ	bīta hua
permanent (adj)	स्थायी	sthāyī
personal (adj)	व्यक्तिगत	vyaktigat

polite (adj)	विनम्र	vinamr
poor (not rich)	गरीब	garīb
possible (adj)	संभव	sambhav
present (current)	वर्तमान	vartamān

principal (main)	मूल	mūl
private (~ jet)	निजी	nijī
probable (adj)	मुमकिन	mumakin
prolonged (e.g., ~ applause)	दीर्घकालिक	dīrghakālik
public (open to all)	सार्वजनिक	sārvajanik

punctual (person)	ठीक	thīk
quiet (tranquil)	शांत	shānt
rare (adj)	असाधारण	asādhāran
raw (uncooked)	कच्चा	kachcha
right (not left)	दायां	dāyān

right, correct (adj)	ठीक	thīk
ripe (fruit)	पक्का	pakka
risky (adj)	खतरनाक	khataranāk
sad (~ look)	उदास	udās

sad (depressing)	उदास	udās
safe (not dangerous)	सुरक्षित	surakshit
salty (food)	नमकीन	namakīn
satisfied (customer)	संतुष्ट	santusht

second hand (adj)	इस्तेमाल किया हुआ	istemāl kiya hua
shallow (water)	उथला	uthala
sharp (blade, etc.)	तेज़	tez
short (in length)	छोटा	chhota

short, short-lived (adj)	अल्पकालिक	alpakālik
significant (notable)	महत्वपूर्ण	mahatvapūrn
similar (adj)	मिलता-जुलता	milata-julata
simple (easy)	सरल	saral
skinny	पतला	patala

small (in size)	छोटा	chhota
smooth (surface)	समतल	samatal
soft (~ toys)	नरम	naram
solid (~ wall)	मज़बूत	mazabūt

sour (flavor, taste)	खट्टा	khatta
spacious (house, etc.)	विस्तृत	vistrt
special (adj)	ख़ास	khās
straight (line, road)	सीधा	sīdha
strong (person)	शक्तिशाली	shaktishālī

stupid (foolish)	बेवकूफ़	bevakūf
suitable (e.g., ~ for drinking)	उचित	uchit
sunny (day)	सूरज का	sūraj ka
superb, perfect (adj)	उत्तम	uttam
swarthy (adj)	काले मुँख का	kāle munkh ka

sweet (sugary)	मीठा	mītha
tan (adj)	सांवला	sānvala
tasty (delicious)	मज़ेदार	mazedār
tender (affectionate)	नाज़ुक	nāzuk
the highest (adj)	उच्चतम	uchchatam
the most important	सबसे महत्वपूर्ण	sabase mahatvapūrn
the nearest	निकटतम	nikatatam

the same, equal (adj)	समान	samān
thick (e.g., ~ fog)	घना	ghana
thick (wall, slice)	मोटा	mota
thin (person)	दुबला	dubala
tired (exhausted)	थका	thaka
tiring (adj)	थकाऊ	thakaū
transparent (adj)	पारदर्शी	pāradarshī
unclear (adj)	धुंधला	dhundhala
unique (exceptional)	अद्वितीय	advitīy
various (adj)	विभिन्न	vibhinn
warm (moderately hot)	गरम	garam
wet (e.g., ~ clothes)	भीगा	bhīga
whole (entire, complete)	पूरा	pūra
wide (e.g., ~ road)	चौड़ा	chaura
young (adj)	जवान	javān

MAIN 500 VERBS

252. Verbs A-C

to accompany (vt)	साथ चलना	sāth chalana
to accuse (vt)	आरोप लगाना	ārop lagāna
to acknowledge (admit)	मानना	mānana
to act (take action)	करना	karana
to add (supplement)	और डालना	aur dālana
to address (speak to)	संबोधित करना	sambodhit karana
to admire (vi)	सराहना	sarāhana
to advertise (vt)	विज्ञापन देना	vigyāpan dena
to advise (vt)	सलाह देना	salāh dena
to affirm (assert)	स्वीकार करना	svīkār karana
to agree (say yes)	राज़ी होना	rāzī hona
to aim (to point a weapon)	निशाना लगाना	nishāna lagāna
to allow (sb to do sth)	अनुमति देना	anumati dena
to amputate (vt)	अंगविच्छेद करना	angavichchhed karana
to answer (vi, vt)	जवाब देना	javāb dena
to apologize (vi)	माफ़ी मांगना	māfī māngana
to appear (come into view)	सामने आना	sāmane āna
to applaud (vi, vt)	तालियां बजाना	tāliyān bajāna
to appoint (assign)	तय करना	tay karana
to approach (come closer)	पास आना	pās āna
to arrive (ab. train)	पहुंचना	pahunchana
to ask (~ sb to do sth)	कहना	kahana
to aspire to …	… की महत्त्वाकांक्षा करना	… kī mahattvākānksha karana
to assist (help)	मदद करना	madad karana
to attack (mil.)	हमला करना	hamala karana
to attain (objectives)	पाना	pāna
to avenge (get revenge)	बदला लेना	badala lena
to avoid (danger, task)	टालना	tālana
to award (give medal to)	पुरस्कार देना	puraskār dena
to battle (vi)	झगड़ना	jhagarana
to be (vi)	होना	hona
to be a cause of …	की वजह होना	kī vajah hona
to be afraid	डरना	darana

to be angry (with ...)	क्रोध में आना	krodh men āna
to be at war	युद्ध करना	yuddh karana
to be based (on ...)	आधारित होना	ādhārit hona
to be bored	ऊबना	ūbana
to be convinced	यकीन आना	yakīn āna
to be enough	बहुत हो जाना	bahut ho jāna
to be envious	ईर्ष्या करना	īrshya karana
to be indignant	गुस्से में आना	gusse men āna
to be interested in ...	रुचि लेना	ruchi lena
to be lost in thought	ख़यालों में गुम रहना	khyālon men gum rahana
to be lying (~ on the table)	रखा होना	rakha hona
to be needed	आवश्यक होना	āvashyak hona
to be perplexed (puzzled)	सटपटाना	satapatāna
to be preserved	बचाना	bachāna
to be required	ज़रूरी होना	zarūrī hona
to be surprised	हैरान होना	hairān hona
to be worried	फ़िक्र होना	fikr hona
to beat (to hit)	पीटना	pītana
to become (e.g., ~ old)	हो जाना	ho jāna
to behave (vi)	बरताव करना	baratāv karana
to believe (think)	विश्वास करना	vishvās karana
to belong to ...	स्वामी होना	svāmī hona
to berth (moor)	किनारे लगाना	kināre lagāna
to blind (other drivers)	अंधा करना	andha karana
to blow (wind)	फूंकना	fūnkana
to blush (vi)	चेहरा लाल होना	chehara lāl hona
to boast (vi)	डींग मारना	dīng mārana
to borrow (money)	कर्ज़ लेना	karz lena
to break (branch, toy, etc.)	तोड़ना	torana
to breathe (vi)	साँस लेना	sāns lena
to bring (sth)	लाना	lāna
to burn (paper, logs)	जलाना	jalāna
to buy (purchase)	खरीदना	kharīdana
to call (~ for help)	बुलाना	bulāna
to call (yell for sb)	बुलाना	bulāna
to calm down (vt)	शांत करना	shānt karana
can (v aux)	सकना	sakana
to cancel (call off)	रद्द करना	radd karana
to cast off (of a boat or ship)	फेंक देना	fenk dena
to catch (e.g., ~ a ball)	पकड़ना	pakarana
to change (~ one's opinion)	बदलना	badalana

to change (exchange)	बदलाना	badalāna
to charm (vt)	मोहना	mohana
to choose (select)	चुनना	chunana
to chop off (with an ax)	काटना	kātana
to clean (e.g., kettle from scale)	साफ़ करना	sāf karana
to clean (shoes, etc.)	साफ़ करना	sāf karana
to clean up (tidy)	साफ़ करना	sāf karana
to close (vt)	बंद करना	band karana
to comb one's hair	अपने बालों में कंघी करना	apane bālon men kanghī karana
to come down (the stairs)	उतरना	utarana
to come out (book)	छापना	chhāpana
to compare (vt)	तुलना करना	tulana karana
to compensate (vt)	क्षतिपूर्ति करना	kshatipūrti karana
to compete (vi)	प्रतियोगिता करना	pratiyogita karana
to compile (~ a list)	संकलन करना	sankalan karana
to complain (vi, vt)	शिकायत करना	shikāyat karana
to complicate (vt)	उलझाना	ulajhāna
to compose (music, etc.)	रचना	rachana
to compromise (reputation)	समझौता करना	samajhauta karana
to concentrate (vi)	ध्यान देना	dhyān dena
to confess (criminal)	मानना	mānana
to confuse (mix up)	उलट-पलट करना	ulat-palat karana
to congratulate (vt)	बधाई देना	badhaī dena
to consult (doctor, expert)	सलाह करना	salāh karana
to continue (~ to do sth)	जारी रखना	jārī rakhana
to control (vt)	नियंत्रित करना	niyantrit karana
to convince (vt)	यकीन दिलाना	yakīn dilāna
to cooperate (vi)	सहयोग करना	sahayog karana
to coordinate (vt)	समन्वय करना	samanvay karana
to correct (an error)	ठीक करना	thīk karana
to cost (vt)	दाम होना	dām hona
to count (money, etc.)	गिनना	ginana
to count on ...	भरोसा रखना	bharosa rakhana
to crack (ceiling, wall)	चीर पड़ना	chīr parana
to create (vt)	बनाना	banāna
to crush, to squash (~ a bug)	कुचलना	kuchalana
to cry (weep)	रोना	rona
to cut off (with a knife)	काटना	kātana

253. Verbs D-G

to dare (~ to do sth)	साहस करना	sāhas karana
to date from ...	तारीख़ डालना	tārīkh dālana
to deceive (vi, vt)	धोखा देना	dhokha dena
to decide (~ to do sth)	फ़ैसला करना	faisala karana
to decorate (tree, street)	सजाना	sajāna
to dedicate (book, etc.)	अर्पित करना	arpit karana
to defend (a country, etc.)	रक्षा करना	raksha karana
to defend oneself	रक्षा करना	raksha karana
to demand (request firmly)	माँगना	māngana
to denounce (vt)	आरोप लगाना	ārop lagāna
to deny (vt)	नकारना	nakārana
to depend on ...	निर्भर होना	nirbhar hona
to deprive (vt)	वंचित करना	vanchit karana
to deserve (vt)	लायक होना	lāyak hona
to design (machine, etc.)	डिज़ाइन बनाना	dizain banāna
to desire (want, wish)	चाहना	chāhana
to despise (vt)	नफ़रत करना	nafarat karana
to destroy (documents, etc.)	तबाह करना	tabāh karana
to differ (from sth)	फ़र्क़ होना	fark hona
to dig (tunnel, etc.)	खोदना	khodana
to direct (point the way)	रास्ता बताना	rāsta batāna
to disappear (vi)	गायब होना	gāyab hona
to discover (new land, etc.)	खोजना	khojana
to discuss (vt)	वाद-विवाद करना	vād-vivād karana
to distribute (leaflets, etc.)	बाँटना	bāntana
to disturb (vt)	बाधा डालना	bādha dālana
to dive (vi)	गोता मारना	gota mārana
to divide (math)	विभाजित करना	vibhājit karana
to do (vt)	करना	karana
to do the laundry	धोना	dhona
to double (increase)	दुगुना करना	duguna karana
to doubt (have doubts)	शक करना	shak karana
to draw a conclusion	नतीजा निकालना	natīja nikālana
to dream (daydream)	सपने देखना	sapane dekhana
to dream (in sleep)	सपना देखना	sapana dekhana
to drink (vi, vt)	पीना	pīna
to drive a car	कार चलाना	kār chalāna
to drive away (scare away)	भगा देना	bhaga dena
to drop (let fall)	गिराना	girāna

to drown (ab. person)	डूबना	dūbana
to dry (clothes, hair)	सुखाना	sukhāna
to eat (vi, vt)	खाना	khāna
to eavesdrop (vi)	छिपकर सुनना	chhipakar sunana
to emit (diffuse - odor, etc.)	निकलना	nikalana
to enjoy oneself	आनंद उठाना	ānand uthāna
to enter (on the list)	दर्ज करना	darj karana
to enter (room, house, etc.)	अंदर आना	andar āna
to entertain (amuse)	मन बहलाना	man bahalāna
to equip (fit out)	तैयारी करना	taiyārī karana
to examine (proposal)	विचार करना	vichār karana
to exchange (sth)	बदलना	badalana
to excuse (forgive)	माफ़ी देना	māfī dena
to exist (vi)	होना	hona
to expect (anticipate)	आशा करना	āsha karana
to expect (foresee)	भविष्य देखना	bhavishy dekhana
to expel (from school, etc.)	बरख़ास्त करना	barakhāst karana
to explain (vt)	समझाना	samajhāna
to express (vt)	प्रकट करना	prakat karana
to extinguish (a fire)	बुझाना	bujhāna
to fall in love (with …)	प्रेम में पड़ना	prem men parana
to feed (provide food)	खिलाना	khilāna
to fight (against the enemy)	लड़ना	larana
to fight (vi)	झगड़ना	jhagarana
to fill (glass, bottle)	भरना	bharana
to find (~ lost items)	ढूंढ लेना	dhūnrh lena
to finish (vt)	ख़त्म करना	khatm karana
to fish (angle)	मछली पकड़ना	machhalī pakarana
to fit (ab. dress, etc.)	फिट करना	fit karana
to flatter (vt)	चापलूसी करना	chāpalūsī karana
to fly (bird, plane)	उड़ना	urana
to follow … (come after)	पीछे जाना	pīchhe jāna
to forbid (vt)	मना करना	mana karana
to force (compel)	विवश करना	vivash karana
to forgive (pardon)	क्षमा करना	kshama karana
to form (constitute)	बनाना	banāna
to get dirty (vi)	मैला होना	maila hona
to get infected (with …)	छूत का रोग लगना	chhūt ka rog lagana
to get irritated	नाराज़ होना	nārāz hona

to get married	शादी करना	shādī karana
to get rid of ...	छुटकारा पान	chhutakāra pān
to get tired	थकना	thakana
to get up (arise from bed)	उठना	uthana
to give a bath (to bath)	नहाना	nahāna
to give a hug, to hug (vt)	गले लगाना	gale lagāna
to give in (yield to)	मान जाना	mān jāna
to glimpse (vt)	देख लेना	dekh lena
to go (by car, etc.)	जाना	jāna
to go (on foot)	जाना	jāna
to go for a swim	तैरना	tairana
to go out (for dinner, etc.)	बाहर जाना	bāhar jāna
to go to bed (go to sleep)	सोने जाना	sone jāna
to greet (vt)	स्वागत करना	svāgat karana
to grow (plants)	उगाना	ugāna
to guarantee (vt)	गारंटी देना	gārantī dena
to guess (the answer)	अनुमान लगाना	anumān lagāna

254. Verbs H-M

to hand out (distribute)	बांटना	bāntana
to hang (curtains, etc.)	टांगना	tāngana
to have (vt)	होना	hona
to have a try	कोशिश करना	koshish karana
to have breakfast	नाश्ता करना	nāshta karana
to have dinner	भोजन करना	bhojan karana
to have lunch	भोजन करना	bhojan karana
to head (group, etc.)	संचालन करना	sanchālan karana
to hear (vt)	सुनना	sunana
to heat (vt)	गरमाना	garamāna
to help (vt)	मदद करना	madad karana
to hide (vt)	छिपाना	chhipāna
to hire (e.g., ~ a boat)	किराये पर लेना	kirāye par lena
to hire (staff)	काम पर रखना	kām par rakhana
to hope (vi, vt)	आशा रखना	āsha rakhana
to hunt (for food, sport)	शिकार करना	shikār karana
to hurry (vi)	जल्दी करना	jaldī karana
to imagine (to picture)	सोचना	sochana
to imitate (vt)	नकल करना	nakal karana
to implore (vt)	प्रार्थना करके मनाना	prārthana karake manāna
to import (vt)	आयात करना	āyāt karana
to increase (vi)	बढ़ना	barhana

to increase (vt)	बढ़ाना	barhāna
to infect (vt)	संक्रमित करना	sankramit karana
to influence (vt)	असर डालना	asar dālana
to inform (e.g., ~ the police about)	बताना	batāna
to inform (vt)	ख़बर देना	khabar dena
to inherit (vt)	उत्तराधिकार में पाना	uttarādhikār men pāna
to inquire (about ...)	जानकारी पाना	jānakārī pāna
to insert (put in)	डालना	dālana
to insinuate (imply)	इशारा करना	ishāra karana
to insist (vi, vt)	आग्रह करना	āgrah karana
to inspire (vt)	प्रेरित करना	prerit karana
to instruct (teach)	निर्देश देना	nirdesh dena
to insult (offend)	अपमान करना	apamān karana
to interest (vt)	रुचि लेना	ruchi lena
to intervene (vi)	घुलना-मिलना	ghulana-milana
to introduce (sb to sb)	परिचय कराना	parichay karāna
to invent (machine, etc.)	आविष्कार करना	āvishkār karana
to invite (vt)	आमंत्रित करना	āmantrit karana
to iron (clothes)	इस्तरी करना	istarī karana
to irritate (annoy)	नाराज़ करना	nārāz karana
to isolate (vt)	अलग करना	alag karana
to join (political party, etc.)	जुड़ना	jurana
to joke (be kidding)	मज़ाक करना	mazāk karana
to keep (old letters, etc.)	रखना	rakhana
to keep silent	चुप रहना	chup rahana
to kill (vt)	मारना	mārana
to knock (at the door)	खटखटाना	khatakhatāna
to know (sb)	जानना	jānana
to know (sth)	मालूम होना	mālūm hona
to laugh (vi)	हंसना	hansana
to launch (start up)	शुरू करना	shurū karana
to leave (~ for Mexico)	चला जाना	chala jāna
to leave (forget sth)	छोड़ना	chhorana
to leave (spouse)	छोड़ना	chhorana
to liberate (city, etc.)	आज़ाद करना	āzād karana
to lie (~ on the floor)	लेटना	letana
to lie (tell untruth)	झूठ बोलना	jhūth bolana
to light (campfire, etc.)	जलाना	jalāna
to light up (illuminate)	प्रकाश करना	prakāsh karana
to like (I like ...)	अच्छा लगना	achchha lagana
to limit (vt)	पाबंदी लगाना	pābandī lagāna
to listen (vi)	सुनना	sunana
to live (~ in France)	रहना	rahana

to live (exist)	जीना	jīna
to load (gun)	भरना	bharana
to load (vehicle, etc.)	लादना	lādana

to look (I'm just ~ing)	देखना	dekhana
to look for ... (search)	तलाश करना	talāsh karana
to look like (resemble)	मिलता-जुलता होना	milata-julata hona
to lose (umbrella, etc.)	खोना	khona
to love (e.g., ~ dancing)	अच्छा लगना	achchha lagana

to love (sb)	प्यार करना	pyār karana
to lower (blind, head)	नीचे करना	nīche karana
to make (~ dinner)	बनाना	banāna
to make a mistake	ग़लती करना	galatī karana
to make angry	क्रोध में लाना	krodh men lāna

to make easier	आसान बनाना	āsān banāna
to make multiple copies	ज़ीरोक्स करना	zīroks karana
to make the acquaintance	परिचय करना	parichay karana
to make use (of ...)	उपयोग करना	upayog karana
to manage, to run	नेतृत्व करना	netrtv karana

to mark (make a mark)	चिह्न लाना	chihn lāna
to mean (signify)	अर्थ होना	arth hona
to memorize (vt)	याद करना	yād karana
to mention (talk about)	उल्लेख करना	ullekh karana
to miss (school, etc.)	ग़ैरहाज़िर होना	gairahājir hona

to mix (combine, blend)	मिलाना	milāna
to mock (make fun of)	मज़ाक उड़ाना	mazāk urāna
to move (to shift)	सरकाना	sarakāna
to multiply (math)	गुणा करना	guna karana
must (v aux)	ज़रूर	zarūr

255. Verbs N-R

to name, to call (vt)	नाम देना	nām dena
to negotiate (vi)	वार्ता करना	vārtta karana
to note (write down)	लिख लेना	likh lena
to notice (see)	देखना	dekhana

to obey (vi, vt)	मानना	mānana
to object (vi, vt)	एतराज़ करना	etarāz karana
to observe (see)	देखना	dekhana
to offend (vt)	नाराज़ करना	nārāz karana
to omit (word, phrase)	छोड़ना	chhorana

to open (vt)	खोलना	kholana
to order (in restaurant)	ऑर्डर करना	ordar karana
to order (mil.)	हुक्म देना	hukm dena

to organize (concert, party)	आयोजित करना	āyojit karana
to overestimate (vt)	ज़्यादा आंकना	zyāda ānkana
to own (possess)	रखना	rakhana
to participate (vi)	भाग लेना	bhāg lena
to pass through (by car, etc.)	गुज़रना	guzarana
to pay (vi, vt)	दाम चुकाना	dām chukāna
to peep, spy on	छिपकर देखना	chhipakar dekhana
to penetrate (vt)	घुसना	ghusana
to permit (vt)	अनुमति देना	anumati dena
to pick (flowers)	तोड़ना	torana
to place (put, set)	रखना	rakhana
to plan (~ to do sth)	योजना बनाना	yojana banāna
to play (actor)	अभिनय करना	abhinay karana
to play (children)	खेलना	khelana
to point (~ the way)	दिखाना	dikhāna
to pour (liquid)	डालना	dālana
to pray (vi, vt)	दुआ देना	dua dena
to prefer (vt)	तरजीह देना	tarajīh dena
to prepare (~ a plan)	तैयार करना	taiyār karana
to present (sb to sb)	प्रस्तुत करना	prastut karana
to preserve (peace, life)	बचाना	bachāna
to prevail (vt)	विजयी होना	vijayī hona
to progress (move forward)	आगे बढ़ना	āge barhana
to promise (vt)	वचन देना	vachan dena
to pronounce (vt)	उच्चारण करना	uchchāran karana
to propose (vt)	प्रस्ताव करना	prastāv karana
to protect (e.g., ~ nature)	रक्षा करना	raksha karana
to protest (vi)	विरोध करना	virodh karana
to prove (vt)	साबित करना	sābit karana
to provoke (vt)	उकसाना	ukasāna
to pull (~ the rope)	खींचना	khīnchana
to punish (vt)	सज़ा देना	saza dena
to push (~ the door)	धकेलना	dhakelana
to put away (vt)	रख देना	rakh dena
to put in order	ठीक करना	thīk karana
to put, to place	रखना	rakhana
to quote (cite)	उद्धत करना	uddhat karana
to reach (arrive at)	पहुंचना	pahunchana
to read (vi, vt)	पढ़ना	parhana
to realize (a dream)	पूरा करना	pūra karana
to recognize (identify sb)	पहचानना	pahachānana

to recommend (vt)	सिफ़ारिश करना	sifārish karana
to recover (~ from flu)	ठीक हो जाना	thīk ho jāna
to redo (do again)	दोबारा करना	dobāra karana
to reduce (speed, etc.)	कम करना	kam karana
to refuse (~ sb)	इन्कार करना	inkār karana
to regret (be sorry)	अफ़सोस करना	afasos karana
to reinforce (vt)	दृढ़ करना	drrh karana
to remember (Do you ~ me?)	याद करना	yād karana
to remember (I can't ~ her name)	याद करना	yād karana
to remind of ...	याद दिलाना	yād dilāna
to remove (~ a stain)	धब्बा मिटाना	dhabba mitāna
to remove (~ an obstacle)	हटाना	hatāna
to rent (sth from sb)	किराए पर लेना	kirae par lena
to repair (mend)	ठीक करना	thīk karana
to repeat (say again)	दोहराना	doharāna
to report (make a report)	रिपोर्ट करना	riport karana
to reproach (vt)	ताने देना	tāne dena
to reserve, to book	बुक करना	buk karana
to restrain (hold back)	रोकना	rokana
to return (come back)	लौटाना	lautāna
to risk, to take a risk	जोखिम उठाना	jokhim uthāna
to rub out (erase)	साफ़ करना	sāf karana
to run (move fast)	दौड़ना	daurana
to rush (hurry sb)	जल्दी करना	jaldī karana

256. Verbs S-W

to satisfy (please)	संतुष्ट करना	santusht karana
to save (rescue)	बचाना	bachāna
to say (~ thank you)	कहना	kahana
to scold (vt)	डाँटना	dāntana
to scratch (with claws)	खरोंचना	kharonchana
to select (to pick)	चुनना	chunana
to sell (goods)	बेचना	bechana
to send (a letter)	भेजना	bhejana
to send back (vt)	वापस भेजना	vāpas bhejana
to sense (~ danger)	महसूस करना	mahasūs karana
to sentence (vt)	सज़ा देना	saza dena
to serve (in restaurant)	सेवा करना	seva karana
to settle (a conflict)	सुलझाना	sulajhāna
to shake (vt)	हिलाना	hilāna

to shave (vi)	शेव करना	shev karana
to shine (gleam)	चमकना	chamakana
to shiver (with cold)	कांपना	kāmpana
to shoot (vi)	गोली चलाना	golī chalāna
to shout (vi)	चिल्लाना	chillāna
to show (to display)	दिखाना	dikhāna
to shudder (vi)	सिहर जाना	sihar jāna
to sigh (vi)	आह भरना	āh bharana
to sign (document)	हस्ताक्षर करना	hastākshar karana
to signify (mean)	अर्थ बताना	arth batāna
to simplify (vt)	सरल बनाना	saral banāna
to sin (vi)	पाप करना	pāp karana
to sit (be sitting)	बैठना	baithana
to sit down (vi)	बैठ जाना	baith jāna
to smell (emit an odor)	गंध देना	gandh dena
to smell (inhale the odor)	सूंघना	sūnghana
to smile (vi)	मुस्कुराना	muskurāna
to snap (vi, ab. rope)	फटना	fatana
to solve (problem)	हल करना	hal karana
to sow (seed, crop)	बोना	bona
to spill (liquid)	छलकाना	chhalakāna
to spit (vi)	थूकना	thūkana
to stand (toothache, cold)	सहना	sahana
to start (begin)	शुरू करना	shurū karana
to steal (money, etc.)	चुराना	churāna
to stop (for pause, etc.)	रुकना	rukana
to stop (please ~ calling me)	बंद करना	band karana
to stop talking	चुप होना	chup hona
to stroke (caress)	सहलाना	sahalāna
to study (vt)	पढ़ना	parhana
to suffer (feel pain)	सहना	sahana
to support (cause, idea)	समर्थन करना	samarthan karana
to suppose (assume)	अंदाज़ा लगाना	andāza lagāna
to surface (ab. submarine)	पानी की सतह पर आना	pānī kī satah par āna
to surprise (amaze)	हैरान करना	hairān karana
to suspect (vt)	शक करना	shak karana
to swim (vi)	तैरना	tairana
to take (get hold of)	लेना	lena
to take a bath	नहाना	nahāna
to take a rest	आराम करना	ārām karana
to take away (e.g., about waiter)	ले जाना	le jāna

to take off (airplane)	उड़ना	urana
to take off (painting, curtains, etc.)	हटाना	hatāna
to take pictures	फ़ोटो खींचना	foto khīnchana
to talk to ...	से कहना	se kahana
to teach (give lessons)	सीखाना	sīkhāna
to tear off, to rip off (vt)	फाड़ना	fārana
to tell (story, joke)	बताना	batāna
to thank (vt)	धन्यवाद देना	dhanyavād dena
to think (believe)	सोचना	sochana
to think (vi, vt)	सोचना	sochana
to threaten (vt)	धमकाना	dhamakāna
to throw (stone, etc.)	फेंकना	fenkana
to tie to ...	बांधना	bāndhana
to tie up (prisoner)	बाँधना	bāndhana
to tire (make tired)	थकाना	thakāna
to touch (one's arm, etc.)	छूना	chhūna
to tower (over ...)	ऊँचा होना	ūncha hona
to train (animals)	सधाना	sadhāna
to train (sb)	प्रशिक्षित करना	prashikshit karana
to train (vi)	प्रशिक्षण करना	prashikshan karana
to transform (vt)	रूप बदलना	rūp badalana
to translate (vt)	अनुवाद करना	anuvād karana
to treat (illness)	इलाज कराना	ilāj karāna
to trust (vt)	यकीन करना	yakīn karana
to try (attempt)	कोशिश करना	koshish karana
to turn (e.g., ~ left)	मोड़ना	morana
to turn away (vi)	मुड़ना	murana
to turn off (the light)	बुझाना	bujhāna
to turn on (computer, etc.)	चलाना	chalāna
to turn over (stone, etc.)	उलटना	ulatana
to underestimate (vt)	कम आंकना	kam ānkana
to underline (vt)	रेखांकित करना	rekhānkit karana
to understand (vt)	समझना	samajhana
to undertake (vt)	ज़िम्मेदारी लेना	zimmedārī lena
to unite (vt)	संयुक्त करना	sanyukt karana
to untie (vt)	ढीला करना	dhīla karana
to use (phrase, word)	उपयोग करना	upayog karana
to vaccinate (vt)	टीका लगाना	tīka lagāna
to vote (vi)	मतदान डालना	matadān dālana
to wait (vt)	इंतज़ार करना	intazār karana
to wake (sb)	जगाना	jagāna
to want (wish, desire)	चाहना	chāhana

to warn (of the danger)	चेतावनी देना	chetāvanī dena
to wash (clean)	धोना	dhona
to water (plants)	सींचना	sīnchana
to wave (the hand)	हाथ हिलाना	hāth hilāna

to weigh (have weight)	वज़न करना	vazan karana
to work (vi)	काम करना	kām karana
to worry (make anxious)	परेशान करना	pareshān karana
to worry (vi)	परेशान होना	pareshān hona

to wrap (parcel, etc.)	लपेटना	lapetana
to wrestle (sport)	कुश्ती लड़ना	kushtī larana
to write (vt)	लिखना	likhana
to write down	लिखना	likhana

www.ingramcontent.com/pod-product-compliance
Lightning Source LLC
Chambersburg PA
CBHW071319090426
42738CB00012B/2728